How Persistent Low Returns
Will Shape Saving and Retirement

How Persistent Low Returns Will Shape Saving and Retirement

EDITED BY

Olivia S. Mitchell,
Robert Clark, and
Raimond Maurer

OXFORD
UNIVERSITY PRESS

OXFORD
UNIVERSITY PRESS

Great Clarendon Street, Oxford, OX2 6DP,
United Kingdom

Oxford University Press is a department of the University of Oxford.
It furthers the University's objective of excellence in research, scholarship,
and education by publishing worldwide. Oxford is a registered trade mark of
Oxford University Press in the UK and in certain other countries

First Edition published in 2018

Impression: 1

Published in the United States of America by Oxford University Press
198 Madison Avenue, New York, NY 10016, United States of America

British Library Cataloguing in Publication Data

Data available

Library of Congress Control Number: 2018935371

ISBN 978-0-19-882744-3

Printed and bound by
CPI Group (UK) Ltd, Croydon, CR0 4YY

Preface

Financial market developments over the past decade have undermined what was once thought to be conventional wisdom about saving, investment, and retirement spending. Foremost among these is the depressingly persistent and extended period of low capital market returns, driving concerns about how to rethink saving and investments in what can be called the 'new normal.' Given this challenging backdrop, our new volume in the Pension Research Council/Oxford University Press series identifies several new tools which retirement savers and pension managers will want to explore. The volume will also interest researchers and employers seeking to design better retirement plan offerings.

In preparing this book, many people and institutions have played key roles. Co-editors Robert Clark and Raimond Maurer provided many helpful suggestions as we structured and helped revise the analysis presented herein. We remain grateful to our Advisory Board and Members of the Pension Research Council for their intellectual and research support. Additional support was received from the Pension Research Council, the Boettner Center for Pensions and Retirement Research, and the Ralph H. Blanchard Memorial Endowment at the Wharton School of the University of Pennsylvania. We also offer deep gratitude to Oxford University Press, which publishes our series on global retirement security. The manuscript was expertly prepared and carefully edited by Joseph Brucker and Lauren Sukovich.

Our work at the Pension Research Council and the Boettner Center for Pensions and Retirement Security of the Wharton School of the University of Pennsylvania has focused on aspects of pensions and retirement well-being over 60 years. This volume contributes to our mission, which is to generate research on and engage debate around policy for global pensions and retirement security.

Olivia S. Mitchell
Executive Director, Pension Research Council
Director, Boettner Center for Pensions and Retirement Research
The Wharton School, University of Pennsylvania

Contents

Part I. Origins and Consequences of the Persistent Low Return Environment

Part II. Whither Retirement Strategies?

List of Figures

List of Tables

Notes on Contributors

Daniel B. Berkowitz is an investment analyst at Vanguard. Prior to his work at Vanguard, he was a retirement plan specialist at the Ambrose Group and taught statistics at Cornell University. Daniel earned his bachelor's degree from Cornell University and an M.B.A. with a distinction in finance from the Johnson Graduate School of Management at Cornell.

David Blanchett is head of retirement research for Morningstar Investment Management LLC, where he works in the group's consulting and investment services and conducts research on financial planning, tax planning, annuities, and retirement. He earned his master's degree in financial services from the American College, his master's degree in business administration from the University of Chicago Booth School of Business, and his doctorate in personal financial planning program from Texas Tech University.

Alistair Byrne heads European DC investment strategy for State Street Global Advisors in London. He has also been a senior DC investment consultant at Towers Watson, an investment manager for AEGON UK, and a finance faculty member at the University of Strathclyde and University of Edinburgh business schools. He has a particular interest in the application of behavioral finance to retirement saving and financial planning decisions. Mr. Byrne received his Ph.D. in finance from the University of Strathclyde in Glasgow and he is a Chartered Financial Analyst (CFA)® charterholder.

Kevin E. Cahill is a research economist with the Center on Aging and Work at Boston College and a senior economist at ECONorthwest, an economics and public policy consulting firm based in Portland, Oregon. His research examines labor force withdrawal including bridge job employment and re-entry, retirement income, occupational changes later in life, and the role of employer-provided pensions in the retirement decisions of older workers. Previously he served as an economist at Abt Associates and Analysis Group. He helped found the journal *Work, Aging, and Retirement*. He earned his B.A. in mathematics and economics from Rutgers College, and his M.A. and Ph.D. in economics from Boston College.

Robert Clark is Stephen Zelnak Professor of Economics and Professor of Management, Innovation and Entrepreneurship in the Poole College of Management, North Carolina State University. He is also Research Associate at the National Bureau of Economic Research and a member of the Advisory Board of the Pension Research Council. His research examines retirement decisions, the choice between defined benefit and defined contribution plans, the impact of pension conversions to defined contribution and cash balance plans, the role of information and communications on 401(k) contributions, and government regulation of pensions. He has also evaluated employer-provided financial literacy and retirement planning programs and how these plans affect worker decisions, as well as state and local pensions and retiree health plans. He earned his M.S. and Ph.D. from Duke University, and his B.A. from Millsaps College in economics.

Andrew S. Clarke is a senior investment strategist at the Vanguard Investment Strategy Group, where he researches how ordinary people do (and do not) succeed in meeting their financial goals. Previously he worked at Morningstar. He earned his B.A. from Haverford College and his M.S. from West Chester University. He is a CFA® charterholder.

Peter Conti-Brown is an Assistant Professor at The Wharton School of the University of Pennsylvania. A financial historian and a lawyer, he studies central banking, financial regulation, and public finance, with a particular focus on the history and policies of the US Federal Reserve System. He has published one book, *The Power and Independence of the Federal Reserve,* and has another forthcoming on bank supervision in the United States from the Civil War to Donald Trump. He also has a comprehensive political and institutional history of the US Federal Reserve. He earned his Ph.D. from Princeton University in history, and his J.D. from Stanford. His A.B. is from Harvard College.

Kevin J. DiCiurcio is a senior investment strategist at Vanguard Investment Strategy Group. He earned his M.B.A. in finance from Villanova University and his B.S. in Business Administration (finance) from the University of Richmond. He is a CFA® charterholder.

Jason J. Fichtner is a Senior Research Fellow with the Mercatus Center at George Mason University. His research focuses on social security, federal tax policy, federal budget policy, retirement security, and policy proposals to increase saving and investment. Previously, he worked for the Social Security Administration as Deputy Commissioner of Social Security (acting), Chief Economist, and Associate Commissioner for Retirement Policy. He also served as Senior Economist with the Joint Economic Committee of the US Congress. Currently he also teaches as an adjunct professor at the Georgetown McCourt School of Public Policy, the Johns Hopkins School of Advanced International Studies, and the Virginia Tech Center for Public Administration and Policy, where he offers courses in economics, public finance, public policy process, public management, and public budgeting processes. Dr. Fichtner earned his B.A. from the University of Michigan, his M.P.P. from Georgetown University, and his Ph.D. in public administration and policy from Virginia Tech.

Michael Finke is Dean and Chief Academic Officer of The American College of Financial Services. His research interests include household investment and intertemporal choice, behavioral personal finance, agency costs of financial planning, retirement income planning, risk tolerance assessment, and aggregate trends in household portfolio allocation. He received the 2013 and 2014 Montgomery Warschauer best paper awards from the *Journal of Financial Planning*. He received his Ph.D. in consumer economics from the Ohio State University and also in finance from the University of Missouri.

William G. Gale holds the Arjay and Frances Miller Chair in Federal Economic Policy and is a senior fellow in the Economic Studies Program at the Brookings Institution. His research focuses on tax policy, fiscal policy, pensions, and saving behavior. He is co-director of the Tax Policy Center, a joint venture of the Brookings Institution and the Urban Institute. He is also director of the Retirement Security Project, and he is a member of the Macroeconomic Advisers Board of Advisors. Previously he taught at the University of California, Los Angeles, and he served as a senior economist for the Council of Economic Advisers under President George H.W. Bush. Dr. Gale attended Duke University and the London School of Economics, and he received his Ph.D. in economics from Stanford University.

Natalia Garabato is an economist at Willis Towers Watson. Her interests include labor economics, pension and retirement finance, foundations and endowments asset liability modeling, and access to finance. Previously she worked at the Inter-American Development Bank. She received her Ph.D. in economics from the University of New South Wales (UNSW), Sydney and her B.A. in economics from the Universidad de la Republica, Montevideo.

Jonathan Gardner is a senior economist at Willis Towers Watson. His research interests include pensions, behavioral finance, labor economics, and health economics. Dr. Gardner earned his Ph.D. in economics at the University of Warwick, and his M.Sc. from University College London.

Vanya Horneff is a Ph.D. researcher at the House of Finance, Goethe University of Frankfurt. Her research interests include public finance, public economics, and financial economics. She is a member of the SAFE Research Center at the University.

Antti Ilmanen manages AQR's Portfolio Solutions Group, advising institutional investors and sovereign wealth funds, and he also develops the firm's broad investment ideas. Previously he was a senior portfolio manager at Brevan Howard, worked at Salomon Brothers/Citigroup, and served as a central bank portfolio manager in Finland. He has advised institutional investors including Norway's Government Pension Fund Global and the Government of Singapore Investment Corporation. His publications have received a Graham and Dodd award and Bernstein Fabozzi/Jacobs Levy awards. Dr. Ilmanen received his M.Sc. degrees in economics and law from the University of Helsinki, and his Ph.D. in finance from the University of Chicago.

David C. John is a senior strategic policy advisor at the AARP Public Policy Institute, where he works on pension and retirement savings issues. He also serves as a deputy director of the Retirement Security Project at the Brookings Institution. Previously Dr. John was a senior research fellow at the Heritage Foundation; he also worked for a money center bank, a law firm, a credit union trade association, and for members of the House of Representatives. He is also a member of the National Academy of Social Insurance. He has written extensively on reforming retirement programs, and he co-invented with J. Mark Iwry the Automatic IRA. He earned his A.B.J. in journalism, his M.A. in economics, and his M.B.A. in finance from the University of Georgia.

Raimond Maurer is the Chair of Investment, Portfolio Management, and Pension Finance at the Finance Department of the Goethe University of Frankfurt. He is also Dean of the Faculty of Economics and Business Administration. His research focuses on asset management, life-time portfolio choice, real estate, and pension finance. Previously he visited the Wharton School as a Metzler Visiting Professor, and he serves in several professional capacities including the Union Real Estate Investment Group, the Society of Actuaries (academic chair of AFIR), the Association of Certified International Investment Analysts (academic director and member of the International Examination Committee). He earned his Habilitation, Ph.D., and Diploma in business administration from Mannheim University, and he received an honorary doctorate from the State University of Finance and Economics of St. Petersburg.

Olivia S. Mitchell is the International Foundation of Employee Benefit Plans Professor, as well as Professor of Insurance/Risk Management and Business Economics/Policy; Executive Director of the Pension Research Council; and Director of the Boettner Center on Pensions and Retirement Research, all at the Wharton School of the University of Pennsylvania. Concurrently Dr. Mitchell serves as a Research Associate at the NBER; Independent Director on the Wells Fargo Fund Boards; Co-Investigator for the Health and Retirement Study at the University of Michigan; Member of the Executive Board for the Michigan Retirement Research Center; and Senior Scholar at the Singapore Management University. She also advises the

Centre for Pensions and Superannuation UNSW and is Faculty Affiliate of the Wharton Public Policy Initiative. She received her M.A. and Ph.D. degrees in economics from the University of Wisconsin-Madison, and her B.A. in economics from Harvard University.

Steven A. Nyce is the Director of Willis Towers Watson's Research and Innovation Center where he works on employee attitudes towards benefit programs and their impact on employee behaviors, workforce productivity, and employee well-being. Dr. Nyce also focuses on the US healthcare market and the implications of recent plan design trends and workplace initiatives as well as the emergence of private healthcare exchanges and modeling the buying patterns of employees in a consumer-grade environment. He earned his B.S. degree in economics from LaSalle University, and his M.A. and Ph.D. in economics from the University of Notre Dame.

Wade Pfau is a professor of retirement income in the Ph.D. in Financial and Retirement Planning program at The American College of Financial Services. His areas of expertise are annuities, investments, portfolio management, and retirement planning. His research has earned him two Montgomery-Warschauer Awards, the Academic Thought Leadership Award from the Retirement Income Industry Association, and a best paper award winner from the Academy of Financial Services. He earned his doctorate and master's in economics from Princeton University, and B.A. and B.S. degrees from the University of Iowa. He is also a Chartered Financial Analyst.

Joseph F. Quinn is a professor of economics at Boston College, where he also served as Dean of the College of Arts and Sciences and Interim Provost and Dean of the Faculties. His research interests include the economics of aging, the determinants of individual retirement decisions, recent trends in the retirement patterns of older Americans, and social security reform. He co-chaired (with Olivia Mitchell) the Technical Panel on Trends and Issues in Retirement Savings for President Clinton's Social Security Advisory Council. A founding member of the National Academy of Social Insurance, he was elected to its Board of Directors and served as Vice President. He earned his Ph.D. from the Massachusetts Institute of Technology and his B.A. from Amherst College, where he currently serves as a trustee.

Matthew Rauseo is Vice President of Business Development, Defined Contribution Strategist at AQR Capital Management. His purview is institutional defined contribution plans, where he focuses on asset allocation, portfolio construction, and investment menu design. He holds his B.A. in Business Administration and Management from Northeastern University.

Catherine Reilly is Global Head of Research, Defined Contribution at State Street Global Advisors, where she focuses on global retirement saving and retirement plan design. Previously she was Chief Economist of Pohjola Asset Management in Finland, where she was responsible for advising large institutional clients on asset allocation decisions. She has also worked for McKinsey and Company in Helsinki. Catherine earned her M.P.A. from the Harvard Kennedy School of Government and her M.Sc. in economics and finance from the Helsinki School of Economics.

Jason S. Seligman is an economist with the US Department of the Treasury's Office of Economic Policy, a fellow at the TIAA Institute, and an affiliate of the Center for Financial Security at the University of Wisconsin, Madison. His research focuses on public finance including disability insurance. Dr. Seligman earned his Ph.D. in economics from the University of California, Berkeley.

Yvonne Sonsino is the Innovation Leader at Mercer for the Europe and Pacific Region, exploring the development of new health, wealth, and career solutions to support the workforce of the future. Her research interests include population aging, automation, the future of jobs, and gender parity. Her projects have included pension plan redesign and financing, career framework implementation, and motivation techniques to drive performance. She is the Co-Chair of the UK Government Department for Work and Pensions Business Strategy Group examining how employers can improve the recruitment, retention, and retraining of older workers. She holds two psychology degrees from The Open University, and her M.A. in business research is from Durham University.

Kimberly A. Stockton is an investment research analyst at Vanguard Investment Strategy Group where she conducts investment research to support portfolio construction solutions and the development of new products, tool, services, and strategies. Her published research includes work on passive investing, tactical asset allocation, pension plan investment strategy, and single portfolio solutions methodology. Her M.B.A. in finance is from Villanova University and her B.A. in economics from the University of California Berkeley.

Daniel W. Wallick is a principal in the Vanguard Investment Strategy Group where he is responsible for developing portfolio strategies and overseeing the development of the firm's Capital Markets Model. He has advised pensions, endowments, and foundations and his research focuses on portfolio construction and liability-driven investments. Previously he worked for a public finance investment firm. He earned his B.A. in history from the University of Pennsylvania and his M.B.A. from Harvard University.

Chapter 1

How Persistent Low Returns Will Shape Saving and Retirement

Robert Clark, Raimond Maurer, and Olivia S. Mitchell

Funded pension systems around the world have long relied on relatively high and predictable long-term capital market returns. Yet pension systems today confront a key challenge: namely, how to deal with what appears to be a persistent low return on bonds and equities. The present economic circumstances can greatly shrink retirement saving accounts: thus a 1 percent lower long-term return can reduce final annual pension amounts by approximately 25 percent. Alternatively, low returns will imply that the costs of paying the pension to employers or governments will increase, if benefits are to remain constant. And for some time, many industrialized countries including Japan, Germany, Sweden, and Switzerland, have experienced negative interest rates even for medium-term bonds. This historically low interest rate environment has prevailed since the financial crisis of 2007–08, when central banks employed monetary policy to support their financial sectors and economies. Though we cannot be sure how long such low interest rates will be with us, Japan offers reason for pessimism as interest rates there have been close to zero percent for over 20 years.

For this reason, it will be prudent, and probably necessary, for insurers, plan sponsors, workers, retirees, and policymakers to take concrete steps to prepare for these lower long-term expected rates of return to retirement wealth. In fact, as we show in this volume, a persistent low-interest-rate economy will compel many to revisit how much they save, how they invest, and how long they can afford to live in retirement. This book explores how we arrived at our current state of affairs and what changes need to be made to achieve adequate retirement incomes for future retirees. Each chapter will interest not only average savers, retirees, and plan sponsors, but also policymakers around the world seeking answers to questions about what the future might bring in terms of investing retirement wealth and how to develop policies so that saving can last throughout retirement for most individuals. In the remainder of the present chapter we offer an overview of the themes and ideas deserving particular attention.

Origins and Consequences of a Persistent Low Return Environment

To provide an essential understanding of how the persistent low return economy developed, Peter Conti-Brown begins in Chapter 2 with an explanation of how the US Federal Reserve Bank (the Fed) seeks to manage inflation. In particular, he points to how the Fed has traditionally sought to remain protected from politics when undertaking to achieve its three mandates, namely achieving maximum employment, maintaining stable prices, and moderating long-term interest rates. While countries differ in their central bank structures, they all seek to maintain monetary policies that sustain economic growth while allowing individuals and institutions to save without undue inflation worries.

Until recently, the Fed had gained the reputation of being almost omnipotent, a view prompted by a coalition that transcended political parties. Yet the last decade of very low and even negative real returns has raised questions about the central banks' ability to remain independent. In the United States, the Fed was once quite a popular institution, but now it is widely disliked—almost as much as the federal tax collection authority. It is not surprising, then, that several bills in Congress have been put forth intending to control the Fed, limiting its power and independence. Yet it is unsurprising that the Fed has been caught in the cross-hairs, as it must deal with an increasingly global economy and capital markets. Conti-Brown concludes that the Fed is responsible for now educating the public and informing it that the Fed is no longer the 'economic maestro' of interest rates.

Against the backdrop of low returns, several chapters take up the question of how to save and invest in this 'new normal' era. David Blanchett, Michael Finke, and Wade Pfau note that, in the past, people had grown accustomed to equities bailing them out of poor return choices. By contrast, low expected returns combined with longer lifetimes have doubled the cost of generating $1 of real annual retirement income. Whereas a 25-year old could save 8 percent per annum for retirement in days gone by, 14 percent or more now seems sensible. Another good solution to this retirement saving problem is to work longer and retire later.

The chapter by Daniel W. Wallick, David B. Berkowitz, Andrew S. Clarke, Kevin J. DiCiurcio, and Kimberly A. Stockton argues that three 'levers' may be used, all of which should be taken into account by retirement savers. One is to have people save more; another is to reduce costs associated with portfolio investment; and a third is to take more risk. The chapter then goes on to explore several different approaches to adding risk, including higher allocations to traditional risky assets like global equities; style-factor tilts with an emphasis on equity and fixed-income factors that have historically earned premiums over the broad stock and bond markets; allocations to traditional active equity management; and allocations to alternatives.

In turn, Catherine Reilly and Alistair Byrne address the question of what can be done on the investment and public policy side to make things easier for younger cohorts of retirement savers. The authors argue that saving more can be useful, but working longer can help even more. For instance, deferring retirement from 65 to 70 saves money, as people can save more, earn more, and will need to fund a shorter retirement period. Thus even in a low-interest rate environment, younger generations can achieve reasonable outcomes by starting to save early, saving consistently, and retiring at 70. Of course, some people may be unable to work longer and thus will need to develop an alternative strategy for dealing with low returns. The authors also suggest allowing people to defer social security benefits past 70 at an actuarially adjusted rate so the system could be a true longevity backstop.

In their chapter, Antti Ilmanen and Matthew Rauseo offer hope for defined contribution plan investors whose target is to ensure post-retirement consumption, despite the low expected return environment over the next decade. The authors agree that higher saving rates will be required, along with deferred retirement. In addition, they propose to expand the investment 'toolbox' by moving away from market cap-weighted portfolios. In addition, they see value in risk parity approaches and also long/short portfolios. Limited additional leverage may also help boost expected returns on defined contribution (DC) portfolios. While such strategies may be nontraditional for conventional individual-account retirement plans, they are likely to be appealing for large institutionally managed DC plans having the necessary management capability.

Workers covered by DC plans must recognize that low returns limit their accumulation of retirement wealth while working, and they also directly affect how much a retiree can expect in terms of monthly benefit payments. Low interest rates also imply that purchasing annuities is expensive: the same $1 yields a lower monthly payout than in the past. Defined benefit (DB) plan sponsors face a similar problem, in that low rates restrict the growth of reserves and also reduce the ability to convert retirement funds into annual benefits for retirees.

Whither Retirement Strategies?

The chapter by Joseph Quinn and Kevin E. Cahill reports that people are actually working longer today than compared to 50 years ago. This trend is particularly notable for older men, but older women are working longer as well. The process by which people move into retirement is also changing. Rather than being a one-time event, people can transition from full-time career employment to part-time work, often with the same employer. Next, people tend to take a bridge job, or leave the labor force altogether and then re-enter at a later date. Bridge jobs are the most common, with 50–60 percent of the US working population transitioning to bridge jobs before quitting work altogether. Policymakers may need to consider additional ways to support continued work later in life, to help mitigate the many challenges that an aging society faces in the decades ahead. The good news is that older workers have been flexible to date, but what is not known is how much more they can continue to adapt. The authors conclude that the low-return environment can alter appetites for risk in order to achieve higher returns.

Vanya Horneff, Raimond Maurer, and Olivia S. Mitchell develop and calibrate a theoretical life cycle model in their chapter, which they use to determine how low interest rates influence household saving within and outside tax-deferred retirement plans. Their approach also integrates income tax rates and devotes particular attention to realistically modeled social security benefits. It is interesting that expected life-cycle profiles generated by the model compare well to actual data on claiming behavior of US retirees. Moreover, the authors show that people tend to save less in times of low interest rates, especially in relatively illiquid tax-qualified plans. Low rates also drive later claiming of Social Security benefits, and longer work lives. Finally, the chapter demonstrates that, in a low return environment, people optimally invest less in tax-qualified plans, and more outside their pensions.

Empirical evidence suggests that older households have responded to the new low interest rate environment in various ways, according to Jason J. Fichtner and Jason S. Seligman. Many of them benefited from strong equity returns in the past, yet some lower-wealth households have already depleted their assets, including home equity. Unfortunately, the bottom 10 percent of retirees exhausts its resources 16 years into retirement, while the bottom quarter runs out in year 18. Overall, low returns have resulted in a negative wealth impact, though some high-wealth households have enjoyed strong equity markets. They conclude that inequality could rise in the future.

A similar lesson applies to DB plan sponsors and national social security programs. If retirement can be deferred, this lowers the length of the pension payout period. Consequently, later retirement ages will help restore traditional pensions to a better footing by reducing the assets needed to finance retirement benefits.

New Designs for Pension Plan Sponsors

In her chapter, Yvonne Sonsino argues that some firms value older workers, yet many do not. This is, in part, because myths about older workers persist, and she argues that these need to be evaluated more carefully. This is critical inasmuch as post-Brexit migration will leave the United Kingdom with a shortage of up to 2.5 million employees. Her recommendation is that employers can take a variety of actions to be age ready, including building age-diverse talented teams in the development pipeline. She also addresses financial wellness concepts, noting that deliberate planning for financial security in old age will be greatly valued.

The work of William Gale and David John takes up efforts by state governments in the United States to sponsor retirement saving plans for individuals whose employers do not offer a retirement plan. In the United States, employers offer pensions on a voluntary basis, and low pension participation is concentrated among lower-paid, less-educated, Hispanic/black, and part-time workers. In response, over 30 states have taken action since 2012 to expand pension coverage, while five states (California, Connecticut, Illinois, Maryland, and Oregon) have established a variant of an auto-enrollment Individual Retirement Account (IRA) plan. Typically employers are mandated to offer these with some default contribution rate, say, of 3 percent. As yet the jury is still out on how successful these state-run plans are in terms of enhancing retirement security for the lower half of the pay distribution.

In their chapter, Natalia Garabato, Jonathan Gardner, and Steve Nyce argue that healthcare costs are crowding out other benefit costs throughout the developed world, with the most dramatic impact in the United States. In addition, the lack of wage growth has meant that people now need employer-provided benefits more than they did in the past. The authors delve into what employers of the future may offer in terms of benefits, focusing on the change from benefits as a transaction to benefits as an experience. The authors also emphasize how firms are moving from providing employees less choice to more choice. At the same time, benefit costs are becoming more closely tailored to employee health habits; those who smoke will pay more, and those with a healthy lifestyle will pay less. Benefits delivery systems are also changing, in that people seek to elect benefits from an exchange, akin to a shopping basket with decision support. Previously, workers elected core medical and dental insurance, whereas now they are offered products such as pet insurance, child life insurance, identity theft protection, and disability insurance. The challenge will be to manage the tension between offering flexibility and choice, and ensuring adequate retirement funds. With increasing life expectancy, all countries will struggle to provide adequate healthcare as well as pension income for retirees.

Conclusion

McKinsey & Co. (2016) recently argued that the asset management business faces a crossroads because future equity returns are expected to average

150–400 basis points below those of the past 30 years, and fixed income assets are anticipated to pay 300–500 basis points less than historical rates. Not surprisingly, disappointed retirement savers are becoming increasingly sensitive to investment fees and charges, driving the trend toward lower-cost and passively managed investments. Moreover, the expected low return environment is prompting savers to seek new—and riskier—types of investment, including alternative and less liquid investments. It should also be noted that the digital revolution is becoming an ever-more widespread force for boosting investment efficiency and improving the gains from portfolio management.

These financial market developments, as well as the changes in work and retirement, are certain to reshape conventional approaches to saving, investment, and retirement. Such dramatic changes must also prompt employers to revisit the nature of work, how they hire, train, and retain employees, and what retirement will mean in the future. And clearly policymakers must start planning now for reforms that will allow older people to work longer, and save more, if they are to ensure financial security in retirement. This volume offers lessons toward that end.

References

Blanchett, D., M. Finke, and W. Pfau (2018). "Low Returns and Optimal Retirement Savings," in R. Clark, R. Maurer, and O. S. Mitchell (eds.), *How Persistent Low Returns Will Shape Saving and Retirement*. Oxford, UK: Oxford University Press, pp. 26–43.

Conti-Brown, P. (2018). "Politics, Independence, and Retirees: Long-term Low Interest Rates at the Federal Reserve," in R. Clark, R. Maurer, and O. S. Mitchell (eds.), *How Persistent Low Returns Will Shape Saving and Retirement*. Oxford, UK: Oxford University Press, pp. 11–25.

Fichtner, J. J., and J. S. Seligman (2018). "Retirement Saving and Decumulation in a Persistent Low-Return Environment," in R. Clark, R. Maurer, and O. S. Mitchell (eds.), *How Persistent Low Returns Will Shape Saving and Retirement*. Oxford, UK: Oxford University Press, pp. 132–62.

Gale, W. G., and D. C. John (2018). "State-sponsored Retirement Savings Plans: New Approaches to Boost Retirement Plan Coverage," in R. Clark, R. Maurer, and O. S. Mitchell (eds.), *How Persistent Low Returns Will Shape Saving and Retirement*. Oxford, UK: Oxford University Press, pp. 173–93.

Garabato, N., J. Gardner, and S. Nyce (2018). "Global Developments in Employee Benefits," in R. Clark, R. Maurer, and O. S. Mitchell (eds.), *How Persistent Low Returns Will Shape Saving and Retirement*. Oxford, UK: Oxford University Press, pp. 194–218.

Horneff, V., R. Maurer, and O. S. Mitchell (2018). "How Persistent Low Expected Returns Alter Optimal Life Cycle Saving, Investment, and Retirement Behavior," in R. Clark, R. Maurer, and O. S. Mitchell (eds.), *How Persistent Low Returns Will Shape Saving and Retirement*. Oxford, UK: Oxford University Press, pp. 119–31.

Ilmanen, A., and M. Rauseo (2018). "Intelligent Risk Taking: How to Secure Retirement in a Low Expected Return World," in R. Clark, R. Maurer, and O. S. Mitchell (eds.), *How Persistent Low Returns Will Shape Saving and Retirement*. Oxford, UK: Oxford University Press, pp. 81–98.

McKinsey & Co. (2016). 'Thriving in the New Abnormal: North American Asset Management,' *McKinsey & Co. Financial Services Practice Report*. Philadelphia, PA: McKinsey & Co.

Quinn, J. F., and K. E. Cahill (2018). "Challenges and Opportunities of Living and Working Longer," in R. Clark, R. Maurer, and O. S. Mitchell, (eds.), *How Persistent Low Returns Will Shape Saving and Retirement*. Oxford, UK: Oxford University Press, pp. 101–18.

Reilly, A., and R. Byrne (2018). "Investing for Retirement in a Low Returns Environment: Making the Right Decisions to Make the Money Last," in R. Clark, R. Maurer, and O. S. Mitchell (eds.), *How Persistent Low Returns Will Shape Saving and Retirement*. Oxford, UK: Oxford University Press, pp. 61–80.

Sonsino, Y. (2018). "Helping Employers Become Age-Ready," in R. Clark, R. Maurer, and O. S. Mitchell (eds.), *How Persistent Low Returns Will Shape Saving and Retirement*. Oxford, UK: Oxford University Press, pp. 165–72.

Wallick, D. W., D. B. Berkowitz, A. S. Clarke, K. J. DiCiurcio, and K. A. Stockton (2018). "Getting More from Less in Defined Benefit Plans: Three Levers for a Low-Return World," in R. Clark, R. Maurer, and O. S. Mitchell (eds.), *How Persistent Low Returns Will Shape Saving and Retirement*. Oxford, UK: Oxford University Press, pp. 44–60.

Part I

Origins and Consequences of the Persistent Low Return Environment

Chapter 2

Politics, Independence, and Retirees: Long-term Low Interest Rates at the US Federal Reserve

Peter Conti-Brown

President Donald Trump has frequently compared himself to one of his most important predecessors, Andrew Jackson, and has hung Jackson's portrait in the Oval Office. While Mr. Trump has not elaborated on the comparison, it is not difficult to draw the parallels. Old Hickory is perceived to be the father of populism, an irascible opponent to much of the prevailing political order of his day. Donald Trump sees himself the same way: as an outsider who challenged the existing hierarchy and won.[1]

There is a significant extra dimension to the comparison, though, that points to an important relationship in government that will far outlive the Trump presidency. Jackson was also the sworn enemy of the Second Bank of the United States, a quasi-private institution that functioned as the nation's central bank (as that term was understood at the time). As described in more detail below, different presidents can and do interact with central banking institutions in different ways. That interaction, though, tells us an enormous amount about the ways that interest-rate policies are politicized, and to what ends. This reality for the Federal Reserve (Fed) is no different in the 21st century than it was for the Bank of the United States in the 19th century.[2]

The fact that the Fed is now occupying a front-and-center role in the political arena is not a comfortable place for the central bankers who run it. Nevertheless, this role is not new. Since the global financial crisis of 2008, the Fed has rarely receded from the political maelstrom, for better or worse. This chapter charts this political terrain, focusing on a question that is as much economic as it is political: why are interest rates so low, and what does the Fed have to do with it? Whether the Fed dictates the national (and international) interest rate climate, or is merely a victim to secular economic trends in productivity is an ongoing debate, which I summarize but do not fully engage. Of more pressing interest is how the Fed is perceived politically, as combatant in that process. Low interest rates represent a profound political problem for the Fed. Not only do they arguably violate the Fed's often forgotten third mandate to maintain 'moderate long-term interest rates,' they also scramble the political constituencies that have normally defended the central bank against attempts at political interference. As a result, when political push comes to existential shove, the Fed's monetary policy actions since 2008 risk alienating another important group: pensioners and other retirees who count on higher interest rates for their economic security and who have historically been staunch defenders of an independent central bank.

The members of the Federal Reserve System are some of the best political infighters in Washington. They have survived extraordinary assaults on its independence and structure throughout the last century. Time and time again, the Fed has not only survived, but thrived.[3] But the challenges ahead will be different, and they will require something more than the Fed has done before.

In what follows, the first section discusses the nature of equilibrium interest rates and the Fed's (in)ability to influence them. I also show that the perception that the Fed can control real interest rates is not simply public misinformation; it is also written into law. The second section traces the history of the Fed's own self-description as an independent central bank designed precisely for the purpose of dictating higher interest rates than politicians would prefer. Long-term efforts to push this narrative have now come back to haunt the Fed as it continues to maintain independence while pursuing the central goal of keeping nominal interest rates at historic lows. The third section details the consequences of the 2016 election for low interest rates.

One note on the chapter's US-based focus: though the politics and history described below focus on the Fed, major central banks in other parts of the world are facing very similar dynamics. They have been billed as economically omniscient, but their tools for addressing the most pressing economic realities that affect retirees are limited.

As with so much else about the political environment, uncertainty clouds every informed discussion of the Fed's future—and the future path of interest rates—during the Trump administration and beyond. Yet there are also dynamics at play that could push nominal interest rates down, not up. The focus for academic, policy, and industry commentators will be on these political dynamics.

The Fed's Role in Determining Low Interest Rates and the Forgotten Third Mandate

The US Congress created the Federal Reserve System in 1913 after a century of national experimentation with nearly every aspect of banking and central banking. Today, the Fed has grown into something that its framers would not have predicted: it has become the regulator par excellence not only of the banking system, but also of the macroeconomy itself. It is, as former Fed Chair Paul Volcker once said, the 'only game in town' (Silber 2012: 201). This has led to the present moment, when the Fed has not only changed the way that banks are funded and regulated during and after financial crisis, but also how interest rates have been brought to historically low levels. Indeed, the Fed is now in an unusual position: while it has focused on fighting inflation and stabilizing employment, two of its statutory mandates, it has failed for just the second time in its modern history to deliver on its often forgotten third mandate: to maintain moderate long-term interest rates (see Figure 2.1).

Interest rates are not simply low: they are historically low. This is obviously true for short-term interest rates, which have hovered at or below the zero-lower bound in major economies since the Great Recession. But, as Figure 2.1 illustrates, this is part of a longer trend for short-term interest rates, too. This observation then prompts a new question: why?

This development is part of a longer-term trend that economist Mohamed El-Erian (2016) called the 'new normal,' coming out of the global financial crisis. Most economists (and certainly central bankers) will argue that the Fed has little to do with this phenomenon. The Fed has remarkable authority in

Figure 2.1. Ten-year Treasury constant maturity rate

Source: Board of Governors of the Federal Reserve System (2017).

controlling short-term nominal interest rates by deploying its balance sheets in a variety of different credit markets. But, as former Fed Chairman Ben Bernanke (2015: np) wrote, real interest rates—the rates most relevant for long-term investment decisions—'are determined by a wide range of economic factors, including prospects for economic growth—not by the Fed.'

The problem is that the Fed controls nominal interest rates and, usually, the nominal short-term interest rates at which banks lend to each other. By contrast, it has less control over what is often called the 'Wicksellian interest rate,' or the real interest rate consistent with full employment of labor and capital, named for Swedish economist Knut Wicksell (1936) who advanced the concept in 1898. The idea that the Fed is as much a victim of these trends as the rest of us stems from the idea that the factors determining the full deployment of labor and capital are not for the Fed to decide. Instead, these are a consequence of technological innovation, demographics, even culture, and certainly governmental fiscal policy, social policy, and the robustness of the financial system. In other words, the Fed as the monetary authority has one not-very-useful instrument, namely short-term nominal interest rates. This instrument cannot dictate the Wicksellian interest rate unilaterally; the best the Fed can do is nudge nominal interest rates toward its estimated Wicksellian rate layer. Indeed, once we focus on that real rate—that is, the interest rate minus inflation—the graph would look even worse. If this view is true, then again the question becomes: why?

One explanation comes from a Depression-era theory from Alvin Hansen (1938), one of the economists who first operationalized Keynesian macroeconomic theory. In the middle of the second of the two severe recessions of the 1930s, Hansen hypothesized that the equilibrium interest rate was so low not because of the sudden, idiosyncratic collapse of aggregate demand à la Keynesian theory, but because of something deeper. His analysis of the situation has gained influence lately, but mainly through summaries offered by others. Hansen's original perspective is worth citing in full:

> The business cycle was par excellence the problem of the nineteenth century. But the main problem of our times, and particularly in the United States, is the problem of full employment. Yet paradoxical as it may seem, the nineteenth century was little concerned with, and understood but dimly, the character of the business cycle. Indeed, so long as the problem of full employment was not pressing, it was not necessary to worry unduly about the temporary unemployment incident to the swings of the cycle. Not until the problem of full employment of our productive resources from the long-run, secular standpoint was upon us, were we compelled to give serious consideration to those factors and forces in our economy which tend to make business recoveries weak and anaemic and which tend to prolong and deepen the course of depressions. This is the essence of secular stagnation—sick recoveries which die in their infancy and depressions which feed on themselves and leave a hard and seemingly immovable core of unemployment.   (Hansen 1939: 4)

From Hansen's perspective, then, all recoveries would be weak because something fundamental had changed about the economy. It wasn't a problem of depression; it was a problem of productivity and demographics.

No economist has done more to bring Hansen's perspective back to the debate about the 'new normal' than Harvard economist Lawrence Summers. From his view, Hansen's theory was right but untimely: 'Hansen turned out to be completely wrong but completely wrong in a way that suggests that at some future point he could turn out to be right' (Summers 2016: 96). Today, then, the anemic recovery from the financial crisis of 2008 and the subsequent recession is what we should expect. Low Wicksellian rates are a more-or-less permanent feature of the landscape. Productivity, from this perspective, is a thing of the past.[4]

As far as economic theory goes, the idea of an equilibrium rate over which the Fed has little control is mainstream, even for critics of the Fed's monetary policies. The idea that we are in a period of secular stagnation is not.[5] Yet these debates miss a much more important point when we consider the Fed's role in determining the interest-rate environment. The question is not 'What is the relationship between the Fed and low interest rates?' but, instead, 'How does the public perceive the relationship between the Fed and low interest rates?'

The answer to the first question is the theoretical and empirical question that occupies economists and central bankers; the second is the question of paramount political importance for those who will control the Fed's future. And that second answer takes a very different view of interest rates that is widely accepted by the public, the result of a long-standing public education program by the Fed, extending over decades, that has taken firm root in law, political discourse, and culture. That view has made it difficult to sell the Fed's own efforts to disclaim responsibility for low interest rates.

Public perception of interest rates pays little attention to the distinctions between an equilibrium rate and the nominal rate, the latter of which the Fed does in fact control. The control mechanism has an obvious economic logic, as basic as a supply-and-demand graph from introductory economics. Here, the supply and demand are supply *of* and demand *for* short-term bank loans, a kind of good for which there is a market, just as there are markets for crude oil, pineapples, or squirrel traps. The price of money in these markets is the interest rate, here the Fed's federal funds rate. When the Fed makes money less available to banks to lend to each other, they will pay more for it, and interest rates will rise. When there is more money, people will pay less for it, and interest rates drop. While the difference between the federal funds effective rate and the federal funds target rate is actually more complicated than this simple explanation suggests, the basic reality is that the Fed can and does affect interest rates through open market operations similar to the process described above: by affecting the availability of money, the Fed changes the price of money.[6]

When the availability of resources controlled by the central bank dictates the value of interest rates, the price-theory of nominal interest rates is economically accurate. Nevertheless, it is not helpful for understanding the nature of the equilibrium rate. This difference may not matter much for economic theory, but confusion between the two is a ubiquitous feature of public discourse on the Fed, interest rates, and public accountability. At a 2013 hearing, for example, Republican Senator Bob Corker lambasted Federal Reserve Chairman Ben Bernanke on exactly this theory: the Fed's continued decision to keep interest rates at the zero-lower bound had 'thrown seniors under the bus.' People living on fixed income and depending on more robust interest rates, the Senator said, were run over by the Fed's monetary policies, apparently in service of policy oriented more toward younger generations.[7] Bernanke didn't appreciate the implication, but the idea that the Fed is responsible for the level of moderate long-term interest rates cannot be blamed on any given Senator. Rather, it is written in the Federal Reserve Act itself, in the Fed's 'mandate.'

The idea of a mandate for central banks is an old one, yet in the United States it found its way into the Federal Reserve Act only in 1977. At that point, the US Congress amended the Federal Reserve Act to give the Fed its marching orders. The revised statute is worth quoting in full, largely because it has become a classic in the Mark Twain sense: it is cited often, but never read. The 'mandate' requires:

> The Board of Governors of the Federal Reserve System and the Federal Open
> Market Committee shall maintain long run growth of the monetary and credit
> aggregates commensurate with the economy's long run potential to increase
> production, so as to promote effectively the goals of maximum employment,
> stable prices, and moderate long-term interest rates.   (12 U.S.C. 225a.)

When discussing what the Fed does, the discussion is almost always reduced to a 'dual mandate' of 'price stability' and 'maximum employment.' As Janet Yellen (2017: np) put it, '[n]early 40 years ago, the Congress set two main guideposts for that task—maximum employment and price stability. We refer to these assigned goals as our dual mandate.' But the statute was broader, as it included an important third mandate: 'to promote effectively the goal of . . . moderate long-term interest rates.'

By nearly any definition, the Fed is now failing at that charge. Interest rates at the zero-lower bound are not moderate, no matter how one defines 'moderate.' Again, most economists and most central bankers would say that it has no control over this factor. But the failure is important because, whether true or not, the Fed is perceived by its congressional masters as not only having that power, but having the legal duty to use it. When the legal authority is put in these terms, the relevant question for the Fed and its long-term interest rates is not whether the Fed can unilaterally raise rates.

Instead, the question is why does the public believe the Fed has this ability at all? To address that issue, we must turn to Fed history.

The Fed's Political Independence in History

Although the Fed's mandate was provided through a political system, the institution remains jealous of its prerogatives for determining how to pursue them.[8] In the important conceptualization offered by economists Guy Debelle and Stanley Fischer (1994), the Fed has 'instrument independence,' not 'goal independence.' To prevent the Fed's goals from becoming inordinately politicized, the bank relies on this instrument independence, a loose term that is frequently invoked but rarely explained. In economics, and to a lesser extent in political science, the concept of central bank independence has been so extensively studied as to earn its own acronym: CBI.[9] Alan Blinder (2004), an academic and former central banker, called the study of central bank independence a 'growth industry,' and the growth has only accelerated in the years since.

Although there are about as many definitions of central bank independence as there are authors who describe it, we can gather from these studies a rough consensus of what central bank independence means in reference to the Fed. The consensus goes something like this. Federal Reserve independence refers to the separation, by statute, of the central bankers (specifically the Fed chair) from the politicians (specifically the US President), for purposes of maintaining low inflation. The idea is that citizens in a democracy naturally prefer a prosperous economy. Politicians seek to please the population by giving that prosperity, or at least trying to take credit for it. But when there is no prosperity to be had, politicians will resort to supporting the economy artificially by running the printing presses to provide enough money and credit for all. The short-term result is re-election for the politicians. The long-term result is worthless money that wreaks havoc on our economic, social, and political institutions.

Several widely invoked metaphors of central banking come tumbling forth: in the Homeric epic, the *Odyssey*, when Odysseus (referred to in central banking circles by his Latin name Ulysses) ventured with his men close to the seductive and vexing Sirens, he devised a scheme to allow his men to guide their ship past their seduction in safety, while he experienced the short-term joys of hearing their songs (Elster 1977). Central bank independence is our 'Ulysses contract.' We write central banking laws that lash us (and our politicians) to the mast and stuff bees-wax in the ears of our central bankers. We enjoy the ride while the technocratic central bankers guide the ship of the economy to the land of prosperity and low inflation. (The public, by the way, represents the Sirens in this metaphor.)

The other commonly invoked metaphor is even more colorful. In the oft-repeated words of William McChesney Martin (1955), the longest serving Fed chair in history, the Fed is 'in the position of the chaperone who has ordered the punch bowl removed just when the party was really warming up.' The subjects of the metaphors differ across the millennia, but the idea is the same: the partygoers and Ulysses alike want something in the near term that their best selves know is bad for them in the long term. Central bank independence is the solution.

It is the last feature of the Ulysses/chaperone conception of independence that matters for our understanding of the Fed's 'new normal' of long-term low interest rates: the idea that the Fed can use technocratic expertise to accomplish its goal of price stability. This notion of Fed independence, and the reasons for it, are so entrenched in the academic and public imagination that deviations from this view present complications even in the Fed's own self-image, to say nothing of how the Fed is perceived externally. And now, when the Fed appears to be pursuing a policy of keeping interest rates *low* rather than raising them *high*, then the Ulysses/chaperone model starts to fail.

To understand this dynamic, and where it came from, we need to know more about why the Fed was created and how it changed over time. A conventional retelling of the Fed's history is that it was a response to the problem of JP Morgan's mortality. There was a financial panic in 1907, as there had been so many times throughout the 19th century, and, as he had before, Morgan—the famous head of a banking dynasty—had stepped in to save the day. Afterward, the public and members of Congress decided to do what they had failed to do before: create a central bank that would endure.[10]

The real story of the Fed's founding is much more complex than this. The time between the Panic of 1907 and the Federal Reserve Act of 1913 made a big difference to the shape the Fed ultimately took, including the strange relationship between the Federal Reserve Board and the 12 quasi-autonomous Federal Reserve Banks. But most important for understanding the current context of low interest rates was the political constituencies for having a central bank at all. Farmers and others likely to be chronically indebted were hostile to the idea of banker control over currency and its value; bankers, on the other hand, were not.

Our understanding of the structure of interest rates and central bank influence over interest rates was different, in large part because the world was different. When the Federal Reserve Act was first passed, the United States was on the gold standard and sought to gain access to international markets also on the gold standard (Broz 1997). As the Fed transitioned to playing a greater role in setting national and international macroeconomic conditions, the perception of its role changed, too.

Perhaps the greatest influence on the public perception of the Fed was William McChesney Martin, Jr., Fed Chairman from 1951 to 1970, and author of the 'chaperone' conception of the central bank role. Martin came to the Fed with a long familiarity with its operations, as his father was the Governor of the Federal Reserve Bank of St. Louis. The son had also worked as president of the New York Stock Exchange in the late 1930s, and then as president again of the Export–Import Bank. By 1951, he was the Assistant Secretary of the Treasury for monetary affairs in the Truman administration.[11]

It was an interesting time to be at the Treasury. The United States had recently discovered that the Soviets had successfully tested an atomic weapon, three years sooner than American estimates. Conflict on the Korean peninsula threatened to plunge the world once again into global war. Most importantly for understanding the Fed's political constraints, it was in intense conflict with the US Treasury. The Fed had been subsidizing US government securities since the beginning of World War II and was agitating to stop. The Treasury wanted the subsidy to continue and refused to budge.

Eventually, the conflict came to a head, but not until President Truman had summoned the Federal Open Market Committee to the Oval Office to berate it for the first and last time in history. With Martin as the Treasury's lead negotiator, the Fed and Treasury reached what came to be called the Fed–Treasury Accord of 1951. The Accord was a public announcement that the Federal Reserve and Treasury had agreed that the Treasury would no longer dictate to the Fed the interest rates that Treasury would expect the Fed to support in the public markets. For many, this is considered a 'major achievement' in American history (Meltzer 2003: 711). In fact, the Accord did not do much on its own: it was just a single-sentence announcement. Here it is in full:

> The Treasury and the Federal Reserve System have reached full accord with respect to debt management and monetary policies to be pursued in furthering their common purpose to assure the successful financing of the Government's requirements and, at the same time, to minimize monetization of the public debt.   (Board of Governors 1952).

All this statement says is that the Fed and Treasury agreed on the twin aims of 'successful financing of the Government's requirements' and the minimization of the 'monetization of the public debt.'

Probably as part of the Accord itself, Fed Chairman Thomas McCabe stepped down and Martin replaced him. But soon, Martin took a very different approach to his role and sought not only to balance those two goals: he also declared the Fed independent of the Treasury for purposes of determining monetary policy completely. President Truman, once Martin's patron, now looked at him very differently. On Martin's report, at their next meeting at an event at a New York City hotel, Truman had but one word to say to the affable Martin: 'Traitor!' (Bremner 2004: 91).

Given that so little was determined by the Accord itself, Martin had to use his own leadership to fill in the gaps. Martin accomplished this in various ways, but one of the most important was not via market intervention or political fighting, but by language. It is difficult to overstate Martin's love for metaphors: his public speeches are full of them. The chaperone language was not his only enduring image. He also stated that, 'lean against the winds of deflation or inflation, whichever way they are blowing.' He also argued that the economy was like a river: the Fed's aspiration was for money and credit to 'flow . . . like a stream. This stream or river is flowing through the fields of business and commerce. We don't want the water to overflow the banks of the stream, flooding and drowning what is in the fields. Neither do we want the stream to dry up, and leave the fields parched.'[12]

In practice, Martin was able to use this kind of language to thwart efforts to trim the Fed's sails or be bullied by politicians. After he had accepted one of Lyndon Johnson's infamous invitations to tour the President's Texas ranch at blistering speeds with Johnson driving recklessly, Martin took the opportunity to point out a large boulder interfering with the flow of the river on the property. Martin explained to Johnson that raising the discount rate was like removing that boulder: it would let credit, like water, run more smoothly. When Martin recounted the exchange to Fed staffers, they quickly corrected the Fed Chairman: that's not how discount rates work. Martin responded: 'Well, it did this time.'[13]

Another metaphor was the idea that the Fed could take away the punch bowl, and also decide who should be drinking and when. Central bankers' insistence on their ability to execute this strategy meant, in time, that there was a trust that the Fed would be able to resolve the time inconsistency problem very easily, and always in the direction of the uncomfortably higher interest rates. This conception stands in painful contrast to Bernanke's insistence on Wicksellian interest rates and the central bank's inability to dictate interest rates to the economy. Later historical developments in Fed history only added to the perception of omnipotence, including the fall of Arthur Burns and the rise of the Great Inflation, Paul Volcker and the skyrocketing interest rates that finally broke inflation's back, and Alan Greenspan as the 'maestro' economic tinkerer without peer.

The financial crisis of 2008 was another historical watershed for the Federal Reserve, for many reasons. First, the crisis brought the Fed front and center to the public's attention in largely unfavorable ways. Second, the idea that the Fed bailed out Wall Street through the extraordinary deployment of billions of dollars took root in the public's mind, and not favorably. In other words, the Fed's unconventional monetary policy actions in the aftermath of the crisis occurred when everyone was watching, which prompted a populist backlash not anticipated by Martin's conception of Fed independence. Instead of insisting that the Fed leave the punch bowl on the table, the populist protestors were *opposed* to low interest rates. The debtors who would benefit most from artificially low interest rates were either silent during the political debate, or they misunderstood the ramifications of the Fed's policies. So it was that Texas Governor and presidential contender Rick Perry in 2011 lambasted the Fed with violent imagery: 'Printing more money to play politics at this particular time in American history is almost . . . treasonous,' he said. 'I don't know what y'all would do to him in Iowa, but we would treat him pretty ugly down in Texas' (Zeleny and Calmes 2011: np).

The simultaneous depiction of the Fed as controlling interest rates and using them to abuse those who would require a higher return on their investments is, then, a deeply rooted one. My point is that the Fed itself was the author of this public idea and drove it deeply into the public psyche in the service of preserving its independence. Now that it requires public support for the *opposite* reasons, that support will be difficult to come by. The political alliances that have previously supported the Fed were built on a notion that does not apply when the equilibrium rate is low.

The Fed During the Trump Administration

Prior to the US presidential election of 2016, the prevailing view was that Donald Trump was too toxic to too many political constituencies to win the general election. In central banking circles, the debate about the equilibrium rate was focused on the question of secular stagnation, not on the inflationary pressures that fiscal policy can create.

What a difference a presidential election made! The election of 2016 was a defining moment for the Fed, with potent consequences for both real and nominal interest rates. For real interest rates, if the Trump administration adopts policies that change the underlying nature of the investment climate and the productive deployment of labor and capital, then the equilibrium rate could rise again. The equity markets, at least initially, treated the election as indicative of accelerated growth, with only modest increases in inflation expectations.

How nominal interest rates develop will be a more interesting dilemma. The Fed has accelerated its campaign to tighten interest rates, a process that began in December 2015. If the Fed's expectations are to be heeded—and to be clear, these projections have been chronically off-target—then we should expect to see a federal funds rate in the 3 percent range by 2019.[14] Yet many factors are at play. Not least is how the Fed will be reshaped during the Trump administration, since he has the opportunity to fill several vacancies on the board. Every president has the statutory and constitutional right to make these appointments and uses them to influence his agenda. Trump will be no different.[15]

Predicting President Trump's agenda is no easy matter, and the point of this chapter is not to stay rooted in the present but to articulate broader applications of political dynamics that will extend into the future. Even so, it is useful to think through how the Trump administration's approach to interest rate policies will influence Fed decision-making. In the past, presidents from both parties generally favored central bankers who lowered interest rates for reasons the Ulysses/chaperone conception of Fed independence anticipated: it is helpful to win elections and preserve legacies when the economy is booming, even if that boom is only on the back of cheap currency. Yet during the Obama administration, Republicans consistently criticized the Fed for these very low interest rates. It is unclear whether the Trump coalition will pursue a more hawkish monetary policy consistent with those 2009–2016 critiques, or favor presidential prerogatives, as has been historically true.

Appointments, though, are not the only mechanism that presidents have for influencing the Fed. The other mechanism, used throughout history, is to deploy the many non-legal mechanisms at a president's disposal to influence central bankers. President Trump's decision to appoint Jerome Powell to succeed Janet Yellen as Fed Chair may have reassured some that the Fed will continue to have its independence in determining monetary policy. But President Trump, like so many of his predecessors, may also develop strong ideas about the appropriate direction that interest rates will take. If the Fed engages in tightening interest rates to cool the economy, he may seek to impose political constraints on the Fed preventing it from moving too quickly. In that case, the Fed's nominal interest rates may undershoot the equilibrium rate—and in the process, cause an overheating economy to trigger inflation. If that occurs, it will in fact be the Fed—not the economy—that is keeping interest rates artificially low.

Conclusions

This chapter has argued that the Fed's status as 'chaperone' given independence by Congress for the purpose of constraining inflationary fiscal policy has backfired during times when the Fed has pursued the opposite tack. A Fed trying to keep the party from getting out of control as an omnipotent central banker is an image that has taken hold in the public imagination in a way that few if any governmental agencies can match. That is an altogether different image from a Fed trying to get a bunch of wallflowers to take tequila shots.

It is little wonder, given the decades-long effort to construct an inflation-fighting central bank, that this abrupt change has caused so much backlash. And it is not enough to claim that the public's misunderstanding on these issues reflects a burden that the public itself must correct. The law requires the Fed to pursue moderate long-term interest rates, in an almost always-forgotten third mandate. In any event, the reason the public believes the Fed is an inflation fighter is that the Fed and central bankers who work within it have been pushing this argument for decades.

Historically, this defense of the currency against inflation has put retirees as staunch defenders of an independent central bank. A world of low interest rates credited to the Fed removes this support. Few groups feel the effects of these rates more profoundly than those who depend on more robust interest rates for their economic security. As Wallick et al. in Chapter 4 of this volume have highlighted, the investment environment for low interest rates requires dramatic changes.

The Fed has become a victim of its own success. The Fed's ability to affect the equilibrium rate that reflects the fullest deployment of labor and capital is not absolute, nor even very strong at all. Moreover, its control over nominal interest rates is important but often exaggerated. Presidential administrations play a decisive role in determining how nominal and real interest rates interact, as well as how activist Fed policy and underlying economic realities intersect. Should a president make appointments or otherwise influence central banking policy to be more consistently accommodative than the equilibrium rate suggests, then inflation will be the consequence and the secular trend of low interest rates will become artificial, precisely as the Fed's critics have argued has been true for years. As we look to the future of monetary policy, the question about central banking control and chronic low interest rates will be as much political as it is economic.

Notes

1. For comparisons between Jackson and Trump, see Baker (2017).
2. For more on Jackson and the Second Bank of the United States, see Howe (2007).
3. For more on the Fed's political role, see Kaiser (2013). For the Fed's ability to gain authority after crisis, see Shull (2005).
4. For the deep historical perspective, see Gordon (2016).
5. For the strongest counterpoint to secular stagnation, see Hamilton et al. (2015).
6. This paragraph borrows from arguments made in Conti-Brown (2016: 134).
7. See Davidson (2013) for coverage of the hearing.

8. Drawn from Conti-Brown (2016: 2).
9. For a recent review of this extensive literature, see Fernández-Albertos (2015).
10. For more on this origin story, see Lowenstein (2015) and Bruner and Carr (2009).
11. Bremner (2004) is a superb biography of Martin.
12. Cited by Conti-Brown (2016: 47) from an interview in US News and World Report, February 11, 1955.
13. As recounted in Bremner (2004: 211).
14. For the Fed's projections, see https://www.federalreserve.gov/monetarypolicy/fomcprojtabl20161214.htm.
15. Chang (2003) provides an excellent overview of the dynamic between President, Congress, and the Fed at the appointment level.

References

Baker, P. (2017). 'Jackson and Trump: How Two Populists Compare.' *New York Times*, March 15.

Bernanke, B. S. (2015). 'Why Are Interest Rates So Low?' *Brookings Institution Blog*, March 30.

Blinder, A. (2004). *The Quiet Revolution: Central Banking Goes Modern*. New Haven, CT: Yale University Press.

Board of Governors of the Federal Reserve System (1952). *Thirty-Eighth Annual Report of the Board of Governors of the Federal Reserve System Covering Operations for the Year 1951*. Washington, DC.

Board of Governors of the Federal Reserve System (2017). '10-Year Treasury Constant Maturity Rate.' Washington, DC. https://fred.stlouisfed.org/series/DGS10.

Bremner, R. P. (2004). *Chairman of the Fed: William McChesney Martin Jr. and the Creation of the Modern American Financial System*. New Haven, CT: Yale University Press.

Broz, J. L. (1997). *The International Origins of the Federal Reserve System*. Ithaca, NY: Cornell University Press.

Bruner, R. F., and S. D. Carr (2009). *The Panic of 1907: Lessons Learned from the Market's Perfect Storm*. Hoboken, NJ: Wiley.

Chang, K. (2003). *Appointing Central Bankers: The Politics of Monetary Policy in the United States and the European Monetary Union*. Cambridge: Cambridge University Press.

Conti-Brown, P. (2016). *The Power and Independence of the Federal Reserve*. Princeton, NJ: Princeton University Press.

Davidson, P. (2013). 'Bernanke: Economy Still Needs Fed Stimulus.' *USA Today*, February 26.

Debelle, G., and S. Fischer (1994). 'How Independent Should a Central Bank Be?' Conference on Monetary Policy in a Low Inflation Regime, Federal Reserve Bank of Boston.

El-Erian, M. (2016). *The Only Game in Town: Central Banks, Instability, and Avoiding the Next Collapse*. New York: Random House.

Elster, J. (1977). 'Ulysses and the Sirens: A Theory of Imperfect Rationality.' *Social Science Information* 16(5): 469–526.

Fernández-Albertos, J. (2015). 'The Politics of Central Bank Independence.' *Annual Review of Political Science* 18(1): 217–37.

Gordon, Robert J. (2016). *The Rise and Fall of American Growth: The U.S. Standard of Living since the Civil War.* Princeton, NJ: Princeton University Press.

Hamilton, J. D., E. S. Harris, J. Hatzius, and K. D. West (2015). 'The Equilibrium Real Funds Rate: Past, Present, and Future.' University of California San Diego Working Paper. San Diego, CA: University of California San Diego.

Hansen, A. (1938). *Full Recovery or Stagnation?* New York: W.W. Norton.

Hansen, A. (1939). 'Economic Progress and Declining Population Growth.' *The American Economic Review* 29(1): 1–15.

Howe, D. W. (2007). *What Hath God Wrought: The Transformation of America, 1815–1848.* New York: Oxford University Press.

Kaiser, R. (2013). *Act of Congress: How America's Essential Institution Works, and How It Doesn't.* New York: Knopf.

Lowenstein, R. (2015). *America's Bank: The Epic Struggle to Create the Federal Reserve.* New York: Penguin Press.

Martin, W. M. (1955). 'Address before the New York Group of the Investment Bankers Association of America,' October 19. https://fraser.stlouisfed.org/files/docs/historical/martin/martin55_1019.pdf.

Meltzer, A. H. (2003). *A History of the Federal Reserve. Vol. 1, 1913–1951.* Chicago, IL: University of Chicago Press.

Shull, B. (2005). *America's Fourth Branch: The Federal Reserve's Unlikely Rise to Power and Influence.* New York: Praeger.

Silber, W. L. (2012). *Volcker: The Triumph of Persistence.* New York: Bloomsbury Press.

Summers, L. (2016). 'Secular Stagnation and Monetary Policy.' *Federal Reserve Bank of St. Louis Review* 98(2): 93–110.

Wallick, D. W., D. B. Berkowitz, A. S. Clarke, K. J. DiCiurcio, and K. A. Stockton (2018). "Getting More from Less in Defined Benefit Plans: Three Levers for a Low-Return World," in R. Clark, R. Maurer, and O. S. Mitchell (eds.), *How Persistent Low Returns Will Shape Saving and Retirement.* Oxford, UK: Oxford University Press, pp. 44–60.

Wicksell, K. (1936, first published 1898). *Interest and Prices: A Study of the Causes Regulating the Value of Money.* New York: Sentry Press.

Yellen, J. (2017). 'The Goals of Monetary Policy and How We Pursue Them.' Address before the Commonwealth Club, San Francisco, CA, January 18.

Zeleny, J., and J. Calmes (2011). 'Perry Links Federal Reserve Policies and Treason.' *New York Times*, August 16.

Chapter 3

Low Returns and Optimal Retirement Savings

David Blanchett, Michael Finke, and Wade Pfau

This chapter explores how lower expected returns affect optimal saving and spending during working years, retirement replacement rates, retirement lifestyles, and the cost of bequests. This is important because the prices of bonds and stocks are much higher than in the recent past, suggesting a greater likelihood that portfolio returns will fall below the assumptions commonly used to estimate retirement savings adequacy. Basing retirement planning recommendations on historical returns can provide a misleading picture about what individuals at present will need to do to smooth their lifestyles and fund successful retirements.

We estimate a simple life cycle model to illustrate how lower future asset returns will impact workers. Optimal lifetime spending is sensitive to expected rates of return. Workers will need to save significantly more to smooth spending and they will need to spend less before and after retirement. In a model that incorporates social security, taxes, expected longevity by earned lifetime income, and spending patterns in retirement we find that lower-income workers will need to save about 50 percent more if future asset returns resemble today's low yield environment, and higher-income workers will need to save as much as 100 percent more to retire at age 65. A reasonable alternative to facing a lower level of lifetime spending is delaying retirement.

Investments have Become More Expensive

Lower investment returns must be factored into how workers plan for retirement. Figure 3.1 compares the cost of buying $1,000 of income from a 10-year Treasury Bond, $1,000 of stock dividends, and $1,000 of total corporate earnings, during 20-year time periods beginning in 1955. The figure suggests that it is now more expensive to buy income from investments than in the past, and high asset prices have persisted for a long time. There were a few periods during the 20th century when bond yields fell to a rate similar to the near-zero yields of today, but these were generally caused

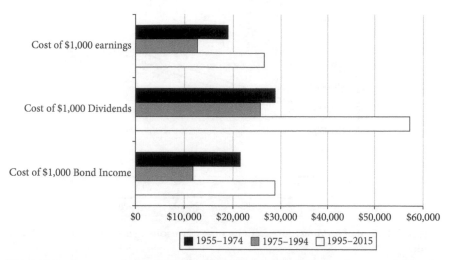

Figure 3.1. Average cost of purchasing $1,000 in ten-year Treasury income, dividends, and corporate earnings

Source: Federal Reserve of St. Louis (2017).

by a flight to safety during each of the World Wars and the Great Depression. The current era is unique in that low bond yields and high stock valuations are occurring in tandem for an extended period. This suggests an increase in demand for all financial assets.

Life Cycle Implications

A reasonable goal for most households is to save and spend in a manner that roughly smooths spending (as a proxy for one's standard of living) over a lifetime, giving rise to retirement saving. Forward-looking workers will understand that their lifestyles cannot be maintained by social security alone, so they will set money aside during their working years to avoid spending reductions in retirement.

Among other factors, decisions about optimal lifetime saving and spending depend on future salary, retirement length, and the investment rate of return. Given a salary profile and length of life, higher investment returns will allow a household to save less while accumulating the same wealth at retirement. For example, if a household earns $50,000 at age 25, expects 3 percent annual salary growth, and seeks $1 million at age 65, this can be achieved with a 10 percent annual savings rate when investments return 5 percent. But if returns are only 2 percent, the required savings rate increases to 18 percent to reach this goal.

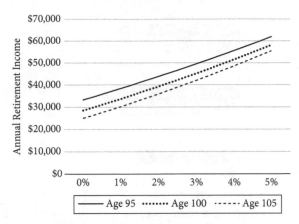

Figure 3.2. Cost of funding retirement income to various ages with a $1 million bond ladder

Source: Authors' calculations.

Lower returns will also reduce the income generated from $1 million from age 65. Figure 3.2 shows the amount of income a retiree can purchase using a bond ladder at real interest rates from 0 to 5 percent for a duration of 30 years (until age 95), 35 years (to age 100), and 40 years (to age 105). Sustainable income falls from $61,954 to only $38,364 as rates fall from 5 percent to 1 percent. Extending the ladder to age 100 or 105 not only reduces the income that can be withdrawn each year at 5 percent ($58,164 and $55,503), but also increases the income spread compared to a 1 percent expected return ($33,667 and $30,154). Longer retirements are particularly hard hit by lower asset returns.

Figure 3.3 shows how optimal spending levels are reduced with lower rates of return, and the varying impact of asset returns on the cost of funding a legacy goal. Because workers need fewer dollars today to fund a dollar of spending in the future, higher rates of return allow a saver to spend more before and after retirement. Although the difference between a 6 percent and a 4 percent real rate of return appears modest, this two-percentage-point drop in returns results in a 9.1 percent decrease in lifetime spending (from $46,938 to $42,653) with no bequest and an 11.6 percent decrease in lifetime spending (from $46,008 to $40,572) with a $500,000 bequest. If real lifetime rates fell to 2 percent, lifetime spending would drop by 22.2 percent ($36,538) compared to a 6 percent real rate of return and by 34 percent ($32,195) with a $500,000 bequest. Low lifetime real rates of return will have a significantly larger impact on the spending of households that hope to leave a bequest.

Income replacement rates at retirement also fall with lower expected returns if the retiree seeks to smooth his lifetime standard of living (see

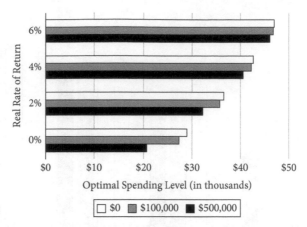

Figure 3.3. Optimal spending by expected real portfolio return and legacy goal

Note: Calculations assume a 30-year career followed by a 30-year retirement, a starting salary of $50,000, and real salary growth of 1 percent. Rates of return are defined in real terms, and retirement spending adjusts for inflation. The legacy goal reflects the value of investment assets targeted to remain at the end of retirement.

Source: Authors' calculations.

Figure 3.4). Planners therefore should consider the need to adjust replacement rates downward if they anticipate a low return environment during the retirement planning process. While optimal replacement rates at a 6 percent real portfolio return are near the 70 percent replacement rate rule of thumb, a 2 percent real portfolio return will result in an optimal replacement rate of about 55 percent when there is no bequest motive. At a 0 percent real portfolio return, the optimal replacement rate is a bit above 40 percent. With a legacy goal of $500,000, the optimal replacement rate falls further to 31 percent.

Finally, a perhaps counterintuitive result of our life cycle simulations in a low-return environment is that households will need to accumulate more wealth by the time they retire in order to maintain even a lower standard of living in retirement—particularly if they hope to leave a legacy. At a 2 percent expected real rate of portfolio return, the household must save just over $1 million by retirement with a $500,000 legacy goal, while a household expecting a 6 percent real rate of return will need to save just over $750,000. The amount of savings required in a low return environment as shown in Figure 3.5 (the difference between income and spending) needs to be much higher to fund a larger nest egg in order to pay for a more expensive retirement. As noted, the amount that the household can spend each year in this more expensive retirement is also more modest.

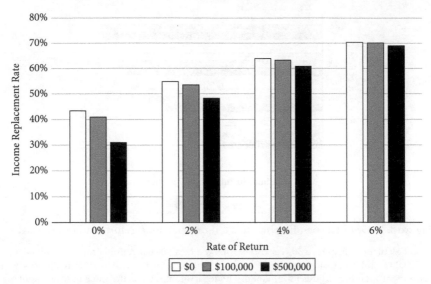

Figure 3.4. Income replacement rates and legacy goal

Note: Calculations assume a 30-year career followed by a 30-year retirement, a starting salary of $50,000, and real salary growth of 1 percent. Rates of return are defined in real terms, and retirement spending adjusts for inflation. The legacy goal reflects the value of investment assets targeted to remain at the end of retirement.

Source: Authors' calculations.

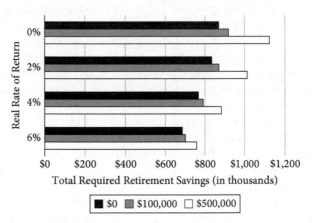

Figure 3.5. Total savings required to fund lifetime spending goal at retirement by legacy goal

Note: Calculations assume a 30-year career followed by a 30-year retirement, a starting salary of $50,000, and real salary growth of 1 percent. Rates of return are defined in real terms, and retirement spending adjusts for inflation. The legacy goal reflects the value of investment assets targeted to remain at the end of retirement.

Source: Authors' calculations.

What is a reasonable portfolio return assumption? From the investor's perspective, the choice should be net of inflation, investment expenses, asset management fees, and taxes. Real interest rates can be found using the yield curve for Treasury Inflation-protected Securities (TIPS). With a 1 percent rate and longer-term maturities, investment and asset management fees may result in negative real returns. Expected real equity returns may be in the range of perhaps 2–4 percent net of asset fees and inflation. It is reasonable to evaluate the planning consequences of a future 0 percent to 2 percent real future portfolio return.

Changes in Longevity

While the length of the retirement life cycle stage is unknown at the time of retirement, the cost of funding an income stream rises as expected longevity rises. A longer lifetime gives workers three choices. They can retire later; they can retire at the same age as yesterday's retiree and spend less; or they can retire at the same age and accept a greater risk of outliving assets while maintaining the same lifestyle. None of these choices results in a better retirement than the high return environment would.

Life expectancies for Americans who reach the age of 65 rose significantly during the twentieth century. In addition, higher-income earners are living longer than lower earners, as indicated in Figure 3.6. This relatively recent trend (Chetty et al. 2016) in which higher-earning Americans are seeing the largest improvements in longevity raises the cost of retirement for those who

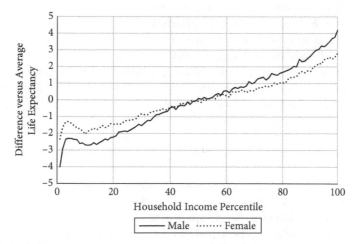

Figure 3.6. Differences in life expectancies by household income for a 65-year-old man and woman

Source: Human Longevity Project (2017).

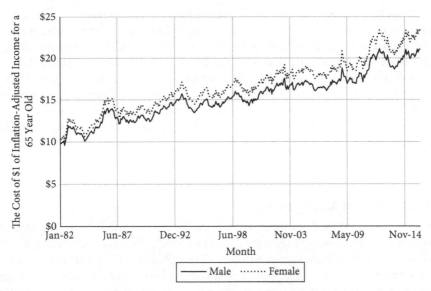

Figure 3.7. The cost of buying $1 in real annuity income at age 65 over time

Source: Blanchett et al. (2017).

rely the most on savings to maintain their spending in retirement. Since social security provides a larger income replacement rate for lower-income workers, increases in longevity raise the cost of retirement for those who need to replace the largest portion of their retirement income with savings.

The simultaneous improvement in longevity coupled with the decline in real interest rates on bonds raise the cost of buying an annuitized income stream in retirement. Figure 3.7 reports the cost of buying $1 in lifetime income via an inflation-adjusted annuity using mortality-weighted net present value of cash flows. Using historical mortality tables from the Social Security Administration (2015), historical bond Treasury yields from the Federal Reserve Bank of St. Louis (2017), and historical implied inflation estimates from the Federal Reserve Bank of Cleveland (2017), we calculate the cost of buying safe real income between 1982 and 2015. Observed annuity payouts offered by annuity companies differ slightly, but they are very similar to the prices of annuities using data from Immediateannuities. com (2017).

Our results show that rising longevity and falling real interest rates have doubled the cost of buying safe income over the last 35 years. In other words, a retiree today who hopes to fund expenses through safe investments will need to save twice as much, all else equal, if he or she expects to retire at age 65.

It may be tempting for retirees to avoid annuitizing wealth at retirement when the cost of buying safe income is so high. In reality, annuitizing safe investments becomes even more important when interest rates are low. This is because building a bond ladder, an alternative to annuitization, is also more expensive when interest rates are low. But the difference between the cost of buying a bond ladder to fund spending, particularly spending in old age, and buying income through an annuity widens as interest rates fall. In other words, the mortality credit that allows a retiree to spend a higher percentage of his or her income than he or she could receive from a bond ladder becomes relatively more important when interest rates are low.

Estimated Increases in Optimal Savings Rates

Many assumptions in this life cycle model are unrealistic. We have not included Social Security income, which provides an income cushion that softens the blow of low asset returns. We also omit differences in taxation before and after retirement, and we do not consider the natural decrease in spending that most retirees experience as their physical and cognitive abilities decline in old age.

To address these complexities, we have built a model to estimate the required savings rate needed to fund a spending amount after tax that smooths consumption immediately after retirement and then maintains a typical retiree's subsequent declining spending path (Blanchett and Idzorek 2015). It also incorporates the impact of progressive taxation at different levels of income before and after retirement, and it estimates the amount of Social Security income that a retiree at different levels of income can expect to receive. We assume that all savings are pre-tax (e.g., in a Traditional 401(k) or IRA). A more detailed description of assumptions is provided in the Appendix.

In line with the observed decline in real spending that occurs during retirement (Blanchett 2014), we assume that real spending needs fall each year in retirement. Earnings paths are based on empirically observed changes in pay by age and level of income. We also assume that the amount of annual savings rises with income over the life cycle. Since longevity is expected to improve for future workers, we assume younger workers will have to fund more years of spending in retirement if they retire at a given age. Since higher-income workers will also live longer, we assume that higher earners will need to fund more years of retirement spending.

American retirees rarely annuitize their savings to provide guaranteed income throughout retirement, and hence, a certain percentage of retirees will outlive their savings. This requires us to establish an acceptable probability of depleting savings during retirement in order to generate a lifetime spending path. Our simulations set this probability at 20 percent. A lower probability would result in higher estimated savings rates. Mortality rates for single households are based on gender-neutral mortality, while mortality rates for a married household assume one male and one female of the same age.

Asset returns are estimated using an autoregressive model (Blanchett et al. 2013), calibrated so that one return series approximates the historical averages; it includes three additional scenarios of low, medium, and high expected returns. The high scenario has returns similar to long-term averages but incorporates today's low bond yields. We also include a 50 bp portfolio fee, so workers will need to save more than our estimates in order to pay higher fees on savings.

Worker's portfolios are assumed to decrease the fraction of risky assets nearing retirement. The allocation is based on the Morningstar Moderate Lifetime Index glide path, which takes into account the present value of human capital as a bond-like asset to generate optimal asset allocations over the life cycle (Morningstar 2015).

We estimate savings rates for scenarios that include low, moderate, and historical asset returns. In the low and moderate simulations, bond yields begin at a 2 percent real rate of return. In the low return scenario, the mean real return starts at 2 percent and follows a random distribution that rises to 3.5 percent at the 75th percentile and 5.25 percent at the 95th percentile (or falls to 1 percent at the 5th percentile). In the moderate return scenario, the real return rises to 4 percent on average. Since rates of return on long-duration corporate securities are currently below the mean expectations in the low return scenario, our projected saving rates using these rates of returns may underestimate the saving needed if the low return environment persists.

Results

Table 3.1 provides results for workers at various age and income levels who intend to retire at age 65. Optimal saving rates using historical data for joint households who start saving at age 25 are between 4.3 percent for low earners ($25,000), up to 9 percent for high earners ($250,000), and between 6.8 percent and 8.8 percent for singles. Higher-income households must save more because Social Security replaces a smaller percentage of income and because of progressive taxation.

We assume moderate returns increase the optimal saving rate by 63 percent, to 7.0 percent for couples with $25,000 of household income, and by 82 percent, to a 16.4 percent savings rate for couples earning $250,000. For most higher-income workers, a persistent low return environment results in workers optimally contributing up to the limit of their employer-sponsored retirement contributions even if they begin saving at a

TABLE 3.1 Target total pre-tax savings rates for various households just starting to save for retirement

25 Years Old

		Single Household					Joint Household		
		Returns					Returns		
		Historical	Low	Mid			Historical	Low	Mid
Household	$25	6.8	11.3	9.0	Household	$25	4.3	7.0	5.7
Income	$50	8.1	14.2	11.2	Income	$50	6.4	10.9	8.6
($0,000s)	$100	8.2	14.9	11.4	($0,000s)	$100	6.9	12.5	9.7
	$150	8.8	15.9	12.1		$150	8.0	14.2	11.2
	$200	9.0	16.4	12.7		$200	8.7	15.6	12.0
	$250	9.3	16.8	13.0		$250	9.0	16.4	12.7

30 Years Old

		Single Household					Joint Household		
		Returns					Returns		
		Historical	Low	Mid			Historical	Low	Mid
Household	$25	7.4	12.2	9.9	Household	$25	4.2	6.6	5.5
Income	$50	9.9	17.0	13.5	Income	$50	7.2	12.1	9.6
($0,000s)	$100	10.1	17.6	14.0	($0,000s)	$100	8.5	14.3	11.5
	$150	11.0	18.7	14.6		$150	9.6	16.9	13.2
	$200	11.4	19.2	15.4		$200	10.6	18.1	14.2
	$250	11.7	19.5	15.7		$250	11.3	18.8	15.0

35 Years Old

		Single Household					Joint Household		
		Returns					Returns		
		Historical	Low	Mid			Historical	Low	Mid
Household	$25	8.9	13.6	11.3	Household	$25	4.2	6.3	5.0
Income	$50	12.1	18.1	15.8	Income	$50	8.6	13.1	11.1
($0,000s)	$100	12.5	20.4	17.1	($0,000s)	$100	10.0	16.8	13.4
	$150	13.2	22.2	17.8		$150	11.8	19.0	15.4
	$200	13.9	23.7	18.4		$200	12.8	21.1	17.4
	$250	14.3	24.1	18.8		$250	13.7	23.5	18.3

40 Years Old

		Single Household					Joint Household		
		Returns					Returns		
		Historical	Low	Mid			Historical	Low	Mid
Household	$25	10.4	14.8	12.8	Household	$25	4.3	6.3	4.9
Income	$50	13.9	19.4	17.5	Income	$50	9.4	12.4	11.2
($0,000s)	$100	16.5	25.6	20.4	($0,000s)	$100	12.6	19.0	16.5
	$150	17.6	26.4	22.8		$150	14.5	23.8	18.6
	$200	18.1	27.3	24.3		$200	16.4	25.5	20.1
	$250	18.5	27.5	24.8		$250	17.6	26.4	22.8

Source: Blanchett et al. (2017).

Table 3.2 Impact of retirement ages on target total pre-tax savings rates for a 35-year-old (%)

		Retire at Age 60							
		Single Household					Joint Household		
		Returns					Returns		
		Low	Mid	Historical			Low	Mid	Historical
Household	$25	21.7	17.8	14.1	Household	$25	18.3	14.9	12.0
Income	$50	24.6	19.1	16.9	Income	$50	21.4	18.2	15.0
($0,000s)	$100	25.9	20.7	16.3	($0,000s)	$100	24.8	19.2	15.0
	$150	25.8	20.1	16.2		$150	25.6	19.6	15.5
	$200	25.9	20.5	16.3		$200	25.9	19.9	16.1
	$250	25.9	20.7	16.4		$250	26.0	20.5	16.4

		Retire at Age 65							
		Single Household					Joint Household		
		Returns					Returns		
		Low	Mid	Historical			Low	Mid	Historical
Household	$25	13.6	11.3	9.1	Household	$25	6.3	5.0	4.3
Income	$50	18.1	15.8	12.3	Income	$50	13.1	11.1	8.9
($0,000s)	$100	20.4	17.1	13.2	($0,000s)	$100	16.8	13.4	10.7
	$150	22.2	17.8	13.8		$150	19.0	15.4	12.1
	$200	23.7	18.4	14.3		$200	21.1	17.4	13.4
	$250	24.1	18.8	14.8		$250	23.5	18.3	14.2

		Retire at Age 60							
		Single Household					Joint Household		
		Returns					Returns		
		Low	Mid	Historical			Low	Mid	Historical
Household	$25	6.2	4.8	4.2	Household	$25	0.0	0.0	0.0
Income	$50	12.7	10.6	8.7	Income	$50	3.8	2.8	2.0
($0,000s)	$100	15.9	12.8	10.3	($0,000s)	$100	9.1	7.4	6.3
	$150	18.3	14.7	11.7		$150	13.8	11.3	9.1
	$200	19.8	16.6	12.8		$200	17.2	13.8	11.1
	$250	21.4	17.6	13.6		$250	18.7	15.4	12.2

Source: Blanchett et al. (2017).

young age. Workers relying on historical returns to estimate optimal savings would believe that they needed to save much less than is needed to preserve their lifestyle after retirement.

The increase in saving needed to fund retirement is even more dramatic if households begin saving for retirement at ages 35 or 40. Now optimal saving rates rise to 24.1 percent, in the low return simulation, versus 14.3 percent using historical returns for a single worker who begins saving at age 35. If the household waits until age 40, the optimal savings rate rises to 27.5 percent. Even in a moderate return scenario, optimal savings rates are 24.8 percent for a single household and 22.8 percent for a couple. Both single and joint households who use historical asset returns to project optimal savings rates would save near the employee contribution limit for those with incomes of $100,000. At lower interest rates, this amount of saving is not nearly enough to sustain a lifestyle for those retiring at age 65.

Fortunately, most workers are able to defer retirement to a later age. This allows them to save less during their working years, resulting in an improved lifestyle both before and after retirement. Despite deferring retirement for a few years, increases in longevity will not necessarily result in fewer years spent in retirement. For this reason, a reasonable alternative is to delay retirement since doing so increases the number of years of savings (and asset growth), reduces expected longevity, and increases Social Security income. Table 3.2 shows how optimal savings can be reduced (or lifestyle today can be improved) by delaying retirement for a household that begins to save at age 35.

A couple earning $250,000 could reduce its saving rate from 26 to 18.7 percent if it deferred retirement from age 60 to 70. The benefits of deferring retirement are even greater in a low return environment. A couple using historical rates would need to save 16.4 percent of income to retire at age 60, versus 12.2 percent if it retired at age 70. Workers who are shown realistic projections of lower expected returns may be more likely to choose a later retirement date, while those who project their retirement savings using historical returns may falsely believe that modest savings rates will allow them to retire at age 65.

Conclusion

In recent decades, prices for stocks and bonds have risen well above their historical averages. Higher asset prices imply lower expected future asset returns, so workers who rely on historical asset returns to project optimal retirement savings are at risk of unexpected shortfalls.[1] Improvements in longevity have also increased the cost of retiring at a given age. Workers, employers, and policymakers who rely on historical asset returns to make saving recommendations may fail to recognize how sensitive optimal savings rates are to persistent low investment returns. Our simple life cycle framework suggests that saving rates would need to rise by roughly two-thirds for most Americans given persistent low returns. Also, higher-income workers are most at risk of under-saving if they use historical asset return projections.

Appendix: Methodology and Data Details

We build on the model of Blanchett and Idzorek (2015) in our analysis.

Retirement income goal. Our model assumes that the individual seeks to maintain his or her level of after-tax (i.e., take-home) pay during retirement, compared to his or her after-tax income immediately before retirement. Retirement is assumed to commence at age 65.[2]

Change in annual retirement income need. Many retirement income models assume that retiree consumption (i.e., the annual retirement income need) increases annually with inflation throughout retirement (i.e., constant real spending), yet Blanchett (2014), among others, suggest that actual retiree spending need not increase by inflation throughout retirement. Our model assumes that retirees tend to decrease spending in retirement in real terms, although the relationship varies by the total level of household spending. In particular, we assume that the annual retirement spending need changes (ΔAS) during retirement for a given age (Age) and for a given target spending level ($SpendTar$) as follows where the maximum annual real change is +1 percent and the minimum annual real change is −1 percent:

$$\Delta AS = 0.00008(Age^2) - (0.0125 * Age) - 0.0066 \ln(SpendTar) + 54.6\% \tag{A1}$$

Figure 3A.1 shows how the real retirement income need changes for three target spending levels: $25,000, $50,000, and $100,000 from ages 65 to 100.

Income growth model. To trace workers' earnings over the life cycle, we have estimated regressions using data from the IPUMS-CPS (Flood et al. 2015). To be included in the analysis, individuals had to be coded as employed, working at least 20 hours a week in all jobs, and have annual total wage compensation of at least $5,000.[3]

It is assumed that an individual in a given earnings percentile (e.g., the 15th percentile) remains in that percentile for his or her entire working career (see Figure 3A.2).

Savings growth model. A common assumption in retirement planning models is that deferral rates remain constant as the individual ages. Nevertheless, this does not track actual investor behavior. Our research suggests that a more realistic accrual path has saving rates increase by approximately 25 percent over 10 years. For example, a 35-year-old saving 10 percent of pay would be assumed to be saving 12.27 percent at age 45, but only 1.56 percent by age 55.

Retirement period. The base mortality table used for this analysis is the Social Security Administration 2013 Periodic Life Table (Social Security

Administration 2015). Mortality rates in the future are assumed to decline based on the G2 projection scale in the Society of Actuaries 2012 Individual Annuity Mortality Table (Society of Actuaries 2012). We further adjust mortality rates by a constant factor so that life expectancies are allowed to vary by income level.

Returns model. Three types of series were created for this analysis: bonds, stocks, and inflation. For bond returns, we first select an initial bond yield (i.e., seed value) for the simulation. This is the bond yield at the beginning of the retirement simulation based approximately on 10-year US bonds. For simulation purposes, the historical yield seed is assumed to be 5 percent.

Yields for subsequent years are based on equation (1.1), where ϵ_{Yld} is an independent white noise that follows a normal distribution with a mean of 0 and a standard deviation of 1.25 percent:

$$Yld_t = \alpha + \beta_1 Yld_{t-1} + \beta_2 Yld_{t-1}{}^2 + \epsilon_Y \qquad [1.1]$$

The resulting annual bond yield (Yld_t) is assumed to be bounded between 1.0 and 10.0 percent.[4]

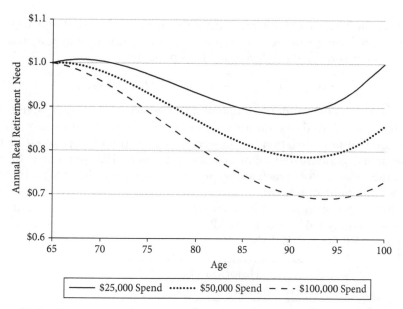

Figure 3A.1. The Spending Smile: lifetime real income target for various spending levels

Source: Blanchett (2014).

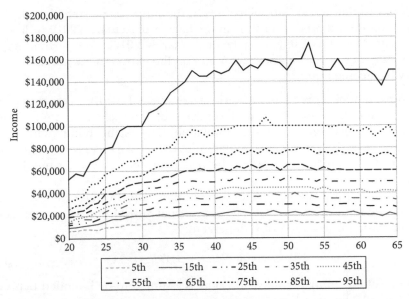

Figure 3A.2. Earnings curves at various income percentiles

Source: Bureau of Labor Statistics (2015).

After the bond yield for a given year is determined, the bond return (r_{bond}) is estimated using equation (1.2), where ϵ_{bond} is assumed to have a mean of 0.0 percent and standard deviation of 1.5 percent:

$$r_{bond} = Yld_{t-1} + -8.0(Yld_t - Yld_{t-1}) + \epsilon_{bond} \qquad [1.2]$$

The 1.5 percent standard deviation for the error term (ϵ_b) is not the assumed standard deviation for the asset class (bonds, in this case); rather it is the standard deviation for the errors around the regression estimates. The actual standard deviation of bond returns of 10.0 percent is higher because other factors (such as the yield and the change in yield) affect the actual variability of returns.

The stock return model is based on the yield for a given year plus the assumed equity risk premium (ERP). Therefore, we assume the following levels of ERP for the analysis:

	Historical	Low	Mid	High
ERP	5.5%	3.5%	4.5%	5.5%

Stock returns each year are based on equation (1.3), where ϵ_{stock} is assumed to have a mean of 5 percent and standard deviation of 20 percent, where Yld_t is the average yield for all years in that scenario:

$$r_{stocks,t} = \frac{\text{—}}{Yld_t} + \epsilon_{stocks} \qquad [1.3]$$

The inflation model is based on the loose historical relation between bond yields and inflation and is depicted in equation (1.4), where ϵ_i is an independent white noise term that follows a standard normal distribution with a mean of zero and a standard deviation of 0.5 percent:

$$r_i = 0.6\% + \ + 0.5 Yld_{t-1} + \epsilon_i \qquad [1.4]$$

Additional structure. Social Security retirement benefits are estimated based on the highest assumed average 35 years of earnings for each simulated participant. Social Security retirement benefits are estimated using the 2015 bend points (bps) and assumed to commence at age 65 on retirement.

The required level of retirement savings is determined using a solver routine, which determines the amount of savings or balance required to achieve an 80 percent probability of success during retirement.[5]

For simplicity, our model assumes that all savings are Roth contributions. For some scenarios, the individual is unlikely to have accounts sufficient to fund the Roth (e.g., if he or she needs to save $50,000). Portfolio allocations follow the Morningstar Moderate Lifetime Index glide path. The portfolio fee is 50 bps.

Notes

1. For a model which endogenizes retirement, work, and saving in a low return environment, see Horneff et al.'s Chapter 8 of this volume.
2. Alternative replacement levels are explored by Aon Consulting (2008) and Blanchett et al. (2013), among others.
3. The income definition is per individual (not household) and it only includes wage income (i.e., it excludes non-wage income such as pension benefits).
4. The coefficients vary by model type, as below:

	Historical	Low	Mid	High
a	0.25%	0.30%	0.30%	0.40%
β_1	0.95	0.55	0.65	0.50
β_2	0.00	0.50	0.50	0.65

5. While 80 percent may seem like a relatively aggressive estimate (e.g., some researchers use probability-of-success metrics that exceed 95 percent), it is important to look at the combined impact of the assumptions, and not to focus on a single assumption in isolation. For example, two of the most important assumptions when

estimating the cost of retirement are the assumed length of retirement and the target safety level (i.e., the target probability of success). Since the length of retirement period is relatively conservative (i.e., much longer than true life expectancy) the target success level need not be as conservative (e.g., it is possible to target an 80 percent chance of success versus a 95 percent chance of success). It is also important not to be too conservative with respect to assumptions (e.g., assuming a 99 percent probability of success), given the potential impact on consumption during retirement. After all, dying at an advanced age with a major portion of savings untouched is another form of retirement 'failure' (except, of course, in the case of a planned bequest).

References

Aon Consulting (2008). 'Replacement Ratio Study: A Measurement Tool for Retirement Planning.' Aon Consulting White Paper. London, UK: Aon Consulting.

Blanchett, D. M. (2014). 'Exploring the Retirement Consumption Puzzle.' *Journal of Financial Planning* 27(5): 34–42.

Blanchett, D. M., M. Finke, and W. D. Pfau (2013). 'Low Bond Yields and Safe Portfolio Withdrawal Rates.' *Journal of Wealth Management* 16(2): 55–62.

Blanchett, D. M., M. Finke, and W. D. Pfau (2017). 'Planning for a More Expensive Retirement.' *Journal of Financial Planning* 30(3): 42–51.

Blanchett, D. M., and T. Idzorek (2015). 'The Retirement Plan Effectiveness Score: A Target Balance-Based Measurement and Monitoring System.' Morningstar White Paper. Chicago, IL: Morningstar.

Bureau of Labor Statistics (2015). Current Population Survey—2015. Washington, DC: BLS. https://www.bls.gov/cps/cps_over.htm

Chetty, R., M. Stepner, S. Abraham, S. Lin, B. Scuderi, N. Turner, A. Bergeron, and D. Cutler (2016). 'The Association between Income and Life Expectancy in the United States, 2001–2014.' *Journal of the American Medical Association* 315: 1750–66.

Federal Reserve Bank of Cleveland (2017). *Inflation Expectations: Historical Data.* Cleveland, OH: Federal Reserve Bank of Cleveland. https://www.clevelandfed. org/~/media/content/our%20research/indicators%20and%20data/inflation% 20expectations/ie%2020170714/ie%2020170714%20xls.xls?la=en

Federal Reserve Bank of St. Louis (2017). *Economic Data Series.* St. Louis, MO: Federal Reserve Bank of St. Louis. https://fred.stlouisfed.org

Flood, S., M. King, S. Ruggles, and J. R. Warren (2015). "Integrated Public Use Microdata Series, Current Population Survey: Version 5.0." Minneapolis, MN: University of Minnesota. https://doi.org/10.18128/D030.V5.0.

Horneff, V., R. Maurer, and O. S. Mitchell (2018). "How Persistent Low Expected Returns Alter Optimal Life Cycle Saving, Investment, and Retirement Behavior," in R. Clark, R. Maurer, and O. S. Mitchell (eds.), *How Persistent Low Returns Will Shape Saving and Retirement.* Oxford, UK: Oxford University Press, pp. 119–31.

Human Longevity Project (2017). *Human Longevity, Inc.* http://www.humanlongevity. com/

Immediateannuities.com (2017). Income Annuity Quote Calculator, (updated August 29, 2017) https://www.immediateannuities.com/

Morningstar (2015). 'Construction Rules for Morningstar Asset Allocation Index Family.' Morningstar Methodology Paper Version 1.2. Chicago, IL: Morning Star.

Social Security Administration (2015). *The 2015 OASDI Trustees Report: Period Life Expectancy*. Washington, DC: SSA. https://www.ssa.gov/oact/tr/2015/lr5a3.html

Society of Actuaries (2012). *2012 Individual Annuity Reserving Report & Table*. Washington, DC: SOA. https://www.soa.org/experience-studies/2011/2012-ind-annuity-reserving-rpt/

Chapter 4

Getting More from Less in Defined Benefit Plans: Three Levers for a Low-Return World

Daniel W. Wallick, Daniel B. Berkowitz, Andrew S. Clarke, Kevin J. DiCiurcio, and Kimberly A. Stockton

As fixed income yields hover near historic lows, defined benefit (DB) pension plan sponsors must grapple with a rise in the present value of their plan liabilities and a fall in prospective investment returns. Our asset class projections illustrate the change. From 1926 through 2016, a portfolio with a 60 percent allocation to global equities and 40 percent to global fixed income generated an annualized real return of 5.5 percent. For the ten years through 2026, we estimate that the median return for the same portfolio will be about two percentage points lower, as illustrated in Table 4.1.

The prospect of lower returns has reshaped retirement plan sponsor expectations. In 2014, 42 percent of corporate DB plans surveyed by Stockton (2016) projected median long-term returns of more than 7 percent.[1] In 2015, only 31 percent expected returns of more than 7 percent.[2] Even as expected returns decline, most plans are underfunded. J.P. Morgan (2015) estimates that DB plans sponsored by companies in the Russell 3000 Index have an aggregate funded ratio of 80.5 percent. The present value of every dollar in pension obligations, in other words, is backed by about 80 cents in assets. Public sector plans face even greater challenges. Aggregate assets in the largest public plans, according to actuary and benefits consultant Milliman, equaled an estimated 69.8 percent of total plan liabilities as of 2016. Novy-Marx and Rauh (2014) explore the funding shortfall through another lens, estimating that state and local pension plans would need to increase contributions over the next 30 years by 2.5 times to fund legacy liabilities and future service accruals.

This chapter examines three levers that plan sponsors can use to improve their funding levels in a lower-return future. Sponsors can either increase contributions, reduce costs, or increase risk. While we explore these levers in the context of a total return investment strategy, we typically encourage well-funded corporate DB plans to adopt a liability-driven investment (LDI)

TABLE 4.1 Future returns may not look like those from the past: Implications for a 60 percent equity/40 percent fixed income allocation

	Historical return (%)		Projected return, 2016–2026 (%)		
	1926–2016	2000–2016	25th Percentile	50th Percentile	75th Percentile
Nominal	8.5	4.9	3.1	5.6	8.1
Real	5.5	2.7	1.2	3.8	6.4

Note: The historical returns for our hypothetical portfolios are based on data for the appropriate market indexes through September 2016. The projected returns reflect the following allocation: 60 percent global equity and 40 percent global fixed income. The subasset allocation for equities is 60 percent US equity and 40 percent global ex-US equity, unhedged in USD, rebalanced annually. The subasset allocation for fixed income is 70 percent US bonds and 30 percent global ex-US bonds, hedged in USD, rebalanced annually. Projected returns at each percentile are based on 10,000 simulations generated by the Vanguard Capital Markets Model®

Source: Authors' computation.

strategy. An LDI strategy changes the concept of risk from a focus on return volatility to a focus on the stability and level of the funded ratio (Stockton 2014). Even so, total return is an important focus for many pension plans. If a plan with a long time horizon can tolerate a total return strategy's attendant contribution volatility, the sponsor can benefit from the potential for lower total contributions over the life of the plan. Cash balance plans and hybrid pension plans, which combine final-pay and cash balance plans, often default to total return strategies, as do most public pension plans.

We evaluate each lever according to its magnitude and certainty of impact. We define 'magnitude' as the change in the expected value of a $100 million portfolio over a ten-year investment horizon. 'Certainty' refers to the change in the projected dispersion of portfolio values. In what follows, we start with an overview of the motivations and investment rationales for each of the three levers and conclude with a hierarchical assessment of their potential impact on portfolio returns, risk, and expected values. We also detail the impact of risk-oriented investment decisions on a hypothetical DB plan's funded ratio.

Increase Contributions for a Significant and Certain Impact on Portfolio Value

An increase in contributions is the most reliable strategy to improve DB plan funding levels. Every additional dollar in contributions immunizes a dollar of future liabilities against the vagaries of capital market returns. The decision to increase contributions must compete with other uses of

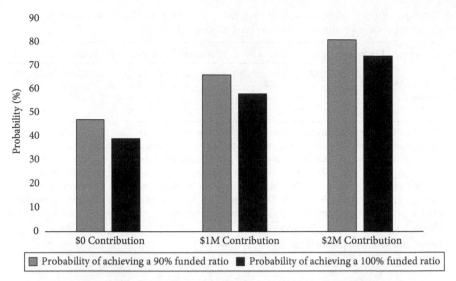

Figure 4.1. The impact of annual contributions on funded ratios

Note: We model three scenarios to show how increased contributions can minimize the risk that a plan sponsor will be unable to meet its pension obligations. We simulate projected funded ratios for a 60 percent equity/40 percent bond portfolio that starts with $60 million in assets and liabilities of $73.4 million. We assume annual contributions of $0, $1 million, and $2 million over a ten-year period. Contributions are made at the end of each year.

Source: Authors' calculations.

corporate cash flow such as capital investment and returns to shareholders, but the benefits to active and retired participants are clear.

Consider a DB plan with $60 million in assets and $73.4 million in liabilities. Its funded ratio is 82 percent. In this simplified illustration, the portfolio manager initially allocates 60 percent of plan assets to global equities and 40 percent to global bonds. We model changes in the portfolio's value over a ten-year period to illustrate the impact of additional contributions.[3] Figure 4.1 presents the probabilities that a portfolio will achieve a 90 percent or 100 percent funded status assuming three levels of annual contribution: $0; $1 million; and $2 million.

Increased contributions have a certain impact, and if the contributions are large enough, the magnitude of impact can be high. Annual contributions of $1 million raise the probability of reaching full funding from 47 percent to 66 percent over a 10-year period. Contributions of $2 million per year yield an 81 percent probability, increasing the sponsor's flexibility to implement LDI strategies that limit the plan's vulnerability to changes in interest rates and asset and liability values.[4] We recognize that competing demands for cash can make higher contributions impossible or unattractive for some plan sponsors, but it is worth remembering that this is a powerful lever.

Reduce Costs for a More Modest but Certain Impact on Portfolio Value

Whether a pension plan retains the services of in-house or external portfolio managers, the only guarantee is that those services have a cost. The future performance delivered by those managers is uncertain. All else equal, reducing costs has a certain and positive impact on the future value of a portfolio. The short-term benefits are relatively modest. Over time, however, a modest reduction in costs can deliver significant long-term benefits as annual savings compound.

Table 4.2 quantifies the impact of costs on a portfolio with an initial value of $100 million. We assume a return of 7 percent per year before fees, a figure consistent with plan sponsors' expectations in Stockton's survey. Net of 100 basis points in annual fees, the portfolio's value would grow to about $178 million after 10 years. If fees had been 50 basis points, however, the portfolio would have accumulated an additional $9 million in assets. Over 30 years, annual savings of 50 basis points would translate into more than $90 million in additional assets.

The concept of reducing costs is simple, yet its impact is surprisingly powerful. This is particularly true for plan sponsors with a long time horizon. The compounded annual savings make bigger dents in funding shortfalls with every passing year. Over 30 years, for example, a 50-basis-point difference in annual costs compounds to more than 9,000 basis points (91 percentage points) in cumulative return.

TABLE 4.2 The black magic of compounding costs: Projected value of a $100 million portfolio

	Portfolio values ($ million)		
Cost (basis points)	10 years	20 years	30 years
0	196.7	387.0	761.3
25	191.9	368.1	706.3
50	187.1	350.2	655.4
75	182.6	333.2	608.3
100	178.1	317.1	564.8

Note: These calculations assume a return of 7 percent per year before fees.

Source: Authors' computation.

Increase Risk for a Potentially Significant but Uncertain Impact

Boosting contributions and cutting costs address inflows and outflows to deliver certain growth in a portfolio's long-term value. Increasing portfolio risk is a different strategy: it seeks to accelerate the rate at which portfolio assets grow.

While increased risk can have a greater impact than increasing contributions and reducing costs, the certainty of success is lower. Among the widely used risk-oriented strategies are: (1) increased allocations to global equities; (2) style factor tilts; (3) allocations to traditional active equity management; and (4) allocations to alternatives.

We assume that an increase in a portfolio's strategic equity allocation would be achieved through passively managed, market capitalization weighted index portfolios. The other options—style factor tilts, traditional active management, and alternatives—represent forms of active management. These strategies introduce active risk, but with the exception of some alternatives, produce no change to a portfolio's broad strategic allocation. We review the investment cases for each risk-oriented strategy.

Higher equity allocation. Raising a plan's strategic equity allocation represents a move along the efficient frontier to a riskier portfolio, with a higher expected return, as illustrated in Figure 4.2. A higher expected return can help a plan close funding shortfalls, but the higher volatility associated with this expected return also diminishes the certainty that this benefit will be realized.

Style factor tilts. A static allocation to style factors seeks to improve the risk and return characteristics expected from a portfolio's allocation to broad asset classes. Although researchers have identified a number of potential style factors, we focus on three—size, value, and credit. Ilmanen (this volume) explores the use of several other factors in retirement-plan portfolios. Size, value, and credit are notable for both the extensive literature documenting each and the empirical research on their performance. Table 4.3 includes possible risk-based or behavioral explanations for the persistence of their excess returns (Banz 1981; Fama and French 1992, 1993; Pappas and Dickson 2015).

Like any active strategy, the use of factor tilts demands both a conviction that the factors represent an enduring opportunity to earn a return premium and the patience to stick with this conviction through factors' inevitable periods of underperformance.[5]

Actively managed equity funds.[6] Traditional active management is another option for plan sponsors. Stockton found that most DB plan sponsors invest a majority of their assets in actively managed portfolios, as is typical for institutional investors.[7] Survey respondents reported that, on

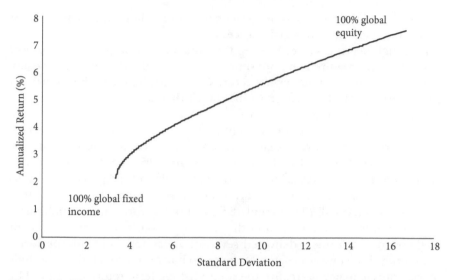

Figure 4.2. The efficient frontier for a portfolio of global equities and global fixed income

Note: Calculations reflect median asset class return projections for the ten years through 2026.

Source: Authors' calculations.

TABLE 4.3 Possible return rationales for select equity and fixed income risk factors

Factor	Risk explanation	Behavioral explanation
Value (equity)	Cyclical risk of positive correlation between economic activity and security's returns.	Recency bias leads to investors shunning distressed firms and overpaying for recent growth.
Size (equity)	Cyclical risk of smaller firms being more exposed to changing, negative economic activity and default risk.	N/A
Credit (fixed income)	Default and downgrade risk; positive correlation to economic activity.	N/A

Sources: Banz (1981); Fama and French (1992, 1993); Pappas and Dickson (2015).

average, 66 percent of equity and 72 percent of fixed income assets were actively managed.

Three elements need to be present for active management to be successful: talent, cost, and patience. Talent is paramount. On average, the odds that an active manager will outperform a relevant benchmark are low. In the 17 rolling 3-year periods for the 20 years ending 2016, only 15 percent of US equity funds, on average, outperformed their benchmarks. When those results are weighted by assets under management rather than the number of funds, the odds improved to 38 percent.

Although talent is key to beating the odds against outperformance, low cost is another requirement, not simply because of the mathematical reality that lower costs equal higher net returns. In an analysis of various portfolio characteristics, Wallick et al. (2015b) found that cost is the most powerful predictor of future outperformance.[8]

Even if an investor identifies talent and secures it at a low cost, success requires patience. Active managers typically produce inconsistent patterns of returns, as illustrated in Figure 4.3. Of the 2,085 US-domiciled active equity funds in existence at the start of 2000, only 552 (26 percent) outperformed their prospectus benchmark over the subsequent 15 years. Of that 26 percent, almost all (98 percent) failed to outperform their benchmarks in at least four calendar years over the 15-year period. More than 50 percent of these top performers delivered seven or more years of underperformance. Only those investors patient enough to hang on through these periods of weakness managed to realize the superior long-term returns delivered by these exceptional managers.

Alternative investments. Alternative investments are widely used in DB plans. These investments include both non-traditional asset classes such as real estate and commodities and specialized investment vehicles such as private equity and hedge funds. On average, plan sponsors allocate 11 percent

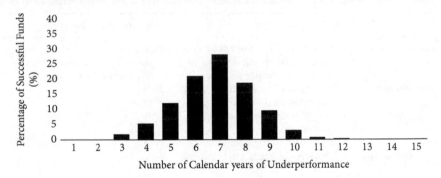

Figure 4.3. Even successful funds had multiple periods of underperformance: Distribution of 552 funds that outperformed their index, 2000–2014

Note: Data are as of December 31, 2015. Successful funds are those that survived for the 15 years and also outperformed their prospectus benchmarks. Our analysis was based on expenses and fund returns for active equity funds available to US investors at the start of the period. When multiple share classes existed, the oldest and lowest-cost single share class was used to represent a fund. Funds that were merged or liquidated were considered underperformers for the purposes of this analysis. The following fund categories were included: small-cap value, small-cap growth, small-cap blend, mid-cap value, mid-cap growth, mid-cap blend, large-cap value, large-cap growth, and large-cap blend.

Source: Vanguard calculations, using data from Morningstar, Inc.

of portfolio assets to alternatives (Stockton 2016). Of the corporate plans that invest in alternatives, 89 percent expected to maintain or increase their allocations; the remaining 11 percent were considering a reduction in these allocations.

We consider two alternative strategies: hedge funds and private equity. Neither is a separate asset class; rather, they are a repackaging of publicly or privately traded traditional asset classes. Both strategies represent a form of active management. As with traditional active management, talent is key because the spread between winners and losers is extreme, as illustrated in Figure 4.4. In alternatives, however, the selection challenge is greater

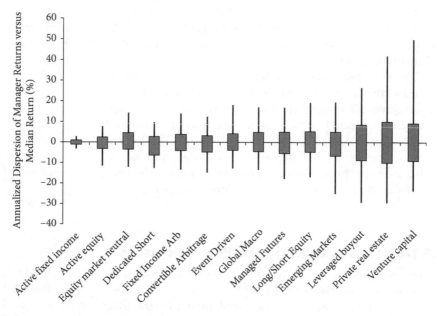

Figure 4.4. Manager dispersion with private alternative investments is significantly higher than with traditional asset classes

Note. Public US active fixed income and active equity distributions were based on data provided by Morningstar, Inc., for mutual funds domiciled in the United States from January 1, 1994, through July 31, 2014. Equity-market neutral, dedicated short bias, fixed income arbitrage, convertible arbitrage, event-driven, global macro, managed futures, long/short equity, and emerging markets' distributions were based on data provided by Lipper TASS, for hedge funds in existence from January 1, 1994, through July 31, 2014. All funds are US-dollar-denominated, adjusting for survivorship bias in each category. Leveraged buyout, real estate, and venture capital distributions based on data provided by Preqin. Each distribution was based on an internal rate of return (IRR) calculation from a series of annual cash flows from each fund. For private equity funds that had not yet distributed 100% of the fund's capital back to the limited partners, IRR calculations were based on an ending net asset value. Each distribution has been adjusted so that the median resides at point zero, to isolate the dispersion.

Source. Authors' calculations, using data from Morningstar, Inc., Lipper TASS, and Preqin.

because of the limited access to many managers and the higher due diligence hurdles for complex (and at times opaque) strategies.

Wallick et al. (2015b) found that hedge funds generally did not deliver long-term outperformance relative to a portfolio balanced between global equities and global fixed income.[9] Their conclusions about private equity were similar. The researchers nevertheless noted that vehicles such as venture capital and leveraged buyout (LBO) funds could deliver a 'liquidity risk premium,' the reward investors expect for locking up their money over a specified period. Absent this expected premium, however, Wallick et al. (2015b) found that the median venture capital fund has trailed the returns of the public equity markets, while the median LBO had more or less matched them. Other researchers have reached similar conclusions. (Moskowitz and Vissing-Jorgensen 2002; Cochrane 2005; Kaplan and Schoar 2005; Conroy and Harris 2007; Phalippou and Gottschalg 2009).

These analyses take place within a total return framework, but the LDI case for alternatives may be no more compelling. Bosse (2012) showed that alternatives allocations (real estate investment trusts and commodities, in particular) funded from a portfolio's fixed income holdings produced a notable increase in funding ratio volatility. If funded from the equity allocation, the alternatives allocation must be significant (24 percent of portfolio assets in the analysis) to produce a modest decline in the volatility of portfolio assets relative to plan liabilities (−3 percent).

A Decision Hierarchy for Plan Sponsors

When we examine increased contributions, reduced costs, and increased risk in a quantitative framework, a decision-making hierarchy emerges. Table 4.4 details the magnitude and certainty of impact for the three levers. Increased contributions deliver the most powerful combination of certainty and impact. Reduced costs have a smaller impact, but a high certainty that the impact will be realized. Cutting costs is a productive strategy in any investment environment. In ideal circumstances, increased risk has a significant and positive impact, but the likelihood of realizing this impact is uncertain.

We test each lever's impact on a $100 million portfolio with an initial allocation of 60 percent global equities and 40 percent global fixed income. For each lever, we generate 10,000 potential portfolio outcomes over a 10-year period, based on asset class projections from the Vanguard Capital Markets Model® (Davis et al. 2014).

Increased contributions. This lever is conceptually simple, though finding the funds for higher contributions can be devilishly difficult in practice.

TABLE 4.4 Quantifying the decision hierarchy for plan sponsors

Panel A. Simulated 10-year performance of a $100 million portfolio with an allocation of 60 percent global equities and 40 percent global fixed income, rebalanced annually.

Expected annualized return (%)	Projected portfolio values ($ million)			
	25th percentile	50th percentile	75th percentile	IQR
5.70	136.0	174.1	220.9	84.9

Panel B. Each lever's incremental impact on portfolio performance.

	Change in median return (pp)	Change in portfolio values ($ million)[g]			
		25th percentile	50th percentile	75th percentile	IQR
Increase contributions[a]					
+$.5 million	–	+5.9	+6.7	+7.7	+1.8
+$1.0 million	–	+11.8	+13.3	+15.6	+3.8
Reduce costs[b]					
−25 basis points	+0.25	+3.3	+4.1	+5.1	+1.8
−50 basis points	+0.50	+6.5	+8.1	+10.0	+3.5
Increase risk					
10 pp increase in equity allocation	+0.52	+1.3	+8.7	+19.9	+18.6
10 pp private equity allocation[c]	+0.33	+3.7	+3.7	+5.8	+2.1
Static factor tilts[d]	+0.12	+2.6	+1.9	+2.2	−0.4
10 pp allocation to active equity[e]	+0.05	+0.9	+0.8	+1.2	+0.3
10 pp hedge fund allocation[f]	−0.38	+1.1	−6.2	−15.0	−16.1

Notes:
[a] We assume that contributions are made into the portfolio annually at the end of each year over the horizon.
[b] We analyze each lever relative to a cost-free portfolio. To evaluate the impact of reducing costs, we model an increase in costs (+25 and +50 basis points) relative to the initial portfolio. An alternative approach would be to assume costs of, say, 75 bps for the original portfolio and then deduct costs of 25 and 50 basis points. The two approaches produce approximately the same results.
[c] We assume that private equity provides a 2-percentage-point liquidity premium relative to public equity. We adjust the strategy's volatility to match the Sharpe ratio of the broad public equity market and assume that private equity returns have a correlation of approximately 0.9 with US equity returns, consistent with Vanguard research.
[d] We replace 10 percentage points of the broad equity allocation with 5-percentage-point long-only allocations to the value and size factors. We replace 10 percentage points of the fixed income allocation with the long-only, cap-weighted credit factor.
[e] We replace 10 percentage points of the broad equity allocation with active equity. We assume excess returns of 0.5 percentage point. Active fund excess return distributions are simulated based on statistical estimations from historical manager excess return data and are added to broad market US equity projections to form an active manager return distribution.
[f] We replace 10 percentage points of the broad equity allocation with 5 percentage point allocations to market neutral and multi-strategy hedge funds.
[g] The 25th, 50th, and 75th percentile columns correspond to terminal asset value distributions for each lever. The interquartile range (IQR) of projected portfolio values measures the dispersion, or degree of certainty, associated with each lever.

Source: Authors' computation.

Increased contributions produce no incremental change in the returns produced by portfolio assets or in the volatility of those returns.

But higher contributions of $0.5 or $1 million have a significant impact on portfolio values. Relative to the original portfolio, annual contributions of $1 million produce a median expected increase in portfolio value of about $13 million at the end of the 10-year period. This lever is the most powerful and predictable of the three levers available to plan sponsors.

Reduced costs. Next, we illustrate the impact of costs by assessing fees of 25 and 50 basis points on the original cost-free portfolio. Lower costs (all else equal) lead to higher returns, with no incremental increase in return volatility. The impact on portfolio value at the end of the 10-year period is more modest. Even so, it is larger than intuition might suggest because of the compounding of annual cost savings. The longer the time period, the greater the power of this compounding benefit.

Increased risk. The impact of increased risk varies by strategy. Compared with increased contributions and reduced cost, the certainty that this impact will be realized is low. To test each approach, we implement a 10 percent allocation to the risk-oriented strategy, funding it from the original portfolio's relevant asset class. Our assumed return premiums are consistent with averages found in empirical research (Wallick et al. 2015a). We review the impact of each risk-oriented strategy, from greatest to least.[10]

Increased equity allocation. A 10-percentage-point increase in the portfolio's strategic allocation to global equities adds an incremental 0.52 percentage point to annualized expected returns and an additional $8.7 million to the portfolio's projected median value at the end of the 10-year period. This move along the efficient frontier also produces higher volatility. In the original portfolio, the difference between simulated terminal values at the 25th and 75th percentiles (the interquartile range, or IQR) is about $85 million. When the equity allocation increases by 10 percentage points, the IQR increases to about $104 million.

Private equity allocation. A 10-percentage-point allocation to private equity has the next greatest impact, adding an annualized 0.33 percentage point to returns and $3.7 million to the median portfolio's terminal value. The dispersion of portfolio values increases modestly, an interquartile range of $87 million, compared with $85 million in the original portfolio. A caution is in order: these summary statistics mask the challenge of selecting private equity funds that can, in fact, deliver these benefits. There is no investable beta for private equity funds—no indexed vehicle that captures the risk and return characteristics of the category. Success depends on picking above-average performers from a category with a high dispersion of outcomes.

Style factor tilts. A 10-percentage-point allocation to equity style factors and a 10-percentage-point allocation to credit in the fixed income allocation increase expected annualized return and modestly reduce the dispersion of returns. (Our analysis is based on long-only implementations of factor tilts.) The benefits reflect the potential persistence of style factor premiums and the factors' less-than-perfect correlation with the broad equity and fixed income markets. The effect is modest, however, and it is important to note that factors' excess returns can be highly cyclical. Plan sponsors must have an ex-ante belief in the persistence of any factor premiums and the patience to pursue these premiums through good periods and bad.

Active equity allocation. A 10-percentage-point allocation to traditional active equity strategies has limited impact on portfolio risk and return. Again, our simulation is based on assumptions about active management as a category. The performance and impact of a given manager can, and does, vary widely.

Hedge fund allocation. We model two widely used hedge fund strategies: market-neutral and multi-strategy. A 5-percentage-point allocation to each, funded from the original portfolio's equity allocation, reduces the portfolio's expected annualized return, while producing a sizable decline in the volatility of returns. The hedge fund allocation reduces the difference between 25th and 75th percentile portfolio values to about $69 million, compared with an IQR of $85 million in the original portfolio.[11]

Commentary

Some plan sponsors will no doubt use return premium assumptions and allocation strategies that differ from those used here. In general, however, we would expect most assumptions to yield similar relative impacts for the risk-oriented strategies. A decision to increase the portfolio's equity allocation is likely to be the most consequential. This conclusion is consistent with Brinson et al. (1986), who found that a broadly diversified portfolio's strategic asset allocation was the primary driver of its performance. Subsequent research by Ibbotson and Kaplan (2000) and Scott et al. (2017) reached similar conclusions.

The other risk-oriented strategies represent portfolio implementation decisions that, on average, will have less impact on performance. It is possible, of course, for an aggressive allocation to an exceptional active manager or private equity fund to have an outsized impact on portfolio performance, but this alluring possibility would be an outlier. Our hierarchical framework can help plan sponsors set reasonable expectations for the potential magnitude and certainty of each risk-oriented strategy.

The Impact of Investment Decisions on DB Plan Funding Ratios

Our decision hierarchy has examined investment returns in a traditional mean-variance portfolio construction framework. Many total-return-oriented plan sponsors also assess the impact of investment decisions on critical pension plan metrics such as the funding ratio.

Table 4.5 presents incremental changes in the expected funding ratio and its dispersion resulting from risk-oriented strategies. Our conclusions are similar to those presented above. An increased equity allocation produces the greatest impact, but with the least certainty. Private equity, factor tilts, and active management produce a more limited increase in the funding ratio and modest changes in the dispersion of the expected funding ratio. Hedge fund strategies reduce the expected funded ratio status, with a decrease in the dispersion of the funding ratio.

Conclusion

It is widely believed that we are in an era of more modest returns than those produced by global equity and fixed income markets over the past few decades. Lower returns intensify pressure on all investors to meet their

TABLE 4.5   Risk-oriented strategies and ten-year change in funded status

Panel A. Projected funded status for portfolio with an allocation of 60 percent global equities and 40 percent global fixed income, rebalanced annually, and an initial funding ratio of 82 percent.

Projected funded status (%)

25th percentile	50th percentile	75th percentile	IQR
66.6	97.5	137.0	70.4

Panel B. Each risk-oriented lever's incremental impact on a portfolio's funded status.

	Change in funded status (percentage points)			
	25th percentile	50th percentile	75th percentile	IQR
10 pp increase in equity allocation	+0.1	+6.2	+15.6	+15.5
10 pp private equity allocation	+2.8	+3.8	+5.5	+2.7
Static factor tilts	+1.0	+1.4	+0.8	−0.2
10 pp allocation to active equity	+0.8	+0.9	+1.4	+0.6
10 pp hedge fund allocation	+1.1	−4.2	−12.2	−13.3

Note. The 25th, 50th, and 75th percentile columns correspond to terminal asset value distributions for each lever. The interquartile range (IQR) of projected funded status measures the dispersion, or degree of certainty, associated with each lever.

Source. Authors' computation.

goals. Blanchett et al. and Reilly and Byrne in their chapters in this volume explore savings, working, and Social Security claiming strategies to help individuals fund retirement liabilities in a lower-return future. The challenges for DB plans may be more daunting because of their relatively inflexible obligations.

Plan sponsors can use three levers to enhance a portfolio's chances of meeting these goals: increased contributions, reduced costs—a smart strategy in any return environment—and increased risk. Many sponsors will need to use a combination of the three levers. Our analysis provides a framework and a reasonable set of parameters for assessing the magnitude and certainty of impact delivered by each.

Notes

1. The survey included responses from 178 corporate DB plan sponsors. Plan size ranged from $20 million to $50 million (11%) to more than $5 billion (8%), with an average plan size of approximately $1 billion and total plan assets across the entire survey of approximately $180.9 billion.
2. The expected return on assets (EROA) for corporate DB plans is a component of pension expense for the sponsor company's income statement. Public plans use EROAs to discount their funded future liabilities. EROAs are intended to be very long-term, typically 30 years, and based on median (expected) results.
3. Reality is more complicated than this hypothetical illustration. Contribution levels are a function of both regulation and plan sponsor goals. For a US corporate plan with a funding deficit, for example, the Pension Protection Act of 2006 mandated a minimum contribution equal to roughly one-seventh of the shortfall.
4. See Sparling (2014) for an overview of derisking strategies triggered by changes in plan funding status.
5. Regarding the uncertainty associated with using factors, Pappas and Dickson (2015) note that there is 'conjecture over whether the historical returns associated with certain factors will persist in the future. For example, Lo and MacKinlay (1990), Black (1993), and Harvey et al. (2014) contend that the empirical evidence is a 'result of data mining' (Pappas and Dickson 2015: 8). Before implementing a tilt using one of these factors, plan sponsors should maintain a clear understanding of either the risk explanation, behavioral explanation, or both. For example, if the behavioral explanation holds for a factor, but the risk explanation does not, the return premium could narrow if investors change their behavior in the future. Factor tilts also raise questions about how to implement that tilt—long-only, or long-short, beyond the scope of this analysis.
6. Our analysis of traditional actively managed strategies does not include fixed income funds. For fixed income, our analysis of risk-oriented strategies uses a static tilt to the credit risk premium. This treatment is consistent with research from Bosse et al. (2013), who found that a 'persistent overweighting to corporate

credit risk, and not dynamic or tactical portfolio management (i.e., alpha, or manager skill), has been the primary driver of performance for funds benchmarked to the Barclays US Aggregate Bond Index.'

7. For example, the NACUBO (2015) Commonfund Study of Endowments found a passive/active mix for domestic equity of 29 percent/71 percent in 2015.

8. Wallick et al. (2015b) analyze the relationship between alpha and various quantitative portfolio characteristics. Only the expense ratio and portfolio turnover provide a statistically significant explanation of alpha. 'More than any other quantifiable attribute we have examined, lower costs are associated with higher risk-adjusted future returns—or alpha' (Wallick et al. 2015a: 1). Simply selecting a fund from the lowest- rather than the highest-cost quartile increased the likelihood of outperforming a relevant index in the subsequent five years by more than 50 percent (a 40% chance versus 26%).

9. Wallick et al. (2015a) analyze funds of hedge funds, because these are professional managers who are paid to construct a high-quality collection of hedge funds for clients. This objective is similar to what numerous institutional investors would be attempting to do for their own portfolio. The authors also analyzed individual hedge funds over the same period using the same database and found that 56 percent outperformed a traditional portfolio of 60 percent equity and 40 percent fixed income.

10. These conclusions reflect our assumptions about the implementation approaches and return premiums associated with the risk-oriented strategies. For plan sponsors that use different assumptions, the results of the analysis may vary. But this framework is not intended to identify an optimal strategy. Rather, it outlines a process that plan sponsors can use to evaluate the various options.

11. Although some hedge fund strategies have less volatility than broad market equities, they introduce consequential new risks such as a high degree of manager risk.

References

Banz, R. W. (1981). 'The Relationship between Return and Market Value of Common Stocks.' *Journal of Financial Economics* 9(1): 3–18.

Black, Fisher (1993). 'Beta and Return.' *Journal of Portfolio Management* 20(1): 8–18.

Blanchett, D., M. Finke, and W. Pfau (2018). "Low Returns and Optimal Retirement Savings," in R. Clark, R. Maurer, and O. S. Mitchell (eds.), *How Persistent Low Returns Will Shape Saving and Retirement.* Oxford, UK: Oxford University Press, pp. 26–43.

Bosse, P. M. (2012). 'Pension Derisking: Diversify or Hedge?' Valley Forge, PA: The Vanguard Group.

Bosse, P. M., B. R. Wimmer, and C. B. Philips (2013). 'Active Bond-Fund Excess Returns: Is it Alpha . . . or Beta?' Valley Forge, PA.: The Vanguard Group.

Brinson, G. P., L. R. Hood, and G. L. Beebower (1986). 'Determinants of Portfolio Performance.' *Financial Analysts Journal* 42(4): 39–48.

Cochrane, J. H. (2005). 'The Risk and Return of Venture Capital.' *Journal of Financial Economics* 75(1): 3–52.

Conroy, R. M., and R. S. Harris (2007). 'How Good Are Private Equity Returns?' *Journal of Applied Corporate Finance* 19(3): 96–108.

Davis, J., R. Aliaga-Díaz, H. Ahluwalia, F. Polanco, and C. Tasopoulos (2014). 'Vanguard Global Capital Markets Model.' Valley Forge, PA: The Vanguard Group.

Fama, E. F., and K. R. French (1992). 'The Cross-Section of Expected Stock Returns.' *Journal of Finance* 47(2):427–65.

Fama, E. F., and K. R. French (1993). 'Common Risk Factors in the Returns on Stock and Bonds.' *Journal of Financial Economics* 33(1): 3–56.

Harvey, Campbell R., Yan Liu, and Heqing Zhu (2014). '. . . and the Cross-Section of Expected Returns.' Working Paper. Durham, NC: Duke University. http://papers.ssrn.com/abstract-2249314.

Ibbotson, R. G., and P. D. Kaplan (2000). 'Does Asset Allocation Policy Explain 40, 90, or 100 Percent of Performance?' *Financial Analysts Journal* 56(1): 26–33.

JP Morgan Institutional Asset Management (2015). *Pension Pulse.* Spring, New York. https://am.jpmorgan.com/gi/getdoc/1383226745018.

Kaplan, S. N., and A. Schoar (2005). 'Private Equity Performance: Returns, Persistence, and Capital Flows.' *Journal of Finance* 60(4): 1791–823.

Lo, A. W., and A. C. MacKinlay (1990). 'Data-Snooping Biases in Tests of Financial Asset Pricing Models.' *Review of Financial Studies* 3(3): 431–67.

Moskowitz, T. J., and A. Vissing-Jorgensen (2002). 'The Returns of Entrepreneurial Investment: A Private Equity Premium Puzzle?' *American Economic Review* 92(4): 745–78.

NACUBO (2015). '2015 Commonfund Study of Endowments.' Washington, DC: National Association of College and University Business Officers.

Novy-Marx, R., and J. Rauh (2014). 'Revenue Demands of Public Employee Pension Promises,' *American Economic Journal: Economic Policy* 6(1): 193–229.

Pappas, S. N., and J. M. Dickson (2015). 'Factor-based Investing.' Vanguard White Paper. Malvern, PA: Vanguard.

Phalippou, L., and O. Gottschalg (2009). 'The Performance of Private Equity Funds.' *The Review of Financial Studies* 22(4): 1747–76.

Reilly, C., and A. Byrne (2018). "Investing for Retirement in a Low Returns Environment: Making the Right Decisions to Make the Money Last," in R. Clark, R. Maurer, and O. S. Mitchell (eds.), *How Persistent Low Returns Will Shape Saving and Retirement.* Oxford, UK: Oxford University Press, pp. 61–80.

Scott, B. J., J. Balsamo, K. N. McShane, and C. Tasopoulos (2017). 'The Global Case for Strategic Allocation and an Examination of Home Bias.' Vanguard Research. Malvern, PA: Vanguard.

Sparling, J. (2014). 'Pension Derisking: Start with the End in Mind.' Valley Forge, PA: The Vanguard Group.

Stockton, K. A. (2014). 'Fundamentals of Liability-Driven Investing.' Valley Forge, PA: The Vanguard Group.

Stockton, K. A. (2016). 'Survey of Defined Benefit Plan Sponsors, 2015.' Valley Forge, PA: The Vanguard Group.

Wallick, D. W., D. M. Grim, C. Tasopoulos, and J. Balsamo (2015a). 'The Allure of the Outlier: A Framework for Considering Alternative Investments.' Valley Forge, PA: The Vanguard Group.

Wallick, D. W., B. R. Wimmer, and J. Balsamo (2015b). 'Shopping for Alpha: You Get What You Don't Pay For.' Valley Forge, PA: The Vanguard Group.

Chapter 5

Investing for Retirement in a Low Returns Environment: Making the Right Decisions to Make the Money Last

Catherine Reilly and Alistair Byrne

At the same time that longevity has been increasing, expected investment returns have fallen below historical levels. Figure 5.1 shows Society of Professional Forecasters' estimates of ten-year real returns on key US assets classes, with forecasts made from 1992 to 2017. Expected bill rates, bond returns, and equities returns are all significantly lower now than in the recent decade. In a lower return environment, markets do less of the work for savers, so contributions need to be higher instead. For Baby Boomers who have enjoyed good returns for most of their careers, this will have little impact. For younger individuals, however, lower future returns are a more significant drag on retirement income prospects.

How to Reach Target Replacement Rates with Defined Contribution Plans

Approach and methodology. One goal of this chapter is to provide participants, plan sponsors, and policymakers with simple guidelines on the strategies that participants can employ to have enough money available in retirement. It seems self-evident that people should save more and expect to work for longer, but how much more do they need to save and at what age should they aspire to retire? The answers to these questions may be different depending on the participant's current age and previous contribution history. Furthermore, because the social security replacement rate varies depending on income level, we also need to take this into consideration.

To do so, we first look at the replacement rate that different age cohorts can expect from their defined contribution (DC) savings. We use identical savings assumptions, so that any differences in outcomes between cohorts are due purely to differences in market returns. We then study the impact that increasing the savings rate or postponing retirement would have on

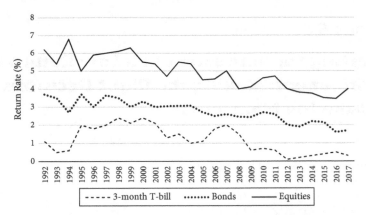

Figure 5.1. Ten-year expected returns from the Society of Professional Forecasters

Note: Returns are deflated with Survey of Professional Forecasters' long-run consumer price index inflation forecast.

Source: Williams (2017).

retirement readiness for the different age cohorts. Unsurprisingly, we find that the outlook for younger generations is considerably more challenging than for older generations who have benefited from stronger historical returns. Of course, in addition to their DC savings, most participants will also receive income from social security in retirement and some will also have income from defined benefit (DB) plans.

Second, we investigate the outlook for different income groups, taking into account both differences in life expectancy and social security replacement rates. Primarily due to the progressive nature of social security, low income cohorts will need lower DC savings rates to achieve retirement readiness than will higher earning cohorts. Finally, we study the strategies that late starters (i.e., 45- and 55-year-old participants without accumulated savings balances) can employ to improve their ability to retire in comfort. By employing aggressive savings rates (over 15 percent) and working to 70 or beyond, these groups are likely to achieve reasonable retirement outcomes.

Challenges for different age cohorts. To calculate outcomes by cohorts, we assume that all the individuals invest in identical portfolios consisting of 80 percent S&P500 stocks and 20 percent US government bonds throughout their working lives. While this portfolio is undeniably simplified and may not be the investment vehicle of choice for current cohorts, we choose it because something like it has been available to all the different cohorts (unlike e.g., target date funds, first launched in the mid-1990s). This also provides a reasonable approximation of the average equity/bond split of a target date fund during the accumulation phase. We assume that all participants join the plan at the age of 22 and invest the same amount of their salary (in our base case, 9 percent) in the portfolio, and they also experience the same nominal wage growth (2 percent per annum) throughout their careers. The nine-percent contribution rate is our base case because the median employee contribution rate is about six percent and the most common employer matching contribution is three percent (Vanguard 2016). For older participants, their returns are based mainly on realized historical returns; for younger participants, their portfolio growth is based mainly on forecasted future returns based on Monte Carlo simulations using asset class return forecasts from State Street Global Advisors' Investment Solutions Group. We take into account that life expectancy will continue to rise, so that someone who is now 25 years old will have higher life expectancy at age 65 than someone now 60 years old. We calculate the replacement rate that each age cohort can expect at retirement, based on the returns that their portfolios have delivered over their savings periods and their life expectancies at retirement.

We show that there is wide variation in outcomes by cohort (see Figure 5.2). A hypothetical individual currently 60 years old and who retires at age 65,

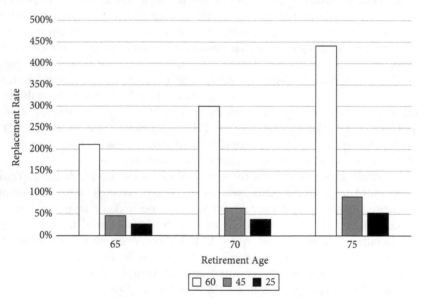

Figure 5.2. Expected replacement rate by current age of participant and retirement age, 9 percent contribution rate

Source: Authors' calculations, based on Investment Security Group (ISG) asset class forecasts and UN population projections. The drawdown rate assumes that 90 percent of the assets will last until at least five years beyond median life expectancy for each cohort (equivalent to approximately the 75th percentile).

having been saving since age 22, could expect to achieve a 211-percent replacement rate from his DC savings alone. In addition, he can expect to receive social security and may well have some DB benefits as well. (While few 60-year-olds may have been in a DC plan since the age of 22, they could have made contributions to a retirement savings account by themselves.) By contrast, an individual currently 25 years old and who employs the same saving strategy could expect to achieve a 27-percent replacement rate if he was to retire at age 65. Furthermore, the younger individual is unlikely to have any DB entitlements and faces more uncertainty regarding the amount of social security that he will receive. A 45-year-old individual can expect better outcomes than the 25-year-old but is also clearly disadvantaged compared to the 60-year-old.

Due to these lower expected returns, younger cohorts are clearly at a disadvantage to older workers. The most obvious tactics that younger workers could adopt to improve their situation are to contribute more and to work for longer. Yet the real questions is: how much more and how much longer? We also seek combinations that are feasible: savings rates that are affordable, and working patterns that are manageable.

For example, let us assume that our worker aspires to achieve a 40-percent replacement rate from his DC plan (while relying on social security and other sources of income for the rest of his retirement income). Depending on his desired retirement age, he will have a menu of action plans to choose from (here, we assume in all cases that he employs the same savings rate throughout his working life). A 25-year-old could reach a 40-percent replacement rate by contributing about 13.5 percent and working until age 65; by contributing slightly above 10 percent and working to age 70, or by contributing about 7 percent and working to age 75 (see Table 5.1 below). The 35- and 45-year-olds benefit from stronger historical returns, so they can achieve the target replacement rate at slightly lower contribution rates.

It is encouraging to see that these contribution rates seem feasible. Yet it is important to note that this assumes consistent savings behavior during the entire working life, no career breaks, and no leakage from retirement savings. In fact, however, leakage can be a significant drag on savings accumulation (Munnell and Webb 2015). Moreover, those who start to save later or aspire to retire earlier will require higher savings rates. In sum, financial advisers' often-quoted rule of thumb of 12–15 percent of income seems surprisingly realistic (Munnell et al. 2014).

Challenges for computations by income: differences in life-expectancy and social security replacement rates. Participant income levels are relevant to our computations for reasons over and above the fact that those with more income will be more able to save. First, public social security or pension benefits tend to be (fairly) flat, meaning that replacement rates from state

TABLE 5.1 Expected replacement rate by retirement age and contribution rate

25-year-olds	Retirement age		
Contribution rate (%)	65 (%)	70 (%)	75 (%)
3	9	13	18
6	18	26	35
9	27	38	53
12	36	51	71
15	45	64	89
35-year-olds			
3	11	15	22
6	22	31	44
9	33	46	66
12	44	62	88
15	55	77	110
45-year-olds			
3	15	21	30
6	31	43	60
9	46	64	90
12	62	86	120
15	77	107	150

Notes: The drawdown rate assumes a 90% probability that the assets will last until at least five years beyond median life-expectancy for each cohort (equivalent to approximately the 75th percentile).

Source: Authors' calculations, based on Investment Security Group (ISG) asset class forecasts and UN population projections.

pensions are higher in percentage terms for lower earners. Second, life expectancies are correlated with income levels, in that higher earners tend to live longer. Both factors will influence our retirement income calculations.

An often-cited rule of thumb suggests a two-thirds or 70 percent income replacement target, but this is rather imprecise. In reality, the required replacement rate depends on a variety of factors including household size, home equity, region, and so on (MacDonald et al. 2016). Broadly speaking, a lower earner will need a higher replacement rate in percentage terms (to cover essential expenditures) compared to a higher earner, though the latter may have higher aspirations.

There will also be differences in social security entitlements and other sources of income. Lower-paid individuals are likely to receive relatively high replacement rates (in percentage terms) from social security. Nevertheless, percentages can be misleading, as people on very low incomes may need close to a 100-percent replacement rate simply to meet their basic needs, especially if they have few other financial resources. Those on lower incomes also typically have poorer health and lower life expectancies, reducing their ability to extend their working life. Indeed only about 30 percent of males in the lowest income quintile are still in full-time employment at age 60, compared with almost 80 percent in the highest income quintile (Gorodnichenko et al. 2013). Yet this also reduces the number of years in retirement that lower-income persons need to fund.

Higher-income individuals will receive considerably lower replacement rates from social security, but they are more likely to be able to manage with the often-quoted 70-percent replacement rate or even less. They are also more likely to own their own homes and have other sources of income in addition to social security. Extending their working lives may also be more feasible, and indeed more necessary, since their higher life expectancies mean that they will have a longer retirement period to fund. In order to achieve a given replacement rate target, higher earners must also generate a higher replacement rate from their DC savings. Table 5.2 shows social security replacement rates by income levels for individuals retiring either at age 65 or 70 (the latter being the current maximum age for claiming social security). It illustrates the progressive nature of social security bene-fits. For example, a low earner can expect a 49-percent replacement rate from age 65, whereas someone earning at the contribution cap would have a replacement rate of only 24 percent at that age.

There is also substantial evidence that high-income individuals have longer life expectancies than the lower-income groups (see Table 5.3). This disparity has risen for several decades, and adding race and education to the computation makes the disparity even more striking. The life expect-ancy for white American males with 16 years or more of schooling in 2008 was 14.2 years more than for black American male with fewer than 12 years of education (Olshansky et al. 2012).

Accordingly, higher earners also expect to spend a longer period in retirement, while receiving a lower replacement rate from social security.

TABLE 5.2 US social security replacement rates by income level and retirement age

Earnings group (2014)	Ending salary (2014, $)	Retirement age	
		65 (%)	70 (%)
Low	21,176	49.0	60.8
Medium	47,125	36.3	45.0
High	75,393	30.1	37.3
Max	114,391	23.9	29.6

Note. Benefit adjustments calculated for persons born in 1960 or later.

Source. Authors' calculations, based on social security replacement rate data consistent with Office of the Chief Actuary (2014).

TABLE 5.3 Difference in life expectancy for male Social Security-covered workers, by age between selected earnings groups for the period 1999–2000 (in years) at different ages between top and bottom income quartiles

	Top half minus bottom half	Top quarter minus bottom quarter
60	2.6	3.3
65	1.9	2.3
70	1.2	1.3
75	0.5	0.3
80	0	−0.4
85	−0.4	−0.9

Source: Waldron (2007).

This means that in order to achieve a given target replacement rate, higher earners must save a higher proportion of their incomes than low-income earners, or live on relatively less in retirement.

In our next round of calculations, we examine the case of a 25-year-old at the start of their career. We add our DC replacement rate calculations to the expected social security replacement rates for different income cohorts to assess how much individuals in different income cohorts would need to save in order to achieve a target income replacement rate when retiring at age 65 or 70.

To illustrate, we assume that all households target a 70-percent replacement rate at retirement. As Figure 5.3 shows, the mix of DC savings and social security that provides this replacement rate varies by income group. A low earner retiring at age 70 would be able to rely entirely on social security to provide a 70-percent replacement rate, whereas a maximum earner retiring at 65 would need to generate a 46-percent replacement rate from his DC savings. The maximum earner here is an individual earning the maximum wage on which social security contributions are paid (currently $127,000); individuals earning higher salaries will need to generate an even higher proportion of retirement income from their DC savings.

Moreover, higher earners must save considerably higher shares of their salaries than do the low earners. If we exclude the very lowest income group, people aspiring to retire at age 65 should save between 11 and 15 percent of their salary; those planning to defer retirement until 70 should save between four and eight percent (see Figure 5.4).

Two interesting implications arise from this analysis. First, even in the low return environment, people who save systematically for retirement should be well equipped to retire even at fairly modest deferral rates (we reiterate that these are total savings rates including an employer matching contributions). Participants wishing to retire at 65 need to save almost twice

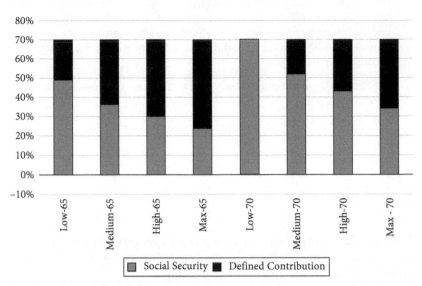

Figure 5.3. Getting to a 70-percent replacement rate: different strategies by earnings groups

Source: Authors' calculations.

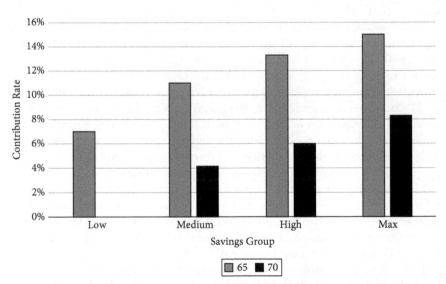

Figure 5.4. Required defined contribution rates to achieve 70-percent replacement rate target, by earnings group and retirement age

Source: Authors' calculations.

as much of their salary as those planning to retire at 70. Our model assumes that participants keep the same 80/20 portfolio until retirement; this is more aggressive than most people are likely to do, and may slightly overstate the investment gains during the last years of working life. Accordingly, these should be interpreted as minimums rather than recommended rates. Yet this does not change the conclusion that postponing retirement has a very positive impact on retirement readiness, not least through its impact on the replacement rate offered by social security.

Second, because the low earners receive a high replacement rate from social security, they only need to save a fairly small proportion of their salaries. If they are able to work until age 70, they may not need to save much at all. This has interesting implications for the potential introduction of automatic enrollment schemes targeted at uncovered employees, such as state plans in the United States (see Gale and John's chapter in this volume) or automatic enrollment in the United Kingdom. Employees at the lower end of the earnings spectrum are also less likely to be offered retirement plans by their employers than those at the higher end, and automatic enrollment plans often have quite modest total contribution rates (a total rate of 8 percent in the United Kingdom, while the Oregon State plan targets at 6 percent). These rates are likely to be inadequate for higher earners, but as we have demonstrated, they are probably ample for the low paid. Requiring people on low incomes to save more could be counter-productive, as it may lead them to opt out altogether. Since optimal savings rates will differ by earning levels, one potential solution could be to have different automatic enrollment rates for employees by income level. Alternatively, communication and engagement could focus on encouraging higher earners to save more, though plan sponsors will need to be aware of the powerful influence of inertia in preventing action.

Challenges for late starters. In the previous section, we showed that participants who systematically save for retirement throughout their careers can reach reasonable outcomes with fairly low savings rates, despite the low expected market returns. Yet many people reach middle age without having saved significant amounts for retirement. What strategies can these individuals employ to maximize their chances of attaining financial security in retirement?

We study a 45-year-old and a 55-year-old who start saving for retirement, and first evaluate the impact of different contribution rates (10, 15, 20, and 25 percent) and alternative retirement ages. We then study how working part time in retirement (from 65 to 70 or from 70 to 75) could affect expected replacement rates. For such late starters, we assume that they make their contributions to an age-appropriate target date fund. Again, assumed investment returns are based on State Street Global Advisors' asset class return forecasts, and in retirement, the same drawdown rates are used as in the previous section.

Participants who start the retirement saving journey late do face more challenges, yet they can also significantly improve their retirement readiness with a disciplined approach to saving and by postponing retirement. Figure 5.5 shows the DC replacement rates that an individual starting to save at age 45 or 55 can expect to achieve, depending on his contribution rate and retirement age. Unsurprisingly, even at these relatively high contribution rates, outcomes are considerably poorer than for early starters. Previously we showed the combinations of contribution rate and retirement age, that would lead to a 40-percent DC replacement rate. Here, by contrast, we see that even a 20-percent contribution rate and working until age 70 provides only a fraction of this target.

Figure 5.6 shows expected total replacement rates for late starters at different contribution rates, including social security. The first calculation assumes a medium earner who saves 15 percent and retires at age 65. He can expect a replacement rate of just over 50 percent; by delaying retirement to age 70, he could achieve a total replacement rate of 70 percent. Those on higher salaries will have lower social security replacement rates at all ages.

Potential policy reforms. As evident, postponing retirement is an extremely powerful tool for improving retirement outcomes. In fact, retiring at age 70

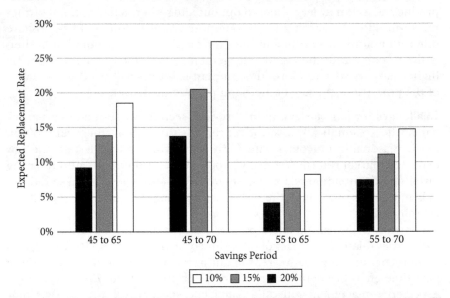

Figure 5.5. Expected DC replacement rates for individuals starting to save at 45 or 55 and working until 65 or 70 by contribution rate

Source: Authors' calculations.

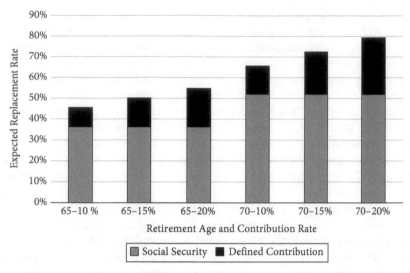

Figure 5.6. Expected total replacement rate for a medium earner who started saving at age 45, by retirement age and contribution rate

Source: Authors' calculations.

or even 75 would improve retirement readiness for all cohorts, but particularly for late starters and higher earners. Though some people may not be physically able to work full time that late, part-time work may be feasible for many.

Another consideration is that social security payments currently start at the latest at age 70, and there is no option for 'partial retirement.' One alternative policy would be to allow individuals to take out partial social security benefits rather than obliging them to always take the full benefit. For example, in Sweden, people who have reached the minimum age of eligibility for social security (62) can take a 25 percent, 50 percent, 75 percent, or 100 percent benefit, and modify this percentage when desired at an actuarially fair rate. There is also no maximum age by which full payments must start (Pensions Myndigheten 2016). Such a flexible option could be particularly useful for people who start saving for retirement later in life.

Another option would be to give people a choice to defer the start of social security benefits beyond age 70, to make the most efficient use of its cost-efficient longevity insurance. This would make it possible to use social security as a longevity backstop, providing the main source of income in late life, rather than a steady source of income throughout retirement. For example, in Australia, eligibility for the Age Pension is based on an asset test (reassessed annually) rather than retirees' age. People are not eligible for the Age Pension until they have drawn their assets down to a minimum level, after which they receive the flat rate Age Pension for the rest of their lives. Johnson (2016) suggests a similar modification to the UK State Pension, postponing the start of payments to age 80 but doubling the payment.

If it were possible to defer social security payments until age 75 at an actuarially fair rate, this would substantially increase replacement rates. Some people might find it preferable to run down their DC balances first, in order to maximize the benefit from social security by claiming at a later date. The ability to postpone payments and receive higher benefits for a shorter period could be particularly valuable for higher earners, who would now actually receive meaningful income and valuable longevity insurance from social security. Table 5.4 calculates the social security replacement rate for starting payments at age 75 by assuming that this would lead to the same increase as deferring from 65 to 70. As a matter of fact, this understates the actuarially fair increase, as mortality credits would accumulate faster between open 70 and 75 than between 65 and 70. Nevertheless, a flat rate has the benefit of simplicity and is used in a number of countries. For example, the UK uses a flat rate increase of 5.8 percent per annum for deferring the state pension.

Another policy alternative would be to offer people a lump sum rather than a higher annuity payment as a means to encourage people to defer retirement. Maurer et al. (2016) found that offering a lump sum incentive rather than a higher monthly payment after the Early Retirement Age (62) induced people to voluntarily claim 6–8 months later that they otherwise would. In essence, offering lump sum incentives builds on the behavioral reluctance of people to annuitize. The fact that those who currently claim at the youngest ages were also most responsive to the lump sum offer indicates

TABLE 5.4 How would allowing deferral to age 75 affect social security replacement rates for different income cohorts?

Income level	Claiming age		
	65	70	75
Low	49%	70%	100%
Medium	36%	52%	74%
High	30%	43%	62%
Max	24%	34%	49%

Note: For simplicity we have adjusted the benefit to age 75 using the same increase as from age 65 to 70; in reality, the actuarially fair adjustment would be higher, as mortality credits would accrue more rapidly at more advanced ages.

Source: Authors' calculations.

that this could be an effective incentive, particularly for the less financially literate sections of the population. Maurer et al. (2017) also found that lump sums of 85–90 percent of the actuarially fair amount were still effective in encouraging later claiming.

As the population approaching retirement is becoming increasingly heterogeneous, it may also be necessary to offer different incentive structures for different groups. For example, offering lump sum incentives could be an effective and equitable way of encouraging lower earners to defer claiming social security. As lower earners have lower life expectancies, they expect to derive less benefit from deferring social security for a higher payment than higher earners. Offering them a lump sum would allow them to reap the full benefit of deferring retirement.

We have also modeled what would happen if employees had the option of taking out 50 percent social security at ages 65 or 70. For those who work part time from 65 to 70, we calculate the social security benefit by assuming that at age 65 they receive 50 percent of the benefit payable at 65; from age 70, they receive 50 percent of the benefit payable at 65 and 50 percent of the benefit payable at age 70. We follow an equivalent procedure for those who work part time from 70 to 75. We model the income stream that they would receive by subtracting the DC contribution rate from the wage income (hence the 85-percent replacement rate while in full time work).

Figure 5.7 shows that for the participant who started saving at age 45, working part time in retirement until age 70 would get him to a replacement rate slightly higher than 60 percent. While this may not be optimal, it is still a 10-percentage-point improvement compared to completely retiring at age 65 (Figure 5.6). The participant who did not start saving until age 55 only achieves a 55-percent replacement rate because of his limited DC savings (Figure 5.8).

Late starters aiming for higher replacement rates could also benefit from working part time from 70 to 75, as they would reap the benefit of higher social security payments and a longer savings period (Figures 5.9 and 5.10). The income stream in these calculations is rather uneven; one solution would be to start drawing down some DC savings at age 70 to generate a smoother income stream.

This hypothetical delayed social security payment is not currently available, yet the simulations illustrate how powerful delaying retirement and the start of social security payments can be. Even with the current system, it can be beneficial for employees with limited savings to use their DC balances to delay taking social security as long as possible, rather than to use them to supplement their social security payments. Offering more flexibility to defer social security payments could further enhance the value of this benefit and allow individuals to optimize the value of their DC savings.

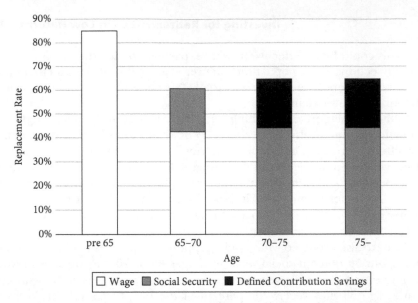

Figure 5.7. Income stream for a medium earner participant who started saving at age 45 at 15 percent, who works halftime and takes half his social security between 65 and 70 years old

Source: Authors' calculations.

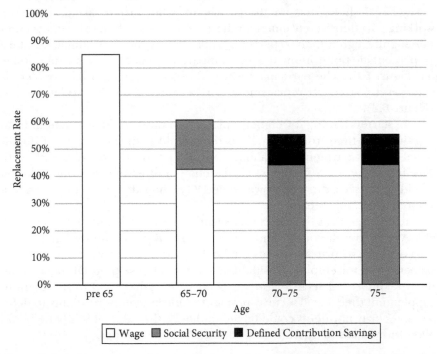

Figure 5.8. Income stream for a medium earner participant who started saving at age 55 at 15 percent, who works halftime and takes half his social security between 65 and 70 years old

Source: Authors' calculations.

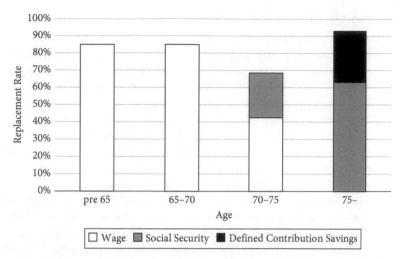

Figure 5.9. Income stream for a medium income participant who started saving at age 45 at 15 percent, who works halftime and takes half his social security between 70 and 75 years old

Source: Authors' calculations.

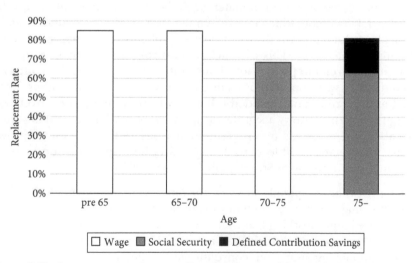

Figure 5.10. Income stream for a medium income participant who started saving at age 55 at 15 percent, who works halftime and takes half his social security between 70 and 75 years old

Source: Authors' calculations.

Altering the Choice Environment

Incentives for saving. These approaches require individuals to save consistently over their working lives, and there is a range of behavioral interventions ('nudges') that can help people save more to generate better replacement rates. It is now fairly well established that automatic enrollment can boost pension participation rates. Automatic enrollment is now mandated in the UK and achieving opt outs of only around 5–15 percent (Department for Work and Pensions 2014). Many large US DC plans also use automatic enrollment (Vanguard 2016) and the approach is under consideration for improving participation in Ireland. Australia and Chile go even further with compulsory retirement plan participation for all employees.

It has also been shown that 'save more tomorrow' approaches—involving automatically escalating contribution rates—can be effective in boosting contribution rates over time (Benartzi and Thaler 2007). This can allow for participants to be introduced to retirement saving at a low rate, avoiding adverse reaction to reductions in take-home pay, before being raised to the long-term required levels. This approach is in use in a growing number of large US plans (Vanguard 2016), and in the UK and Australia automatic enrollment and autoescalation have been introduced.

Matching contributions can also be used to encourage voluntary contributions to the match threshold. This can be employer contributions in response to employee contributions, or tax relief for employee contributions which may be presented as a form of matching (relief from 20 percent tax can be recast as 1:4 matching, which may be simpler for participants to understand.)

Finally, reducing pre-retirement 'leakage' of retirement assets will help enhance savings rates. This can include ensuring accumulated assets roll over into a retirement plan on job change rather than being cashed out, and avoiding early withdrawals. For example, the UK 'pension freedoms' abolished annuitization and provided full access to retirement assets from age 55. Early evidence shows a significant number of participants taking withdrawals in their 50s for non-retirement reasons (leisure, home improvement) with relatively little consideration for the impact on longer-term retirement income (State Street Global Advisors 2016).

Making it easier for people to work for longer. As the calculations above show, creating a better retirement income system in the face of low returns will require longer working lives. This means creating incentives for individuals to stay employed (which may mean reskilling or re-engineering job roles), and moving away from conventional retirement ages.

Another important question is how employers will facilitate and value older workers. Some firms already employ them as a source of competitive advantage: for example, B&Q, a home improvements store chain in the UK, is known to employ retirees who are able to advise customers with a lifetime of experience of household maintenance. Yet other firms are not ready for the increasing number of older workers (see Sonsino's chapter in this volume). There may also be regulatory barriers such as compulsory retirement ages to be overcome. For example, both Sweden and the UK have abolished the compulsory retirement age for most positions. Additionally, policymakers may need to take steps to encourage the hiring of older workers, e.g. by subsidizing healthcare costs or reducing employment protections.

Another way to make retirement systems more sustainable is to raise the retirement age. Yet a uniform increase in the minimum retirement age risks may be seen as unfair to low earners who have lower average life expectancies and likely to be employed in jobs where extending the work life is challenging (Belbase et al. 2016). Many low earners also start their working careers earlier than those with higher levels of education, so asking everyone to extend their working lives could be seen as inequitable (Sanzenbacher et al. 2015). One answer might be to link the minimum eligibility for retirement benefits to years of work rather than age; as many low earners start work earlier than their college-educated contemporaries, the former would then qualify for retirement benefits at a younger age. Such an approach was considered by a recent UK review of state pension age (Cridland 2016), though no recommendation or policy change to that effect has been made as yet.

Conclusions

Increasing longevity and low expected returns confront today's workers with a more challenging environment in retirement saving than previous generations. Yet, if they save systematically throughout their careers and extend their working lives to age 70, a 10-percent contribution rate should be sufficient for most wage earners to achieve a reasonable replacement rate in retirement. Those aiming to retire earlier will obviously need to contribute more.

When considering appropriate contribution rates and retirement ages, it is necessary to take into account life expectancy differentials and the progressive replacement rate structure of state entitlements. Two implications for policymakers are relevant. First, rather than linking a right to receive the state pension to a uniform minimum age, one could link it to a minimum number of years of contributions. Second, those on very low incomes can achieve a reasonable replacement rate in retirement with savings rates in the low single digits, whereas those on higher incomes will require 12–15 percent saving rates. Policymakers considering introducing auto-enrollment regimes should think carefully about how high to set the default enrollment rates, because setting too high a rate may cause low earners to opt out. Yet a rate appropriate for low earners will be too low for those in higher wage groups. One possibility could be to have different auto-enrollment rates for different income cohorts.

For those who have started saving for retirement late, deferring retirement is an extremely powerful tool for improving retirement readiness. Not only does it shorten the time in retirement and increase the period of contributions and investment returns, it also significantly increases the income that participants can expect from social security. Participants who do not start saving until later in their working lives should plan to work until at least age 70.

Removing the maximum age for claiming social security benefits would likely benefit high earners the most, while providing lump sum incentives to defer claiming benefits could be more effective in encouraging low-income earners to delay retirement. While this analysis has focused mainly on retirement savings and social security claiming behavior, other strategies are worthy of future research. For instance, housing equity can be used to support retirement income. Our discussion has also ignored other strategies that could be used to boost investment returns (e.g. additional diversification or investing in illiquid assets) or to increase sustainable withdrawal rates (such as full or partial annuitization). Other chapters in this volume take these up (see Ilmanen and Rauseo; and Fichtner and Seligman).

References

Belbase, A., G. T. Sanzenbacher, and C. M. Gillis (2016). 'How do Job Skills that Decline with Age Affect White-Collar Workers?' Center for Retirement Research Working Paper Number 16–6. Boston, MA: Boston College.

Benartzi, S., and R. Thaler (2007). 'Heuristics and Biases in Retirement Savings Behavior.' *Journal of Economic Perspectives* 21(3): 81–104.

Cridland, J. (2016). *State Pension Age Independent Review: Interim Report*, London, UK: Department for Work and Pensions.

Department for Work and Pensions (2014). *Automatic Enrolment Opt Out Rates, Department for Work and Pensions*. London, UK: DWP.

Fichtner, J. J., and J. S. Seligman (2018). "Retirement Saving and Decumulation in a Persistent Low-Return Environment," in R. Clark, R. Maurer, and O. S. Mitchell (eds.), *How Persistent Low Returns Will Shape Saving and Retirement*. Oxford, UK: Oxford University Press, pp. 132–62.

Gale, W. G., and D. C. John (2018). "State-sponsored Retirement Savings Plans: New Approaches to Boost Retirement Plan Coverage," in R. Clark, R. Maurer, and O. S. Mitchell (eds.), *How Persistent Low Returns Will Shape Saving and Retirement*. Oxford, UK: Oxford University Press, pp. 173–93.

Gorodnichenko, Y., J. Song, and D. Stolyarov (2013). *Macroeconomic Determinants of Retirement Timing.* Bonn, Germany: Institute for the Study of Labor (IZA).

Ilmanen, A., and M. Rauseo (2018). "Intelligent Risk Taking: How to Secure Retirement in a Low Expected Return World" in R. Clark, R. Maurer, and O. S. Mitchell (eds.), *How Persistent Low Returns Will Shape Saving and Retirement.* Oxford, UK: Oxford University Press, pp. 81–98.

Johnson, M. (2016). 'The State Pension: No Longer Fit for Purpose.' *Centre for Policy Studies.* London, UK: CPS. http://www.cps.org.uk/publications/the-state-pension/

MacDonald, B. J., L. Osberg, and K. D. Moore (2016). 'How Acurately Does 70% Final Employment Earnings Replacement Measure Retirement Income (In)adequacy? Introducing the Living Standards Replacement Rate (LSSR).' *Astin Bulletin* 46(3): 627–76.

Maurer, R., O. S. Mitchell, R. Rogalla, and T. Schimetscheck (2016). 'Will They Take the Money and Work? People's Willingness to Delay Claiming Social Security Benefits for a Lump Sum.' NBER Working Paper No. 20614. Cambridge, MA: National Bureau of Economic Research.

Maurer, R., O. S. Mitchell, R. Rogalla, and T. Schimetscheck (2017). 'Optimal Social Security Claiming Behavior under Lump Sum Incentives: Theory and Evidence.' NBER Working Paper No. 203073. Cambridge, MA: National Bureau of Economic Research.

Munnell, A., and A. Webb (2015). 'The Impact of Leakages from 401(k)s and IRAs.' Center for Retirement Research at Boston College Working Paper No. 2015–2. Boston, MA: Center for Retirement Research.

Munnell, A., A. Webb, and W. Hou (2014). 'How Much Should People Save?' Center for Retirement Research at Boston College Working Paper No. 14–11. Boston, MA: Center for Retirement Research.

Office of the Chief Actuary (2014). 'Annual Scheduled Benefit Amounts (with Replacement Rates for Retired Workers with Various Pre-retirement Earnings Patterns Based on Intermediate Assumptions.' Social Security Administration. http://crr.bc.edu/data/frd/

Olshansky, S. J., T. Antonucci, R. H. Binstock, A. Boersch-Supan, J. T. Cacioppo, B. A. Carnes, L. L. Carstensen, L. P. Fried, D. P. Goldman, J. Jackson, M. Kohli, J. Rother, Y. Zheng, and J. Rowe (2012). 'Differences in Life Expectancy Due to Race and Educational Differences are Widening, and Many May Not Catch Up.' *Health Affairs* 31(8): 1803–13.

Pensions Myndigheten (2016). *Du Bestammer Sjalv nar du Vill ta ut Pension.* Stockholm, Sweden: Swedish Pensions Authority. https://www.pensionsmyndigheten.se

Sanzenbacher, G. T., A. Webb, C. M. Cosgrove, and N. S. Orlova (2015). 'Calculating Neutral Increases in Retirement Age by Socioeconomic Status.' Center for Retirement Research Working Paper No. 2015–22. Boston, MA: Boston College.

Sonsino, Y. (2018). "Helping Employers Become Age-Ready," in R. Clark, R. Maurer, and O. S. Mitchell, (eds.), *How Persistent Low Returns Will Shape Saving and Retirement.* Oxford, UK: Oxford University Press, pp. 165–72.

State Street Global Advisors (2016). 'New Choices: Big Decisions.' State Street Global Advisors SSGA White Paper. Boston, MA: State Street Global Advisors.

Vanguard (2016). *How America Saves 2016: Annual Report on Trends in Retirement Saving*. Malvern, PA: Vanguard. https://pressroom.vanguard.com/nonindexed/ HAS2016_Final.pdf

Waldron, H. (2007). 'Trends in Mortality Differentials and Life Expectancy for Male Social Security-covered Workers, by Socioeconomic Status.' *Social Security Bulletin* 67(3): 1–28.

Williams, J. (2017). *Three Questions of R-star*. San Francisco, CA: Federal Reserve Bank of San Francisco. http://www.frbsf.org/economic-research/publications/economic-letter/2017/february/three-questions-on-r-star-natural-rate-of-interest

Chapter 6

Intelligent Risk Taking: How to Secure Retirement in a Low Expected Return World

Antti Ilmanen and Matthew Rauseo

Low market yields on stocks and bonds have historically led to depressed prospective returns for both asset classes. Today's low return environment makes it challenging for investors to meet their future liabilities. While this is true for all investors, from the most sophisticated institutions to individual investors saving for retirement, the impact of this low return environment on securing retirement is far less well understood.

In simplest terms, the liabilities of defined benefit (DB) pension plans can be thought of as what sponsors need to have on hand to meet the future retiree obligations. For decades, professional investors have been managing DB plan assets with an eye to meeting future liabilities. By contrast, the same foresight has not always been used for employee-directed plans such as defined contribution (DC) plans. The liability that DC investors should be concerned with is their post-retirement consumption. DC plans are financed over time by a combination of employee and employer contributions as well as real investment returns on those contributions. Nevertheless, a secure retirement is the sole responsibility of the employee, not the retirement plan sponsoring the program. In our previous work we have explored ways DC plans might become more like DB plans in addressing this challenge (Ilmanen et al. 2017).

The economics of retirement saving are well established. Post-retirement consumption is a function of three drivers: time, savings, and real investment returns. Time represents the length of a participant's accumulation period, beginning when she starts saving for retirement and concluding when retirement begins. Time may also include the decumulation period of an uncertain length. (This chapter will not cover decumulation strategies, mortality pooling, and related important topics.) Savings represent the periodic contributions made by both the participant and the plan sponsor. Savings can be expressed in dollars or in a rate (say, as a percentage of income). Finally, the driver we focus on here is the real investment return generated by the investor's portfolio. This return reflects both portfolio holdings and market outcomes.

Of course, there is no single DC portfolio, as participants have the ability to construct their own given the investment options their plan sponsor makes available. That said, DC portfolio strategies have tended to become more similar in the United States since the Pension Protection Act of 2006, which allowed for automatic enrollment into qualified default investment alternatives. These are typically a pre-constructed diversified portfolio, resulting in a step toward better design and more efficient investing in DC plans. While Target Date Funds (TDFs) have shortcomings (Dhillon et al. 2016), this chapter focuses on intelligent ways to take investment risk in an effort to improve a DC portfolio's real investment return. Ultimately, the goal is to meet a participant's liability, which is his or her target for post-retirement income.

A Percent Saved is not a Percent Earned

Our examination of how capital market returns shape a DC investor's ability to consume in retirement is informed by previous research (Ilmanen et al. 2016). There we showed that capital market returns have an outsized impact on saving accruals. Figure 6.1 shows the amount of DC savings needed to

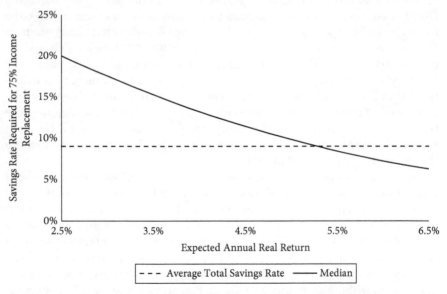

Figure 6.1. Savings rate required for 75-percent income replacement in a range of market environments

Source: Authors' calculations using AQR data. This assumes investment in a stock/bond glidepath, which transitions from a 90/10 stock/bond mix to a 50/50 split at retirement over a 40-year working period. Average contribution and employer match statistics (total savings rate) is according to the Cerulli Retirement Markets Report (2015).

generate a 75-percent income replacement ratio (as a fraction of the final salary),[1] which is our proxy for a comfortable retirement at the typical retirement age of 65. Results cover a range of capital market environments. As one would expect, higher capital market expectations translate to lower required savings rates; however, the trade-off is not one-for-one. The amount of additional savings required to offset a one-percentage-point reduction in capital market expectations varies depending on the initial return expectations. For example, a decrease in returns from 5.5 to 4.5 percent requires a savings increase of 3 percent, while a decrease from 4.5 to 3.5 percent requires 4 percent additional savings to meet the same income replacement goal of 75 percent.

The key point here is not the nonlinearity, but the steep negative slope. Although these are estimates, the takeaway is that participants would have to save meaningfully more to achieve the same goal, all else equal, in order to compensate for the prospectively low capital market returns. Based on today's typical 9 percent savings rate among DC savers, participants need to achieve a real return in excess of 5 percent annually on their investment portfolios to retire comfortably. Much of the DC literature in the past has happily assumed such return prospects because they were broadly consistent with past realized return experience. But looking ahead, such 'rearview mirror' expectations ignore the fact that starting yields are much lower today. Moreover, both past stock and bond returns have been boosted by windfall gains in recent decades (and since 2009). Additionally, low expected returns may have greater consequences than reduced savings accruals. Quinn and Cahill in their chapter in this volume explore how lower future returns may lead to higher savings in non-retirement accounts and Social Security benefits being claimed later in people's life.

What Returns Will the Future Hold?

Predicting future market returns is notoriously difficult, and even the most reliable forecasting methods have limited predictive power (Zhou 2010). Therefore, a healthy dose of skepticism should be present when considering return forecasts over a 40- or 60-year period. That said, we believe that at current market yields and valuations, it is unlikely that DC portfolios will achieve a real return close to what was experienced in the past and is needed for participants saving 9 percent annually over the course of their careers to generate adequate consumption in retirement, especially when investing in traditional DC portfolios.

Figure 6.2 shows the prospective real yield on a US 60/40 stock and bond portfolio going back through time. We believe this is a reasonable proxy for long-term real returns. This estimate of the real equity return is a simple average of the Shiller earnings yield (which uses smoothed ten-year earnings)

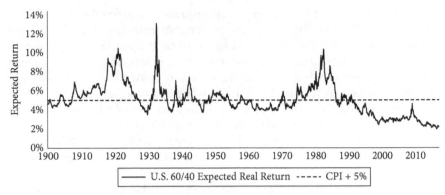

Figure 6.2. Expected return of US 60/40 stock/bond portfolio, January 1900 to
March 2017

Source: Authors' calculations using AQR data.

and an estimate based on a basic dividend discount model (the sum of
dividend yield and 1.5 percent to account for the trend real rate of growth
of dividends per share, assuming no change in valuations). The real bond
yield is the ten-year Treasury yield adjusted for expected inflation (based on
economist consensus forecasts in recent decades and based on statistical
estimates before survey data is available). During much of the 20th century,
expected as well as realized, long-term real returns for a 60/40 portfolio
frequently exceeded the 5 percent return required for today's savings environment. But today's expected real returns fall short of the 5-percent bogey,
and they are among the lowest seen in history (at 2.2 percent, as shown in
Figure 6.2).

While we believe that such current yield measures have limited ability to
predict near-term returns, they may be reasonable anchors for realized
future returns over the next decade. Extrapolating our view for the next
decade to accommodate an entire savings and retirement window, we anticipate that future returns will be closer to 3.5 percent for a global 60/40 stock
and bond portfolio. This multi-decade expectation assumes some increase in
starting yields beyond the next decade. Even for the first decade, our
expected returns could be somewhat higher than shown in Figure 6.2,
because non-US stocks have higher yields than US stocks, and global fixed
income should include credit spreads on non-government bonds as well as
so-called rolldown gains.

Savings, Time, and Returns

For DC investors to achieve a comfortable retirement in a world with around
3.5 percent expected real return, they need to be saving at least 15 percent[2]

rather than the 9 percent participants are currently saving, on average.[3] When post-retirement consumption is the objective, either savings rates must be raised, the length of time participants contribute and earn investment returns must be lengthened, or investment returns must be increased. We next briefly summarize how the inputs related to each have changed in recent years, to improve participants' potential for retirement income.

Time. Retirement plan sponsors have recently sought to lengthen the accumulation phase through automatic enrollment, which allows employers to automatically place new employees in a retirement plan. As a result, the percentage of plans adopting auto-enrollment increased from 10 percent in 2006 to 41 percent in 2015 (Vanguard 2016). For participants who start active retirement saving late in life, other strategies may be needed, including making the most of their Social Security benefits.[4]

Savings. Retirement plan sponsors have also begun taking advantage of findings from behavioral finance that help encourage participants increase savings (Wurtzel 2015). Despite these efforts, however, participant savings rates have not improved much. Indeed, savings rates inclusive of the matching contribution have fallen from 10 percent to 9 percent since 2011 (Vanguard 2016; Blanchett et al., this volume).

Investment returns. There has also been some limited innovation related to TDFs. From a broad asset allocation perspective, the asset class allocation along the glide path has been largely unchanged. Slight increases in equity exposure have been seen for mid-career investors, but young savers and near-retirees have not changed their asset allocation much. Few enhancements have been added to date to the investment strategies in TDFs, such as alternative asset classes or strategies adopted by institutional pension plans and endowments (Morningstar 2017). Thus, it seems that investment returns are one area ripe for innovation.

Examining the DC Investors' Tool Box

Investors have a broad range of tools available to harvest returns, with the most recognized being the traditional asset classes of stocks and bonds. Stocks can harvest the equity risk premium, and bonds capture the term and credit premium. These traditional asset classes have long dominated DC investors' asset allocations in traditional ways. Fund menus include market cap-weighted, benchmark-centric strategies, that are either passively managed or utilize discretionary active managers. They are most frequently funded by cash rather than taking advantage of more capital-efficient techniques such as leverage. These traditional ways also limit holdings exclusively to long positions, rather than taking advantage of the ability to express negative views on securities by selling them short. Importantly, this no-shorting constraint rules out the ability to utilize market-neutral strategies designed to generate absolute returns without exposure to general equity and fixed income markets.

Such traditional investments implemented in traditional ways generate several benefits. Their efficacy as return drivers has been understood for decades, so they are the most conventional way to harvest risk premia. They are also relatively liquid and in this modern age of index funds, they can be accessed at very low cost to the investor. Indeed, cap-weighted indices are the only strategies that can be held by everyone at the same time.[5] Additionally, stock and bond returns are often only loosely correlated, providing solid building blocks for a portfolio.

Yet this approach also has several disadvantages. One is that, when combined in any typical equity-centric portfolios, the resulting asset allocation is undiversified. Superficially, this may not seem true when viewed through the lens of how the capital is allocated. But viewed through a risk allocation lens, a 50/50 capital split between stocks and bonds loads most of the portfolio risk onto equities. This is because equities usually have three times more volatility than bonds. So what may appear to be diversified may, in fact, imply extreme risk concentration and occasionally sharp drawdowns. Bad times, such as those in 2008, can, in turn, lead retirement savers to capitulate near the market bottom. Better risk diversification allows for higher risk-adjusted returns (Sharpe ratios) and can reduce the likelihood of ill-timed capitulations. The benefits of a higher Sharpe ratio portfolio can be realized either through the same expected return and lower corresponding portfolio volatility, higher expected return, and the same corresponding portfolio volatility, or some mixture of the two.

In the current low expected return environment for stocks and bonds, in which a 5 percent real return would require holding a highly risky all-equity portfolio, it arguably makes more sense to take Sharpe ratio improvements in the form of higher expected returns, while maintaining the same aggregate portfolio risk. In other words, the question is how investors might take risks more intelligently and efficiently when seeking to earn the 5 percent annual real return they need for a comfortable retirement at current savings rates.

Incorporating Intelligent Investing

We challenge the traditional approach to DC investing so as to improve expected return by (1) examining ways to allocate to traditional assets classes beyond market cap-weighted exposure, (2) more fully realizing the benefits of diversification by incorporating leverage, and (3) increasing the opportunity set by allowing for the shorting of unattractive securities (e.g. allowing for market-neutral strategies). To do so, we consider three additional types of investment strategies for inclusion in a DC investor's asset allocation.

Long-only style-tilted strategies. Sometimes referred to as 'smart beta,' this approach is based on well-known and generally accepted styles that have been shown in and out of sample to outperform market cap-weighted portfolios. It as an integrated strategy that overweights securities based on the attributes or styles that research has been shown to deliver positive excess return over time. In addition to positive excess return, these classic style exposures are backed by strong economic reasoning and out of sample evidence. For equities, those styles are value, momentum, and defensive. For fixed income, we also include carry. It may be reasonable to expect lower excess returns in the future from these tilts than historical evidence suggests. Specifically we assume that global style-tilted equities provide 1 percent incremental net return relative to cap-weighted global equities, while global style-tilted fixed income can outpace issuance-weighted global fixed income by about 0.75 percent net (Frazzini et al. 2013; AQR Capital Management 2016).

Risk parity strategies. Risk-based diversification seeks to generate both higher and more consistent returns across potential economic environments compared to a traditional portfolio. A risk parity approach allocates equal risk weight to each of the underlying asset classes, which for a DC portfolio can include global stocks, global bonds, and inflation-sensitive assets (both commodities and inflation-linked bonds). Risk parity is based on the observation that the risk-adjusted returns of traditional asset classes are more similar than they are different, so investing in each asset class is beneficial because each offers complementary performance in different economic environments. Risk parity portfolios hold a better combination of market exposures by including greater nominal exposure to low-risk asset classes and then moderately levering the portfolio to the desired risk level. Acknowledging the low expected return environment, we assume that a risk parity portfolio with 10 percent volatility will earn 4.6 percent annual real return net of fees over the long run, and the gross leverage utilized will be 2.25, on average (Hurst et al. 2010).

Alternative risk premia. The alternative risk premium approach is a cousin to long-only styles. As before, it seeks to capture exposure to the classic styles discussed above. But instead of holding a long-only portfolio where the style exposure is blended with traditional market beta, it involves a long/short portfolio applied in a more balanced way, across a diversified set of asset classes including stocks, bonds, equity indexes, and currencies. The advantage of capturing long/short style exposures is that the resulting portfolio can be engineered to be market-neutral, with each independent style and asset class combination having low correlation to the others. These low correlations provide an exceptional diversification benefit that has been shown in and out of sample to deliver consistent long-term performance unrelated to traditional stocks and bonds. The styles utilized are value, momentum, carry, defensive, and trend. A diversified portfolio of market-neutral style premia can be especially resilient across a range of macro-economic environments. In contrast, long-only portfolios (such as 60/40) tend to perform well amidst strong growth and low inflation, but they underperform in times of weak growth and high inflation (Ilmanen et al. 2014). It is again reasonable to expect somewhat lower future returns than historical evidence suggests. We assume that a portfolio of integrated long/short styles applied across the above set of asset classes with 9 percent volatility will generate 6.2 percent real return net of fees per year and utilize gross leverage of 5.75, on average (Moskowitz et al. 2012; Asness et al. 2015).

About Leverage

US DC plan sponsors have typically been leverage averse.[6] Nevertheless, other institutional investors have embraced moderate use of leverage as a valuable portfolio management tool to improve portfolio performance by increasing returns and/or by improving diversification and reducing risk concentration. That said, the use of leverage comes with risks that must be considered. Leverage magnifies exposures, and transaction costs can be high when bid-ask spreads are wide. Additionally, if an investor has inadequate cash reserves amidst falling asset prices, collateral requirements may force the investor to unwind the positions at inopportune times. Derivatives, which are often the type of security utilized to gain leveraged exposure, introduce risks of their own, specifically counterparty risk. This is the risk that the counterparty on the other side of the trades' credit deteriorates, or they cannot make good on their obligations; the use of exchange-traded futures can mitigate this risk.

These risks can be kept manageable by holding sufficient uninvested cash and sound risk management practices in levered strategies, and by applying leverage only on part of the overall portfolio. While these risks are real, prudent use of leverage through commonly traded derivatives can help investors achieve a more efficient risk diversification. Given that many investors tend to desire little or no leverage, we will only consider portfolios with limited embedded (that is, asset manager use of) leverage—gross holdings comprising less than twice the portfolio's unlevered assets—and recognize that even this may be difficult for many investors to pursue given leverage constraints (Asness et al. 2010).

Analysis of Stepwise Portfolio Improvements

To illustrate these concepts, we assume that the baseline DC portfolio has a global 60/40 stock and bond allocation. While this is a simplification, we note that most DC plan sponsors utilize TDFs as Qualified Default Investment Alternatives, and TDFs are the fastest-growing investment option within DC plans. Target Date Funds are typically multi-asset class portfolios diversified between stocks and bonds, with large allocations to stocks in the early years of a person's working life and gradually raising fixed income allocations later in life. While the exact composition of these funds varies by provider, a dollar-weighted average of the asset mix is generally close to a 60/40 portfolio.[7]

It should be noted that all the enhancements we consider can also be incorporated into a TDF menu with similar benefits to the investor. In fact, a global 60/40 portfolio is generally very similar to a 2025 vintage TDF, since that vintage's asset allocation holds roughly 61 percent equity and 39 percent fixed income (Morningstar 2017). Our goal is to show how the three types of investment strategies described above can help participants improve their outlook for adequate consumption in retirement, while targeting the same aggregate portfolio volatility as the baseline DC portfolio. We show how adding long-only style tilts to a cap-weighted portfolio improves the portfolio's expected real return. Then we examine how further additions of risk parity and alternative risk premia improve the portfolio's expected real return. In each case, we will constrain the amount of leverage utilized in an attempt to account for DC plan sponsors' inability or unwillingness to incorporate leverage. Finally, we solve for a portfolio that minimizes leverage while achieving a 5 percent expected rate of real return and is consistent with what a DC plan participant needs to earn over a life cycle to achieve a comfortable retirement while saving 'only' 9 percent of salary income. We believe a 3.4 percent expected real return is a reasonable approximation of what may be earned over multiple decades if a DC portfolio is invested in market cap-weighted equity index funds and issuance-weighted fixed income index funds. The assumptions used for all portfolio combinations can be found in Table 6.1. These stylized assumptions represent plausible estimates for a well-executed strategy in each context.

In the event a plan sponsor believes it can identify active managers who have the skill to generate alpha, the 3.4 percent real return can be augmented. Nevertheless, alpha is often elusive, expensive, and derived from an idiosyncratic investment process whose merits are hard to identify in advance. Each of our three proposed solutions represents ways to potentially generate additional return, so they are 'alpha' to the investor as long as they are underrepresented exposures within their portfolios; yet they are not idiosyncratic return sources. Rather, they are backed by scientific evidence

TABLE 6.1 Asset classes and investment strategies assumptions

	Net Real Return (%)	Expected Volatility (%)	Net Sharpe Ratio	Fees (%)
Global Equity	4.95	15.0	0.33	0.05
Global Fixed Income	0.95	5.0	0.19	0.05
Global Style-Tilted Equity	5.95	15.0	0.40	0.35
Global Style-Tilted Fixed Income	1.70	5.0	0.34	0.25
Risk Parity	4.60	10.0	0.46	0.40
Alternative Risk Premia	6.20	9.0	0.69	1.10

Note: Expected Sharpe ratio assumes zero real rate for cash and thus is the ratio of expected real return (net of fees) to expected volatility.

Source: Authors' calculations using AQR data. Expected real return assumptions are based on yield-based estimates for equities and bonds and for alternative risk premia and style tilts, a combination of discounted hypothetical performance and judgment. For cash, we assume a 0-percent real return, reflecting the current low-yield environment with some expectation of normalization. Volatilities are based on hypothetical and proxy index performance, rounded. Global equity is based on the MSCI World Index (cap-weighted); global fixed income is based on the Barclays Global Aggregate Index (hedged); global style-tilted equity is based on the MSCI World Index (style-tilted); global style-tilted fixed income is based on the Barclays Global Aggregate Index (hedged, style-tilted); risk parity is based on a global risk parity strategy comprised of equity, interest rate and inflation risk; alternative risk premia is based on a hypothetical multi-asset long/short style strategy.

identifying each of these premia as persistent and systematic sources of return that we believe can be harvested over the long term.

To demonstrate the possible performance impact for investors from the three proposed solutions, we first add long-only style-tilted strategies to replace the market cap-weighted equity index funds and issuance-weighted fixed income index funds. This maintains the same 60/40 allocation between stocks and bonds, resulting in estimated portfolio volatility of 9.4 percent and an expected real return of 4.3 percent. In this portfolio, while maintaining the no-leverage and no-shorting constraints, we have enhanced annual returns by 0.9 percent net of fees. These results appear as Portfolio 1 in Table 6.2.

Next, for Portfolio 2, we relax the no-leverage constraint and allow risk parity to be included within the solution. To do this, we run an optimization to maximize expected real return while maintaining the same 9.4 percent expected portfolio volatility and constraining gross leverage to 1.25. Under these conditions, a 51 percent allocation to style-tilted equities, a 29 percent allocation to style-tilted fixed income, and a 20 percent allocation to risk parity improves expected annual real returns to 4.4 percent net of fees. (The optimal allocation for risk parity would be higher, were it not for the leverage constraint.)

TABLE 6.2 Summary statistics of stepwise portfolio improvements

	DC Portfolio	Portfolio 1	Portfolio 2	Portfolio 3	Portfolio 4
		Add Style-Tilts	Add Risk Parity	Add Alternative Risk Premia	5% Real Return
Global Equity	60%	–	–	–	–
Global Fixed Income	40%	–	–	–	–
Global Style-Tilted Equity	–	60%	51%	55%	52%
Global Style-Tilted Fixed Income	–	40%	29%	26%	17%
Risk Parity	–	–	20%	11%	19%
Alternative Risk Premia	–	–	–	8%	12%
Total	100%	100%	100%	100%	100%
Expected Volatility	9.4%	9.4%	9.4%	9.4%	9.4%
Expected Real Return	3.4%	4.3%	4.4%	4.7%	5.0%
Expected Sharpe Ratio	0.36	0.45	0.47	0.50	0.53
Estimated Gross Leverage	1.00	1.00	1.25	1.50	1.82

Note: Expected Sharpe ratio assumes zero real rate for cash, thus is the ratio of expected real return (net of fees) to expected volatility.

Source: Authors' calculations using AQR data.

For Portfolio 3, we further relax the leverage constraint and also allow for short sales. In addition to risk parity, the alternative risk premia approach is also allowed. To do this, we again run an optimization to maximize expected real returns while maintaining the same 9.4 percent expected portfolio volatility. Portfolio leverage is constrained to 1.5 gross instead of 1.25. The constrained optimal portfolio includes 55 percent style-tilted equities, 26 percent style-tilted fixed income, 11 percent risk parity, and 8 percent alternative risk premia. It generates an expected 4.7 percent annual real return net of fees.

This illustrates in a stepwise fashion how participants may generate incremental return as they seek to finance their future retirement consumption. But constraining the gross leverage to 1.5 of unlevered long assets still produces a return shortfall for those seeking 5 percent real return. The expected returns for our three modified proposals are illustrated in Figure 6.3.[8]

Accordingly, we propose a fourth portfolio that takes a different approach. Rather than optimize returns while constraining leverage, the optimizer is asked to minimize the use of leverage while solving for a 5 percent expected

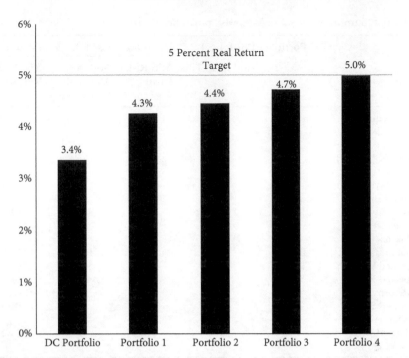

Figure 6.3. Expected real returns versus return target

Source: Authors' calculations using AQR data.

real return target based on return assumptions. Results in Figure 6.4 show a portfolio that generates an expected 5 percent real return (by construction), while still staying below embedded gross leverage of 2 (at 1.82). The final asset allocation is 52 percent style-tilted equities, 17 percent style-tilted fixed income, 19 percent risk parity, and 12 percent alternative risk premia. While this portfolio may at first seem materially more risky than the initial portfolio, it is important to keep in mind that the expected portfolio volatility is unchanged, since maintaining the same expected portfolio volatility is a condition of the optimization. A benefit of this approach is that, while portfolio volatility is the same throughout, the sources of that volatility are different and more diversified.

The top panel of Figure 6.4 shows that better diversification across strategies results in a higher return for the same level of portfolio volatility as long as leverage is allowed to convert higher risk-adjusted returns into higher raw returns. The bottom panel decomposes portfolio risk by showing the shares of key risk sources for total portfolio volatility (that is, summing up their volatilities and then computing volatility shares, ignoring correlations). In the traditional 60/40 portfolio, equity risk dominates with an

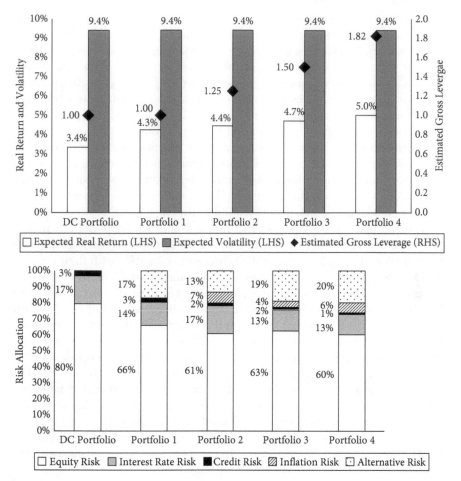

Figure 6.4. Expected return and risk of different portfolios and their portfolio risk allocation

Source: Authors' calculations using AQR data.

80 percent risk share (and higher if we calculate risk contributions including correlations), while equity share of risk falls to 60–66 percent in all other portfolios. Equity risk is replaced by 'alternative risk' from long-only style tilts and long/short alternative risk premia as well as by 'inflation risk' mainly from commodities (in risk parity).

The lesser risk concentration as we move from left to right in Figure 6.4 improves the portfolio's risk-adjusted return (Sharpe ratio), which we convert to higher expected return through some use of leverage instead of smoothing the ride by lowering portfolio volatility. Even at the same portfolio volatility, the ride may be mildly smoother since higher expected returns should cushion drawdowns, and more balanced risk sources often imply more balanced outcomes across different macroeconomic environments. But the main trade-off is between the concentrated risk exposure in the conventional equity-dominated portfolio, and the more diversified exposure to many return sources in an approach that involves embedded leverage and shorting to give a bigger role for market-neutral strategies. Any unconstrained mean-variance optimizer will favor portfolios with higher Sharpe ratios and thus the latter choice, even if, in practice, leverage or conventionality constraints keep many investors away from the efficient frontier. Investors who do not tolerate any embedded leverage may still consider Portfolio 1, which provides exposure to historically rewarded systematic tilts, but does not improve risk diversification as much.

Here we leave aside the question of the shape of the glidepath in our proposal: that is, we do not examine how investors should use the diversifying return sources (alternative risk premia and risk parity, with their embedded leverage) over their life cycles. One possibility would be to combine a typical TDF structure, where the allocations typically shift from stocks to bonds as the saver ages (in this case using style-tilted stocks and bonds), with a constant allocation to risk parity and alternative risk premia strategies. Better risk diversification could be especially important when retirement is approaching and the savings pot is large. In fact, one could propose increasing allocations to risk parity and alternative risk premia with age, but the flipside of better risk diversification is greater use of embedded leverage. While we believe that tools like leverage and shorting are intelligent ways to improve retirement portfolio risk-adjusted returns, whether to use them at all and whether to use them more at a later age must depend on investors' beliefs, preferences, and constraints. In practice, investor sophistication and familiarity with the pros and cons of leverage matter.

Other Paths to a 5-percent Solution

To augment returns today, many DC plans choose more traditional sources of alpha, most frequently in the form of traditional discretionary stock pickers who select securities that they believe will outperform a selected benchmark. Systematic managers seek to achieve the same goal by applying publicly known factors (style tilts and alternative risk premia), more proprietary alpha signals, or some combination of the two. Though we are not impartial observers on this topic, the systematic approach has attracted increasing institutional investor interest, reflecting some disappointment in the performance and relatively higher fees of traditional active management.

For investors willing to relax the leverage and shorting constraints but in a more limited way than required in full market-neutral strategies, relaxed constraint strategies such as 130/30 may be an attractive approach. These allow active managers more flexibility to implement their views by taking larger positions in attractive securities and short selling securities that are unattractive, while maintaining a market beta of one. An additional element that may make these types of strategies appealing to DC portfolios is that they are most frequently benchmarked to the same, or largely similar, indices already being used for DC portfolios.

Taking even more conventional risk is another possibility. Given our assumptions, the traditional way to achieve a 5 percent real return with passive indices would require an all-equity portfolio throughout the life cycle: a permanently high and flat glidepath in TDF jargon. But a meaningful equity market drawdown could then trigger even more ill-timed capitulations than seen in 2008 when investors near retirement held close to 50/50 portfolios.

An additional source of return worth investigating by DC plan sponsors is the illiquidity premium, which is often accessed by institutional investors through private equity investments. Private equity returns mainly reflect a combination of equity premia and illiquidity premia (and hopefully some manager alpha), so they may help boost the returns of a DC portfolio. Yet, unlike risk parity and alternative risk premia strategies, there is limited diversification benefit, especially when returns are adjusted for smoothing. Further, the need for daily pricing and daily liquidity makes implementation challenging within a DC plan.

A logical final question to pose is which investors may be interested in these proposed approaches, acknowledging that they do not have unlimited capacity? It is safe to say that, while these strategies are transparent and well documented, they are not easily understood by the layperson. These strategies are probably most appropriate for institutional DC plans with experience in underwriting complex investments, access and skill to identify the most competent managers, and scale to negotiate appropriate terms including fees.

Conclusion

In a world of low expected returns and inadequate savings, generating sufficient post-retirement income is difficult. DC plan sponsors have taken steps in recent years to boost saving levels, yet saving rates have remained stubbornly stable. And with greater longevity and lower expected market returns, it is unlikely that these changes will be sufficient to fund a secure retirement. Accordingly, it is logical to look for ways to enhance portfolio return.

By taking advantage of decades of experience and theory, it appears that expected returns can be boosted to cover participants' post-retirement needs. Doing so may not require increasing total portfolio risk, but it does require taking more intelligent risk and relaxing self-imposed constraints. We have shown that the prudent use of leverage, derivatives, and shorting can lead to portfolios that may deliver the required rate of 5 percent real return, without increasing the expected volatility of the portfolio. Further, this portfolio is more diversified across various systematic return sources, which may lead to more consistent performance across different economic environments and therefore better enables the investor to weather tough times.

Acknowledgments

The authors thank Jordan Brooks and Rodney Sullivan for helpful comments, and Max Freccia for excellent research assistance.

Notes

1. See Ilmanen et al. (2016) for details. The most important auxiliary assumptions include 30 percent of the replacement ratio coming from savings outside the DC plan (say, from Social Security or home ownership), and real income growing by 2 percent p.a. over a 40-year working life (reflecting both per-capita economic growth and wage growth from increasing experience/seniority).
2. We say at least 15 percent since this coincides with the median required savings rate. The mathematics of median indicates that 50 percent of the time the 15 percent savings rate will provide sufficient retirement income. Savers who want to self-insure against worse market outcomes than the base case in a low expected return world may need to save closer to 20 percent of their income. Thus, it is arguably better to think of 15 percent as a floor rather than a target.
3. This is an estimate that depends on assumptions used. In Ilmanen et al. (2016), we found that the broad conclusions were robust using a simple 60/40 portfolio or a more complex portfolio evolving along the typical TDF glidepaths used by the largest providers, as well as a reasonable range of auxiliary assumptions. Blanchett et al. in this volume explore the impact of expected return levels, as well as other parameters, on required savings rates and find comparable central estimates to ours.
4. For more details see Wallick et al.'s chapter in this volume.
5. Other strategies, including those suggested below, can help only a subset of investors. The fact that a market cap-weighted stock/bond portfolio does not offer 5 percent real return today means that, if subjective expectations remain anchored at such high levels, most investors will be disappointed in the future.

And it is hardly clear that DC savers as a group will be in the subset earning above-market returns through more risky or more intelligent choices.

6. While DC plan sponsors have been averse to leverage, it is rarely a binding constraint. For example, many DC plans use mutual funds as the underlying investment vehicle, and regulations do allow mutual funds to utilize leverage even though many do not. Some of the best-known fixed income mutual funds have long advocated and taken advantage of leverage as a portfolio management tool.

7. For example, assuming a salary growth of 2 percent, a savings rate of 9 percent, and a glidepath that gradually de-risks from 90 percent equities to 50 percent equities over 40 years, a real return assumption of 5 percent for stocks and 1 percent for bonds results in a dollar-weighted equity allocation of 62 percent, on average.

8. Even a 5 percent solution does not quite get us to 9 percent savings rate being sufficient, though it is close. In reality, some further increases in savings or reduced expectations of retirement security will be needed. (Also recall from our discussion of Figure 6.2 that for the next decade we expect baseline DC portfolio real returns below 3 percent, not 3.5 percent, so the prospect of any portfolio reaching 5 percent real return over this period is lower.)

References

AQR Capital Management (2016). 'Alternative Thinking: Style Investing in Fixed Income.' AQR White Paper. Greenwich, CT: AQR.

Asness C., D. Kabiller, and M. Mendelson (2010). 'Using Derivatives and Leverage to Improve Portfolio Performance.' Investors Archive, *Institutional Investor.* May 13: http://www.institutionalinvestor.com/Article/2486929/Investors-Archive/Using-Derivatives-and-Leverage-To-Improve-Portfolio-Performance.html#.WYtB9-mQyUk.

Asness C., A. Ilmanen, R. Israel, and T. Moskowitz (2015). 'Investing with Style.' *Journal of Investment Management* 13(1): 27–63.

Blanchett, D., M. Finke, and W. Pfau (2018). "Low Returns and Optimal Retirement Savings," in R. Clark, R. Maurer, and O. S. Mitchell (eds.), *How Persistent Low Returns Will Shape Saving and Retirement.* Oxford, UK: Oxford University Press, pp. 26–43.

Cerulli (2015). 'Retirement Markets 2015: Grown Opportunities in Maturing Markets.' *The Cerulli Report.* https://www.cerulli.com/vapi/public/getcerullifile?filecid=Cerulli-INFO-PACK-RQU-2015.

Dhillon J., A. Ilmanen, and J. Liew (2016). 'Balancing on the Life Cycle: Target Date Funds Need Better Diversification.' *Journal of Portfolio Management* 42(4): 12–27.

Frazzini A., R. Israel, T. Moskowitz, and R. Novy-Marx (2013). 'A New Core Equity Paradigm.' AQR Capital Management White Paper. Greenwich, CT: AQR Capital Management.

Hurst B., B. Johnson, and Y. Ooi (2010). 'Understanding Risk Parity.' AQR Capital Management White Paper. Greenwich, CT: AQR Capital Management.

Ilmanen A., D. Kabiller, L. Siegel, and R. Sullivan (2017). 'Defined Contribution Retirement Plans Should Look and Feel More Like Defined Benefit Plans.' *Journal of Portfolio Management* 43(2): 61–76.

Ilmanen, A., T. Maloney, and A. Ross (2014). 'Exploring Macroeconomic Sensitivities.' *Journal of Portfolio Management* 40(3): 87–99.

Ilmanen A., M. Rauseo, and L. Truax (2016). 'How Much Should DC Savers Worry about Expected Returns?' *Journal of Retirement* 4(2): 44–53.

Morningstar (2017). '2017 Target-Date Fund Landscape.' Chicago, IL: Morningstar. https://corporate1.morningstar.com/ResearchLibrary/article/803362/2017-target-date-fund-landscape/.

Moskowitz T., Y. Ooi, and L. Pedersen (2012). 'Time Series Momentum.' *Journal of Financial Economics.* 104(2): 228–50.

Quinn, J. F., and K. E. Cahill (2018). "Challenges and Opportunities of Living and Working Longer," in R. Clark, R. Maurer, and O. S. Mitchell (eds.), *How Persistent Low Returns Will Shape Saving and Retirement.* Oxford, UK: Oxford University Press, pp. 101–18.

Vanguard (2016). *How America Saves 2016, Vanguard 2015 Defined Contribution Plan Data.* Malvern, PA: Vanguard. https://pressroom.vanguard.com/nonindexed/HAS2016_Final.pdf.

Wallick, D. W., D. B. Berkowitz, A. S. Clarke, K. J. DiCiurcio, and K. A. Stockton (2018). "Getting More from Less in Defined Benefit Plans: Three Levers for a Low-Return World," in R. Clark, R. Maurer, and O. S. Mitchell (eds.), *How Persistent Low Returns Will Shape Saving and Retirement.* Oxford, UK: Oxford University Press, pp. 44–60.

Wurtzel M. (2015). 'From Academia to Plan Design.' *Pensions and Investments,* October 19: http://www.pionline.com/article/20151019/PRINT/151019912/from-academia-to-plan-design.

Zhou, G. (2010). 'How Much Stock Return Predictably Can We Expect from an Asset Pricing Model?' *Economic Letters* 108: 184–6.

Part II
Whither Retirement Strategies?

Chapter 7

Challenges and Opportunities of Living and Working Longer

Joseph F. Quinn and Kevin E. Cahill

Older persons contemplating retirement today are more exposed to market forces and financial insecurity than were their predecessors, due to demographic change, the trend to defined contribution plans, and macroeconomic volatility (Quinn and Cahill 2016). With public sector budgets also strained, many older individuals must either extend their working lives or reduce their standards of living in retirement. The financial well-being of older households now appears to be more cyclical than in the past, with the outlook for retirement income security being stable or improving in a strong macroeconomic climate, but becoming unstable and declining during and following economic downturns. This choice presents older workers and their employers with both challenges and opportunities.

In response to these changes, some Americans are adapting, although the adequacy of their preparations remains to be seen. A century-long trend toward earlier retirement came to a halt in the 1980s and now has reversed, although the rate of reversal may now be slowing down (Quinn et al. 2011; Munnell 2015a). The rise in labor force participation at older ages is all the more notable because it is occurring while labor force participation among male and female workers aged 25 to 54 has declined steadily since 2000 (Hipple 2016). Older Americans represent a flexible workforce that is willing to change employers, occupations, and work intensity late in life (Johnson et al. 2009; Cahill et al. 2015a). This flexibility may serve as an antidote to the retirement income security challenge lying ahead (Smyer et al. 2009; James et al. 2016).

For the foreseeable future, individuals are likely to play a more central role in determining their own financial security in old age. Policymakers need to focus on the incentives facing older individuals and evaluate how these incentives can encourage continued work later in life among those who can do so, while protecting those who cannot. In this chapter we discuss important changes in the retirement environment, how older workers have been responding to these changes, and the significant challenges still ahead.

Policy Concerns Regarding Retirement Security

Both long-term trends in demographic aging and the current macroeconomic environment challenge our ability to maintain living standards as we age. Moreover, there are legitimate concerns regarding the income sources on which retirees have to rely.

Nearly two-thirds of older persons' income comes from sources about which potential retirees might be concerned: social security, pension benefits (including annuities), and asset income (US Social Security Administration 2016a). For those age 65+ in the lowest three income quintiles, the reliance is even higher: 85, 91, and 83 percent of total income comes from these three sources, with social security by far the most important (see Figure 7.1 and Table 7.1).

Social Security. The progressive nature of social security's benefit calculation formula disproportionately rewards those with lower lifetime earnings, providing lower absolute benefits but higher replacement rates. Yet the system and its recipients face many concerns ahead. The permanent benefit reduction for claiming at the Earliest Age of Eligibility—still age 62—will

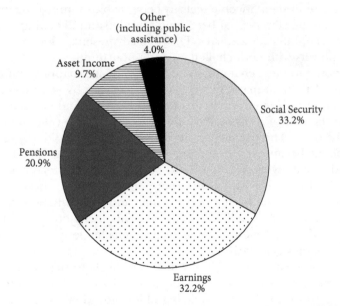

Figure 7.1. Shares of aggregate income for aged units 65+, by source (2014, %)

Note: Totals do not necessarily equal the sum of the rounded components. Aged units include married couples with a least one person aged 65 or older and non-married persons aged 65 or older.

Source: US Social Security Administration (2016a).

TABLE 7.1 Shares of aggregate income by source and quintile of total money income (2014)

Source	Bottom Quintile (%)	Second Quintile (%)	Middle Quintile (%)	Fourth Quintile (%)	Top Quintile (%)
Social Security	80.7	80.5	61.2	39.4	15.4
Earnings	3.0	5.3	12.6	23.7	45.2
Pensions	3.0	7.6	17.8	26.0	22.3
Asset income	1.8	2.4	4.1	5.7	14.0
Other	11.5	4.3	4.4	5.3	3.1

Source: US Social Security Administration (2016b).

increase from 20 to 30 percent, as the Full Retirement Age (FRA) rises from 65 to 67 for those born after 1959 (Board of Trustees of OASDI 2016).[1] This higher offset for those who claim benefits early disproportionately affects lower-income workers and those in physically-demanding occupations who may find it difficult to postpone benefit receipt until their FRA or beyond (Rutledge and Coe 2012).

Social security replacement rates (the ratio of benefits to prior earnings) for the average earner retiring at age 65 will decline from 42 percent in 1985 to a projected 36 percent in 2030.[2] In addition, the Medicare Part B premiums that are subtracted from social security benefits are rising faster than the cost of living, and more recipients will find part of their benefits subject to federal income taxation in the future.[3] When these two additional factors are considered, according to Munnell (2015b), the average replacement rate will drop even further, to 31 percent.

These pessimistic calculations assume that future social security benefits will be paid according to the current scheduled benefit formula, an optimistic assessment. This may well not occur because Social Security faces substantial long-term funding issues. Annual expenditures already exceed (non-interest) revenues, and without reform on the revenue and/or the expenditure side, the Social Security (OASDI) Trust Fund will be depleted by 2034. At that point, Social Security will be able to pay less than 80 percent of promised benefits (Board of Trustees of OASDI 2016). While reforms may occur in the interim, many proposed options spell trouble for future retirees since they involve benefit reductions, either explicitly or implicitly, through additional delays in the FRA.[4] The last major reform, in 1983, did just that, moving the FRA from 65 to 66, and then to 67, thereby lowering the benefits received at any given age.[5]

Employer pensions. About half of all employees in the private sector are covered by an employer pension on their current jobs and about 44 percent of those aged 65+ currently receive income from a pension other than Social

Security (US Social Security Administration 2016b). Although pension coverage has remained steady over time, the type of pension coverage provided has changed significantly, from traditional defined benefit (DB) to defined contribution (DC) plans.[6] DB pensions provide a defined monthly benefit at retirement (as does Social Security, a public DB plan), typically based on earnings and tenure with the firm.[7] By contrast, in a DC plan, the employer's only obligation is to make specified contributions to an account designated by the employee. The size of the account at retirement depends on the amount of these contributions and how these investments perform over the years.

In the United States, the percentage of workers with DB plans has plummeted from 88 percent in the early 1980s (including 26 percent who had both a DB and a DC plan) to only 30 percent in 2013 (including 13 percent with both). Over the same time, DC coverage only has risen from 12 to 71 percent (or including those covered by both from 38 to 84 percent; Munnell 2014). Nevertheless, accumulations in DC accounts remain relatively small. In 2013, for example, workers aged 55–64 with a DC plan had median 401(k) and individual retirement account (IRA) accumulations of about $110,000, enough to purchase a joint and survivor annuity of only about $500/month (Munnell 2014; Dushi et al. 2015).[8] Mean retirement account savings in 401(k)s, IRAs and Keogh plans do rise with age, as expected, averaging about $125,000 for those aged 50–55, and $164,000 for those 56–61 (see Figure 7.2). Because nearly half of American families

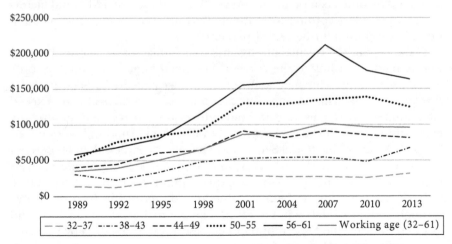

Figure 7.2. Mean retirement account savings of families by age (1989 to 2013)

Note: Figures in 2013 dollars. Retirement account savings include 401(k)s, IRAs, and Keogh plans.

Source: Morrissey (2016).

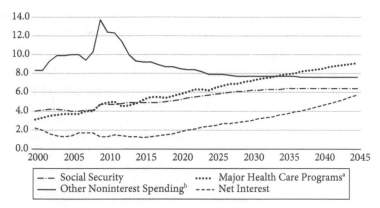

Figure 7.3. Federal spending as a percentage of GDP, by component (2000 to 2045)

Notes:

ᵃ Consists of spending on Medicare (net of offsetting receipts), Medicaid, and the Children's Health Insurance Program, as well as outlays to subsidize health insurance purchased through the marketplaces established under the Affordable Care Act and related spending.
ᵇ Consists of all federal spending other than that for Social Security, the major health care programs, and net interest.

Source: Derived from Congressional Budget Office (2010).

have no retirement account savings at all, the median (50th percentile) value among those aged 32–61 is only $5,000, and is under $10,000 for all except the oldest age group (56–61), whose median was only $17,000 (Morrissey 2016).[9] These amounts are modest at best, especially considering the likelihood of financial shocks in retirement.

Medicare and Medicaid. The fiscal challenges facing Social Security are modest and manageable compared to those facing Medicare and Medicaid. Social Security (OASI) reforms confront political resistance since many politicians do not want to be on record supporting increases in social security taxes or decreases in benefits, especially when Social Security is likely to meet its full obligations for the next 15 years or so. By contrast, Medicare and Medicaid reforms are much more difficult, because they involve not just checks to recipients but rather the provision of healthcare to the elderly. Federal spending on healthcare is projected to rise to almost 8 percent of GDP by 2040, and then head still higher, while social security benefit payouts reach a maximum of about 6 percent of GDP (see Figure 7.3).

Medicare's Hospital Insurance Trust Fund (Medicare Part A) is currently projected to be depleted by 2028, compared to 2034 for OASDI (Board of Trustees, Federal Hospital Insurance and Federal Supplementary Medical Insurance Trust Funds 2016).[10] Moreover, Medicaid costs are already burdening state budgets. For those contemplating retirement, the pending insolvency of Medicare and Medicaid is additional cause for concern.

Savings. Few older Americans have saved much for retirement. Nearly 60 percent of American workers (and over 40 percent of those age 45+) own less than $25,000 in financial assets, excluding the value of their primary residence and DB pension plans (Helman et al. 2016). Since life expectancy at 65 is currently about two decades, decades in which out-of-pocket medical expenses will increase for many, these modest assets provide very little financial cushion late in life.

Effects of the Current Low-Return Environment

The current low-return environment is exacerbating these challenges for older individuals. One downside of a low-return environment is lower returns on assets. Yet this has also been accompanied by lower rates of inflation (Federal Reserve Bank of St. Louis 2016; US Bureau of Labor Statistics 2016). Since social security retirement benefits are indexed for inflation, many older persons will not be affected. Nevertheless, timing issues can still be a concern. Retirees who lock in to annuities during a low-return period stand to lose if interest rates rise, while those who bought annuities during the earlier higher-return environment gain as the nominal returns on their assets are maintained when interest rates decline.[11]

The low return environment could also impact some older workers' decisions about when to leave the labor force and claim benefits. Overall, asset income provides about 10 percent of income for Americans aged 65+. That percentage rises slightly with age and dramatically by income quintile, from less than 3 percent for those in the bottom two quintiles to 14 percent for those in the top quintile, many of whom are still working (US Social Security Administration 2016b). The persistence of the low-return environment could very well deter retirement for these workers. Other individuals might choose to take on more financial risk to achieve higher average returns, at the cost of higher variation in returns.

Another important consequence of low returns is the impact on incentives to save and to take on debt, especially for younger Americans. The Federal Reserve Bank has kept interest rates at historical lows since the Great Recession, in part to induce spending and spur economic growth (Board of Governors of the Federal Reserve System 2016; Conti-Brown, this volume). Yet increased spending implies lower savings, and low interest rates can encourage individuals to incur debt. In turn, such changes in behavior can alter the financial outlook for younger and older workers alike, at a time when household financial security is already a real concern.

Retirement Preparedness

Taking into account each of these threads, it is of interest to assess the retirement preparedness of older households. One approach is to estimate household replacement rates, the ratio of income post- versus pre-retirement, assuming retirement at age 65 (Munnell et al. 2014). Those who fall more than 10 percent below what is required to maintain their prior standard of living are judged to be at risk and inadequately prepared for retirement. Figure 7.4 shows the results across time. In 2010 and 2013, more than half of American households had accumulated less than 90 percent of what they needed to maintain their pre-retirement standard of living.[12] The index jumped by 20 percent from pre- (2007) to post- (2010) recession, but this continued a long-term trend, up from near 30 percent in the 1980s to the high 30s in the 1990s to the mid-40s just before the recession. The index showed little improvement between 2010 and 2013, and it will be interesting to see the extent of the recovery (a decline in the index) when new data become available.

An alternative and more optimistic view is presented by Schieber (2015), who argues that workers will have larger defined contribution balances at retirement than do current retirees. Yet even so, he concludes that 'many low earners face retirement with inadequate resources to provide an income that will allow them to maintain either a socially acceptable standard of living or one that matches that achieved while they were working' (Schieber 2015: 16).

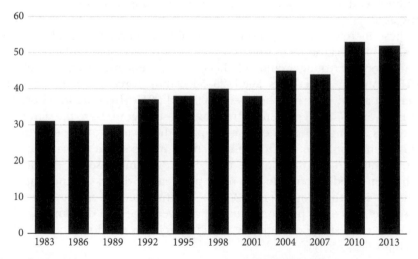

Figure 7.4. The national retirement risk index (1983 to 2013, %)

Source: Munnell (2015b).

What Might Concerned Potential Retirees Do?

Later in life, as people approach traditional retirement ages, the options are limited. An answer for many is simple—either consume less during retirement, or work longer before retirement. The latter can be either on a career job, or on one or more post-career bridge jobs, before complete labor force withdrawal.

Working longer provides additional lifetime earnings and the opportunity for incremental saving, augments the size of eventual pension and social security benefits (especially if receipt of social security benefits, which rise by about 8 percent per year of delay, are postponed while working), and also reduces the number of years of retirement during which these augmented assets will be consumed. The numerator (retirement resources) increases while the denominator (years of retirement) declines. This message has already hit home, since a trend toward delayed labor-force withdrawal has been underway for three decades.

Retirement trends: when do people retire? As seen in Table 7.2, the labor force participation rate of men aged 62 increased between 1985 and 2016 by nearly 20 percent (from 51 to 60 percent) after a century of decline. For men age 65, 68, and 70, the changes were even more dramatic, increasing by approximately 50, 60, and 70 percent over the past three decades.[13] For older women, the increases are even larger. Since 1985, the labor force participation rate of women aged 62 has risen by over 60 percent (from 32 to 51 percent), and for those age 65, 68, and 70, the rates have approximately doubled. Older Americans are already working longer than they did a short time ago.

These increased participation rates of older Americans are all the more remarkable because they came at a time when participation labor market attachment of younger and middle-aged workers has declined (Hipple 2016). Among Americans aged 25–54, labor force participation rates declined about 4 percent between 2000 and 2015 (from 92 to 88 percent for men, and 77 to 74 percent for women), in stark contrast to the significant increases among older Americans. In part, the reversal of the early retirement trend could be due to the reductions in the social security earnings test, eliminated for those above their FRA, and increases in the delayed retirement credit from 3 to 8 percent per year of delay. On the employer pension side, the move from DB to DC plans removed strong retirement incentives, since DB pensions often paid lower expected discounted values after the earliest age of eligibility. This implicit pay cut does not occur in a DC plan.

Retirement patterns: How do people retire? Recent cohorts have redefined the meaning of the term 'retirement.' Three common pathways from career

TABLE 7.2 US labor force participation rates by age and sex (1985 to 2016, %)

	55	60	62	65	68	70	72
				Men			
1985	83.7	71.0	50.9	30.5	20.5	15.9	14.9
1990	85.3	70.5	52.6	31.9	23.4	17.1	16.4
1995	81.1	68.9	51.3	33.5	22.4	20.6	16.0
2000	79.8	66.2	53.0	35.9	28.1	20.2	18.5
2005	80.6	67.7	57.7	39.7	32.2	23.8	21.6
2010	82.2	69.0	59.0	42.7	33.4	24.7	23.9
2015	80.6	70.3	60.5	44.8	32.6	27.3	22.7
2016	80.2	70.9	60.1	46.3	32.6	27.1	23.2
% Change 1985–2016	-4	0	18	52	59	70	56
				Women			
	55	60	62	65	68	70	72
1985	55.5	41.9	31.5	16.2	12.1	9.0	8.2
1990	59.8	44.8	34.9	20.6	15.2	11.7	8.0
1995	64.6	49.2	36.3	22.3	15.2	10.7	9.8
2000	65.2	51.5	38.7	23.2	16.6	10.9	10.8
2005	69.8	55.7	44.6	28.3	20.6	16.7	11.8
2010	72.8	61.0	49.7	33.7	23.7	17.3	14.6
2015	70.2	57.6	50.1	35.6	24.4	18.7	13.9
2016	68.0	58.6	50.7	35.0	24.3	18.1	14.5
% Change 1985–2016	23	40	61	116	101	101	77

Source: US Bureau of Labor Statistics (2017).

employment to complete labor force withdrawal have been identified: phased retirement (a reduction in hours with one's current employer), bridge employment (a job change following career employment, with or without a change in hours), and job re-entry (a subsequent return to the labor force following 'retirement'—sometimes known as 'unretirement') (Kantarci and van Soest 2008; Maestas 2010; Cahill et al. 2015b; 2016). These retirement patterns are usually studied subsequent to career employment (full-time work for a significant duration), but job changes later in life are also common among those who have never had a career job (Cahill et al. 2012).

Bridge employment is the most prevalent form of gradual retirement among those with career jobs (Quinn 1999; Cahill et al. 2006, 2015b). An analysis of three cohorts of older Americans from the Health and Retirement Study (HRS) over a 20-year period showed that between 50 and 60 percent of older career workers moved to a bridge job following career employment. The majority of career workers did not follow a 'traditional' pathway directly from career employment to complete labor force withdrawal. Re-entry was the next most common form of gradual retirement. About 15 percent of career workers who were out of the labor force for at least two HRS survey waves years later returned to paid work (Cahill et al. 2011).

The least prevalent form of gradual departure was phased retirement, with only 10 percent of workers reducing their hours on a career job by 20 percent or more (Cahill et al. 2015b). Phased retirement would seem to be a preferable exit route since workers could continue to capitalize on accumulated specific human capital in a familiar environment. Factors on both the supply and demand sides of the labor market help explain its low prevalence. On the labor supply side, individuals might choose to change employers to alter the type or intensity of the work they do, or prefer to move to warmer climes or closer to grandchildren. Lower hours on a career job might decrease subsequent pension benefits if they are based on the last few years of earnings. The concept of 'encore jobs'—those with a social impact—is also attractive to many (Johnson et al. 2009; Quinn 2010; Alboher 2012), and surveys show that older Americans care about the non-financial aspects of their work (AARP 2014).

On the demand side, legal and regulatory requirements can present obstacles for some employers. Regulations designed to restrict tax-deferred benefits for highly compensated individuals seem to have limited the possibility of phased retirement for older workers. Rules regarding pension distributions can also complicate phased retirement offerings (Johnson 2011). When faced with the choice between full-time work or changing employers, some workers might decide to leave the labor force entirely, and retain the option of labor market re-entry as a contingency plan.

Another important barrier to continued work later in life on a career job or elsewhere is physical or mental health. Increases in longevity and improvements in overall health have reduced the percentage of workers for whom physical health presents a barrier to continued work, while a shift away from physically demanding jobs over time has also expanded options for older workers (Steuerle et al. 1999; Penner et al. 2002; Munnell et al. 2004). Nonetheless, it is important to keep in mind that continued work later in life may be difficult for a portion of the labor force.

Future retirement trends. One might expect the retirement patterns of future retirees to differ from those of the past for at least three reasons in addition to those already mentioned: the impacts of the 2008–2009 Great Recession, the subsequent sluggish recovery (Desilver 2014), and the persistent low-return environment. Older Americans who had planned to live on investment asset returns may alter their retirement plans. While equity returns since 2010 have been strong (Wall Street Journal 2016), older Americans relying on investments are exposed to financial losses in the event of another market downturn.

A preview of future retirement trends is available from the HRS. We have compared the retirement patterns of the Early Boomers (aged 51–56 in 2004) and Mid-Boomers (aged 51–56 in 2010), to those of two older HRS cohorts, the HRS Core (aged 51–61 in 1992) and the War Babies (aged 51–56 in 1998). In each cohort we selected individuals working at a full-time career (FTC) job at the time of their first interview.[14] We then followed these people over time and used each respondent's work history to identify his pathway to retirement (directly, or via phased retirement, bridge job, or job re-entry). We found that bridge employment continues to be the most common gradual retirement pathway for Early and Mid-Boomers, among those who left career employment (see Table 7.3). Few Early Boomers reduced hours in career employment by 20 percent or more.

In other words, the latest data available suggest that recent cohorts are following the same pathways to retirement as did their predecessors, despite their exposure to market fluctuations and the low return environment since 2008. The concept of retirement as a one-time, permanent event does not apply for most older Americans today and has not for decades.[15] This observed flexibility of older workers is good news and offers opportunities to address the challenges of societal aging.

Conclusion

The persistent low-return environment appears to be influencing older individuals' decisions to hold and take on additional debt. The percentage of individuals aged 65 and older with debt increased from 30 percent in 1998 to 43 percent in 2010, with the average leverage ratio—total household debt divided by total household assets—doubling over the same period from 6 percent to 13 percent (Karamcheva 2013). Further, 11 percent of Middle Boomers are now in debt; i.e., have negative net worth (The Center for Retirement Research 2017). More research is needed to understand the degree to which older Americans with sizable debt are vulnerable to a rise in interest rates. Those relying on financial assets in a low-return environment may be tempted to increase asset returns by accepting more investment risk, as well as work longer to supplement their retirement savings. Lusardi and Mitchell (2017) also show that older American women have more debt today than did previous cohorts, and this is positively associated with older women being more likely to work currently, as well as plan to continue to work in the future. To the extent that workers are physically able to work longer, their additional labor supply can be beneficial to these individuals, to their employers, and to society as a whole, as more goods and services are produced to be distributed over an aging population.

TABLE 7.3 Prevalence and part-time status of bridge employment, phased retirement, and re-entry by sex and health and retirement study cohort

	n[a]	Still on or last observed on career job (%)	Moved to bridge job (%)[b]	Moved to no job (%)	Don't know (%)	Bridge job /(bridge job + no job) (%)	PT bridge job (%)[c]	SE bridge job (%)[d]	Reduced FTC job hours >/= 20% On FTC (%)	Reduced FTC job hours >/= 20% Moved (%)	Reentered (%)[e]
Men											
HRS Core	1,417	36	33	27	4	56	40	17	12	7	7
War Babies	586	39	34	23	4	60	40	16	10	8	8
Early Boomers	656	38	32	26	3	55	26	14	10	5	6
Mid Boomers	759	77	7	9	8	46	60				
Women											
HRS Core	1,145	35	34	28	4	55	55	11	10	10	10
War Babies	406	35	38	22	5	64	47	9	8	7	7
Early Boomers	558	37	37	24	3	61	39	10	9	2	5
Mid Boomers	718	71	12	10	8	55	83				

Notes:

[a] Includes respondents aged 51–56 on a wage-and-salary full-time career (FTC) job at the time of the first interview. Transitions are measured within ten years of the first interview, with the exception of the Mid Boomers for whom transitions are measured within four years of the first interview (i.e., by 2014).

[b] Does not include respondents who were not working for two consecutive waves following FTC employment and who later re-entered.

[c] Percentage of respondents working part-time in bridge employment as a percentage of all individuals who transitioned to a bridge job; part-time employment is defined as working fewer than 1,600 hours per year.

[d] Percentage of respondents who were self-employed in bridge employment as a percentage of all individuals who transitioned to a bridge job.

[e] Percentage of respondents who returned to paid work after not having worked for at least two consecutive waves at some point following career employment.

Source: Authors' calculations.

Notes

1. Johnson et al. (2013) report that social security claiming rates at age 62 have declined over the past decade. Among men born in 1943 and 1944, 45 percent claimed benefits at age 62 compared with 55 percent of those born between 1935 and 1937. Approximately one half of women born in 1943 and 1944 claimed social security benefits at age 62, down from 60 percent among those born between 1935 and 1937.

2. The replacement rates reported by the Board of Trustees of OASDI, and referenced in Munnell (2015b), are based on social security benefit amounts as a percentage of career-average earnings, indexed for wage growth (Board of Trustees of OASDI 2013). Biggs and Springstead (2008) measure pre-retirement earnings in different ways (wage-indexed average earnings, inflation-adjusted average earnings, final earnings (based on a five-year average), and a present value of lifetime earnings), and do so on an individual basis and a shared basis for couples. The latter authors find that replacement rates vary depending on how pre-retirement income is measured. On a shared basis, for example, the median benefit replacement rate varies from 39 percent for wage-indexed average earnings to 55 percent for final earnings among individuals aged 64 to 66 in 2040 in the middle lifetime earnings quintile.

3. Couples with 'combined income' of over $32,000 and individuals over $25,000 pay income tax on 50 percent of their social security benefits. At combined incomes of $44,000 and individual incomes of $34,000, 85 percent of Social Security benefits are taxable. These thresholds are not indexed for inflation, so the percentage of recipients paying taxes on social security benefits will rise over time, from about 10 percent in 1985 to about 40 percent today, and an estimated half of recipient households by 2030 (Munnell 2015b).

4. Waiting longer for a given benefit implies getting a smaller benefit at any given age, which is an across-the-board benefit cut, although it is rarely described that way.

5. Many recent reform proposals do the same. For example, the 2010 Simpson-Bowles report, *The Moment of Truth*, proposed (among other changes) lowering benefits for higher-income recipients, increasing both the FRA and the Early Eligibility Age (which is still 62 for all) in step with future longevity increases, and lowering the annual cost-of-living adustment, all three of which would lower future social security benefits relative to the current provisions (National Commission on Fiscal Responsibility and Reform 2010: 54). The Congressional Budget Office (2010) discussed five categories of Social Security reforms, three of which would lower future benefits, via formula changes to reduce initial benefits, additional increases in the FRA, and reductions in cost-of-living adjustments. In fact, a majorityof the 30 proposals the CBO analyzed would lower future benefits (Congressional Budget Office 2010). While none of these have been implemented yet, they do suggest that reasonable reformers will include benefit cuts in their recommendations.

6. Some analysts disagree with the assessment that coverage has been flat. Munnell (2014), using the 2013 Survey of Consumer Finances (SCF), argued that among prime-age private sector workers, the percent participating in an employer pension on the current job has drifted from 50 percent down to the low 40s. Morrissey (2016), also using the 2013 SCF, estimated that participation by respondents or their spouses declined from 60 percent in 2001 to 53 percent in 2013. In contrast, Dushi et al. (2015) estimated that participation rates increased slightly from 58 percent in 2006 to 61 percent in 2012. While these participation rate estimates differ, there is unanimous agreement about the precipitous decline in traditional DB plans in the private sector.

7. Schieber (2015: 13) pointed out that many DB plans no longer automatically pay monthly benefits, but rather 'have restructured their plans so they also pay benefits at termination in the form of lump sums; most terminating workers . . . choose lump-sum payments over annuities.' Those who do claim lump sums then face the longevity risk facing defined contribution recipients, living beyond one's assets.

8. Ownership of DC assets is highly correlated with income. According to Munnell (2014), two thirds of those aged 55–64 in the fourth and fifth income quintiles had DC accounts, averaging $132,000 and $450,000 respectively. DC participation fell to 22 percent and 48 percent in the lowest two quintiles, and they averaged only $13,000 and $53,000 as they approached retirement (Munnell 2014: see Table 7.2). And many have no DC coverage at all.

9. Not surprisingly, retirement saving accounts are much more prevalent among high-income families. In 2013, only 8 and 30 percent of those in the lowest two quintiles had any such accounts, compared to about half of those in the middle quintile, and nearly 70 and 90 percent of those in the highest two quintiles. While over 60 percent of (non-Hispanic) white families had retirement accounts, only 26 and 40 percent of Hispanics and blacks did (Morrissey 2016, Charts 9 and 10). Schieber (2015) makes this same point, that utilization of retirement savings plans is highly correlated with income, and therefore that high-income workers are more likely to be well prepared to meet retirement needs.

10. Medicare Part A is the only component of Medicare that is funded by the FICA tax and that has a Trust Fund. Parts B (supplementary medical insurance) and D (prescription drug benefit) are funded annually from a variety of other sources.

11. The potential loss of retirement income due to low returns can be substantial. For example, the monthly payment on an annuity with a starting principal of $250,000, an interest rate of 5 percent, and a 20-year period is $1,632. At an interest rate of 2 percent the monthly payment is only $1,263—nearly a quarter less.

12. The Survey of Consumer Finances is conducted every three years. Munnell et al. (2017) compares its estimates of preparedness with the self-assessments of preparedness by the individual households in the 2013 SCF. In aggregate, the news is about the same: the authors found that 52 percent were inadequately prepared

compared to 57 percent of the household themselves. But they were not always the same households. A majority, 57 percent of the households, agreed with the authors' assessment. Others were confident when they should not have been (19 percent; often with a DC plan whose income generating potential they overestimated) or were concerned when the authors forecasted they could generate 90 percent of their pre-retirement income (24 percent; including some who underestimated the income-producing potential of owning a home).

13. The average age of retirement for men, as defined by Burtless and Quinn (2002) also reversed. It declined from 65 in 1976 to 63 in 1980, and then increased, in almost symmetric fashion, back to 65 by 2009.

14. A full-time career job is defined as one with 1,600 or more hours per year and ten or more years of job tenure.

15. Data from the old Retirement History Survey (RHS), conducted from 1969 to 1979, suggest that gradual retirement has been the norm since then (Ruhm 1990).

References

AARP (2014). *Staying Ahead of the Curve 2013: The AARP Work and Career Study: Older Workers in an Uneasy Job Market.* Washington, DC: AARP.

Alboher, M. (2012). *The Encore Career Handbook: How to Make a Living and a Difference in the Second Half of Life.* New York: Workman Publishing.

Biggs, A. G., and G. R. Springstead (2008). 'Alternate Measures of Replacement Rates for Social Security Benefits and Retirement Income.' *Social Security Bulletin* 68(2): 1–19.

Board of Governors of the Federal Reserve System (2016). *How Does Monetary Policy Influence Inflation and Employment?* Washington, DC: Board of Governors of the Federal Reserve System.

Board of Trustees of OASDI (2013). *The 2013 Annual Report of the Board of Trustees of the Federal Old-Age and Survivors Insurance and Federal Disability Insurance Trust Funds.* Washington, DC: US Government Printing Office.

Board of Trustees of OASDI (2016). *The 2016 Annual Report of the Board of Trustees of the Federal Old-Age and Survivors Insurance and Federal Disability Insurance Trust Funds.* Washington, DC: US Government Printing Office.

Board of Trustees, Federal Hospital Insurance and Federal Supplementary Medical Insurance Trust Funds (2016). *The 2016 Annual Report of the Boards of Trustees of the Federal Hospital Insurance and Federal Supplementary Medical Insurance Trust Funds.* Washington, DC: US Government Printing Office.

Burtless, G., and J. F. Quinn (2002). 'Is Working Longer the Answer for an Aging Workforce?' *Issue Brief No. 11.* Chestnut Hill, MA: The Center for Retirement Research at Boston College.

Cahill, K. E., M. D. Giandrea, and J. F. Quinn (2006). 'Retirement Patterns from Career Employment.' *The Gerontologist* 46(4): 514–23.

Cahill, K. E., M. D. Giandrea, and J. F. Quinn (2011). 'Reentering the Labor Force after Retirement.' *Monthly Labor Review* 134(6): 34–42.

Cahill, K. E., M. D. Giandrea, and J. F. Quinn (2012). 'Older Workers and Short-term Jobs: Employment Patterns and Determinants.' *Monthly Labor Review* 135(5): 19–32.

Cahill, K. E., M. D. Giandrea, and J. F. Quinn (2015a). 'Evolving Patterns of Work and Retirement,' in L. George and K. Ferraro (eds.), *The Handbook of Aging and the Social Sciences (8th Edition)*. New York: Elsevier.

Cahill, K. E., M. D. Giandrea, and J. F. Quinn (2015b). 'Retirement Patterns and the Macroeconomy, 1992–2010: The Prevalence and Determinants of Bridge Jobs, Phased Retirement, and Reentry among Three Recent Cohorts of Older Americans.' *The Gerontologist* 55(3): 384–403.

Cahill, K. E., M. D. Giandrea, and J. F. Quinn (2016). 'To What Extent Is Gradual Retirement a Product of Financial Necessity?' *The Gerontologist* 55(2): 794–5.

Congressional Budget Office (2010). *Social Security Policy Options*. Washington, DC: U.S. Government Printing Office. https://www.cbo.gov/publication/21547

Conti-Brown, P. (2018). "Politics, Independence, and Retirees: Long-term Low Interest Rates at the US Federal Reserve," in R. Clark, R. Maurer, and O. S. Mitchell (eds.), *How Persistent Low Returns Will Shape Saving and Retirement*. Oxford, UK: Oxford University Press, pp. 11–25.

Desilver, D. (2014). *Five Years In, Recovery Still Underwhelms Compared with Previous Ones*. Washington, DC: Pew Research Center.

Dushi, I., H. M. Iams, and J. Lichtenstein (2015). 'Retirement Plan Coverage by Firm Size: An Update.' *Social Security Bulletin* 75(2): 41–55.

Federal Reserve Bank of St. Louis (2016). *10-Year Treasury Constant Maturity Rate*. St. Louis, MO: Federal Reserve Bank of St. Louis. https://fred.stlouisfed.org/series/DGS10

Helman, R., C. Copeland, and J. VanDerhei (2016). 'The 2016 Retirement Confidence Survey: Worker Confidence Stable, Retiree Confidence Continues to Increase.' *Issue Brief No. 422*. Washington, DC: Employee Benefit Research Institute. https://www.ebri.org/pdf/briefspdf/EBRI_IB_422.Mar16.RCS.pdf

Hipple, S. (2016). 'Labor Force Participation: What Has Happened Since the Peak?' *Monthly Labor Review*. http://www.bls.gov/opub/mlr/2016/article/labor-force-participation-what-has-happened-since-the-peak.htm

James, J. B., C. Matz-Costa, and M. A. Smyer (2016). 'Retirement Security: It's Not Just About the Money.' *American Psychologist* 71(4): 334–44.

Johnson, R. W. (2011). 'Phased Retirement and Workplace Flexibility for Older Adults: Opportunities and Challenges.' *The ANNALS of the American Academy of Political and Social Science* 638(1): 68–85.

Johnson, R. W., J. Kawachi, J., and E. K. Lewis (2009). 'Older Workers on the Move: Recareering in Later Life.' *Research Report No. 2009–08*. Washington, DC: AARP Public Policy Institute.

Johnson, R. W., K. E. Smith, and O. Haaga (2013). 'How Did the Great Recession Affect Social Security Claiming?' *Brief No. 37*. Washington, DC: The Urban Institute.

Kantarci, T., and A. van Soest (2008). 'Gradual Retirement: Preferences and Limitations.' *De Economist* 156(2): 113–44.

Karamcheva, N. (2013). 'Is Household Debt Growing for Older Americans?' *Brief No. 33*. Washington, DC: The Urban Institute.

Lusardi, A., and O. S. Mitchell (2017). 'Older Women's Labor Market Attachment, Retirement Planning, and Household Debt.' NBER Working Paper No. 22606. Cambridge, MA: National Bureau of Economic Research.

Maestas, N. (2010). 'Back to Work: Expectations and Realizations of Work after Retirement.' *Journal of Human Resources* 45(3): 718–48.

Morrissey, M. (2016). 'The State of American Retirement: How 401(k)s Have Failed Most American Workers.' *Retirement Inequality Chartbook*. Washington, DC: Economic Policy Institute.

Munnell, A. H. (2014). '401(k)/IRA Holdings in 2013: An Update from the SCF.' *Issue Brief No. 14–15*. Chestnut Hill, MA: The Center for Retirement Research at Boston College.

Munnell, A. H. (2015a). 'The Average Retirement Age – an Update.' *Issue Brief No. 15–4*. Chestnut Hill, MA: The Center for Retirement Research at Boston College.

Munnell, A. H. (2015b). 'Falling Short: The Coming Retirement Crisis and What to Do About It.' *Issue Brief No. 15–7*. Chestnut Hill, MA: The Center for Retirement Research at Boston College.

Munnell, A. H., K. E. Cahill, A. Eschtruth, and S. A. Sass (2004). *The Graying of Massachusetts: Aging, The New Rules of Retirement, and the Changing Workforce*. Boston, MA: The Massachusetts Institute for a New Commonwealth.

Munnell, A. H., W. Hou, and A. Webb (2014). 'NRRI Update Shows Half Still Falling Short.' *Issue Brief No. 14–20*, Chestnut Hill, MA: The Center for Retirement Research at Boston College.

Munnell, A. H., W. Hou, and G. Sanzenbacher (2017). 'Do Households Have a Good Sense of Their Retirement Preparedness?' *Issue Brief No. 17–4*. Chestnut Hill, MA: The Center for Retirement Research at Boston College.

National Commission on Fiscal Responsibility and Reform (2010). *The Moment of Truth*. Washington, DC: US Government Printing Office. http://momentoftruthp roject.org/sites/default/files/TheMomentofTruth12_1_2010.pdf

Penner, R. G., P. Perun, and E. Steuerle (2002). *Legal and Institutional Impediments to Partial Retirement and Part-Time Work by Older Workers*. Washington, DC: The Urban Institute.

Quinn, J. F. (1999). 'Retirement Patterns and Bridge Jobs in the 1990s.' *Issue Brief No. 206*. Washington, DC: Employee Benefit Research Institute.

Quinn, J. F. (2010). 'Work, Retirement, and the Encore Career: Elders and the Future of the American Workforce.' *Generations* 34(3): 45–55.

Quinn, J. F., and K. E. Cahill (2016). 'The New World of Retirement Income Security in America.' *American Psychologist*, 71(4): 321–33.

Quinn, J. F., K. E. Cahill, and M. D. Giandrea (2011). 'Early Retirement: The Dawn of a New Era?' *TIAA Institute Policy Brief*. New York: TIAA-CREF Institute.

Ruhm, C. J. (1990). 'Bridge Jobs and Partial Retirement.' *Journal of Labor Economics* 8(4): 482–501.

Rutledge, M. S., and N. B. Coe (2012). 'Great Recession-induced Early Claimers: Who Are They? How Much Do They Lose?' Working Paper 2012–12. Chestnut Hill, MA: The Center for Retirement Research at Boston College.

Schieber, S. J. (2015). 'U.S. Retirement Policy Considerations for the 21st Century.' *The Journal of Retirement* 3(2): 12–33.

Smyer, M. A., E. Besen, and M. Pitt-Catsouphes (2009). 'Boomers and the Many Meanings of Work,' in R. Hudson (ed.), *Boomer Bust? The New Political Economy of Aging* (Volume 2). New York: Praeger.

Steuerle, E., C. Spiro, and R. W. Johnson (1999). *Can Americans Work Longer?* Washington, DC: The Urban Institute.

The Center for Retirement Research at Boston College (2017). 'The Late-1950s Boomers: Hit by Divorce.' *Squared Away Blog.* Chestnut Hill, MA: The Center for Retirement Research at Boston College. http://squaredawayblog.bc.edu/squared-away/the-late-1950s-boomers-hit-by-divorce

US Bureau of Labor Statistics (2016). *Consumer Price Index—All Urban Consumers.* Washington, DC: BLS. http://www.bls.gov/pdq/SurveyOutputServlet

US Bureau of Labor Statistics (2017). 'Labor Force Participation Rates by Single Year of Age and Sex, 1965–2016.' Washington, DC: BLS (unpublished).

US Social Security Administration (2016a). *Income of the Aged Chartbook: 2014.* Washington, DC: SSA. https://www.ssa.gov/policy/docs/chartbooks/income_aged/2014/iac14.pdf

US Social Security Administration (2016b). *Income of the Population 55 and Older: 2014.* Washington, DC: SSA. https://www.ssa.gov/policy/docs/statcomps/income_pop55/2014/incpop14.pdf

Wall Street Journal (2016). *Dow Jones Industrial Average—Historical Prices.* New York: Dow Jones & Company. http://quotes.wsj.com/DJIA/Index-historical-prices#

Chapter 8

How Persistent Low Expected Returns Alter Optimal Life Cycle Saving, Investment, and Retirement Behavior

Vanya Horneff, Raimond Maurer, and Olivia S. Mitchell

Low interest rates are now a reality not only in the United States but around the world, as recently noted by former Federal Reserve Chairman Ben Bernanke (2015). In the US, the government can borrow for a decade at a yield of only 2.3 percent, while in Switzerland, government bond yields are negative out to 50 years (Lewin 2016; Zeng 2017). Our chapter explores how this environment of persistent low returns is likely to influence saving, investing, and retirement behaviors, compared to what in the past were deemed more 'normal' financial conditions.

The persistence of low returns has implications for many aspects of the financial market. In the case of defined benefit (DB) pensions, a permanently low interest rate can render the DB plan underfunded, particularly when actual returns prove to be below those assumed when discounting future payouts. In the case of defined contribution (DC) plans, which are now the norm in the United States, the implications are more complex. In particular, persistent low returns can compel workers to save more and invest differently when allocating across stocks and bonds. Moreover, the low interest rate environment can also change retirement decisions, especially regarding how long to work and when to claim social security benefits.

This chapter builds on a number of studies using a life cycle framework to model and evaluate how individuals respond to a range of environmental shocks. The workhorse model of Cocco et al. (2005) and Gomes and Michaelides (2005) was extended by Love (2010) and Hubener et al. (2016), who showed how family shocks due to changes in marital status and children alter optimal consumption, insurance, asset allocation, and retirement patterns. In Horneff et al. (2015), we demonstrated how capital market surprises can influence saving and portfolio allocation patterns, and in Chai et al. (2011) we showed how flexible work patterns can help people hedge both earnings and capital market risk. In the present chapter, we evaluate how people might optimally respond to a *persistently* low return environment by adjusting their consumption, saving, investment, and retirement patterns compared to what used to be perceived as the 'normal' environment. Our chapter therefore builds on and extends the recent life cycle model developed by Horneff et al. (2016). In contrast to that study, we do not include annuity purchases but we do allow flexible work effort and endogenous claiming of social security benefits.[1]

In what follows, we develop and calibrate a life cycle model that embeds stock market and labor market uncertainty, as well as stochastic mortality. We also incorporate US tax rules and minimum distribution requirements for 401(k) plans, as well as real-world social security benefit formulas. We then show that our calibrated life cycle dynamic model produces realistic results that agree with observed saving, work, and claiming age patterns of US households. In particular, our model generates a large peak at the earliest benefit claiming age at 62, as in the data. Also in line with the evidence, our baseline results show a smaller second peak at the (system-defined) Full Retirement Age (FRA) of 66. In the context of a zero-return environment, we show that workers devote more of their savings to non-retirement accounts and less to 401(k) accounts since the relative appeal of investing into taxable versus tax-qualified retirement accounts is lower in a low return setting. Finally, we show that people claim social security benefits later in a low interest rate environment. A short discussion concludes.

The Consumer's Life Cycle Problem: Model and Calibration

In this section we build and calibrate a dynamic consumption and portfolio choice model for a utility-maximizing individual over the life cycle.

Preferences. We work in discrete time and assume that the individual's decision period starts at $t = 1$ (age of 25) and ends at $T = 76$ (age 100); accordingly, each period corresponds to one year. The household has an uncertain lifetime whereby the probability to survive from t until the next year $t + 1$ is denoted by p_t. Preferences in each period is represented by a Cobb Douglas function $u_t(C_t, l_t) = \frac{(C_t l_t^\alpha)^{1-\rho}}{1-\rho}$ based on current consumption C_t and leisure time l_t normalized as a fraction of total available time. The parameter α measures leisure preferences, ρ denotes relative risk aversion and β is the time preferences factor. The recursive definition of the value function is given by:

$$J_t = \frac{(C_t l_t^\alpha)^{1-\rho}}{1-\rho} + \beta E_t(p_t J_{t+1}), \tag{1}$$

with terminal utility $J_T = \frac{(C_T l_T^\alpha)^{1-\rho}}{1-\rho}$ and $l_t = 1$ after retirement. Following prior research in Horneff et al. (2016), the baseline calibration sets $\rho = 5$ and $\beta = 0.96$ for both males and females. The survival rates entering the value function are taken from the US Population Life Table (Arias 2010). We calibrate the leisure parameter α in such a way that our results match empirical claiming rates reported by the US Social Security Administration. This matching procedure produces leisure preference parameters of $\alpha = 0.9$ for males and $\alpha = 1.1$ for females.

Time budget, labor income, and social security retirement benefits. Our model allows for flexible work effort and retirement ages. The worker has the opportunity to allocate up to $(1 - l_t) = 0.6$ of his available time budget (assuming 100 waking hours per week and 52 weeks per year) to paid work. Depending on his work effort, the uncertain yearly pre-tax labor income is given by:

$$Y_{t+1} = (1 - l_t) \cdot w_t \cdot P_{t+1} \cdot U_{t+1} \tag{2}$$

Here w_t is a deterministic wage rate component, which depends on age, education, sex, and if the individual works overtime, full time, or part time. The variable $P_{t+1} = P_t \cdot N_{t+1}$ is the permanent component of wage rates with independent lognormal distributed shocks $N_t \sim LN(-0.5\sigma_P^2, \sigma_P^2)$ with a mean of one and volatility of σ_P^2. In addition $U_t \sim LN(-0.5\sigma_U^2, \sigma_U^2)$ is a transitory shock with volatility σ_U^2 and uncorrelated with N_t.

The wage rate calibration builds on Horneff et al. (2016), who estimated the deterministic component of the wage rate process w_t^i and the variances of the permanent and transitory wage shocks N_t^i and U_t^i using the 1975–2013 waves of the Panel Study of Income Dynamics.[2] These are estimated separately by sex and by educational level, where the latter groupings are less than High School, High School graduates, and at least some college (<HS; HS; Coll+).[3]

Between ages 62 and 70, the worker can retire from work and claim social security benefits, the latter of which depend on his average lifetime 35 best years of earnings. If the individual claims benefits before (after) the system-defined Normal Retirement Age of 66, then his lifelong social security benefits will be reduced (increased) according to pre-specified factors. If the individual works beyond age 62, we require that he devote at least a minimum effort of at least one hour per week; also, overtime work is excluded (i.e., $0.01 \leq (1 - l_t) \leq 0.4$).

Wealth dynamics during the work life. During working life, the individual has the opportunity to use current cash on hand for consumption and investments. Some portion A_t of the worker's pre-tax salary Y_t (up to a limit of \$18,000 per year) can be invested into a tax-qualified 401(k)-retirement plan of the EET type.[4] That is, contributions into the account and investment earnings on account assets are tax-exempt, (E), while withdrawals are taxed (T). In addition, a worker can invest outside his retirement plan in risky stocks S_t and riskless bonds B_t. As such, his cash on hand X_t in each year is given by

$$X_t = C_t + S_t + B_t + A_t \qquad (3)$$

where the usual constraints $C_t, A_t, S_t, B_t \geq 0$ apply. One year later, his cash on hand is given by the value of stocks (bonds) having earned an uncertain (riskless) gross return of R_{t+1} (R_f), plus income from work (after housing expenses h_t), plus withdrawals (W_t) from the 401(k) plan, minus any federal/state/city taxes and social security Tax_{t+1} contributions:

$$X_{t+1} = S_t R_{t+1} + B_t R_f + Y_{t+1}(1 - h_t) + W_t - Tax_{t+1} \qquad (4)$$

We model housing costs h_t as in Love (2010). Our 'baseline' financial market parameterizations assume a risk-free interest rate of 1 percent, and an equity risk premium of 4 percent with a return volatility of 18 percent. In simulations below of the low-yield environment, we vary these assumptions.

During his working life, the individual pays taxes (Tax_{t+1}), which reduce his cash on hand available for consumption and investments.[5] These include the labor income tax at a rate of 11.65 percent (the sum of 1.45 percent Medicare, 4 percent city and state tax and 6.2 percent social security tax). Under the US progressive tax system, the individual must pay taxes on labor income as well as on withdrawals from tax-qualified retirement plans (including a 10 percent penalty tax for withdrawals before age 60), and on returns on stocks and bonds held outside the tax-qualified retirement account. If his cash on hand falls below $X_{t+1} \leq 5,950$ p.a. (an amount also exempt from income taxes), he is supported by the state, so he has a minimum wealth level of 5,950 for the next year.

Prior to the endogenous retirement age $t = K$, the assets in his tax-qualified retirement plan are invested in bonds earning a risk-free gross (pre-tax) return of R_f and risky stocks with an uncertain gross return of R_t. The total value ($F_{t+1}^{401(k)}$) of the 401(k) assets at time $t + 1$, usually held in a 401(account), is determined by the previous period's value minus any withdrawals ($W_t \leq F_t^{401(k)}$), plus additional contributions (A_t), and returns from stocks and bonds:

$$F_{t+1}^{401(k)} = \omega_t^s \left(F_t^{401(k)} - W_t + A_t \right) R_{t+1} + (1 - \omega_t^s) \left(F_t^{401(k)} - W_t + A_t \right) R_f, \textit{for } t < K \qquad (5)$$

We posit that his DC plan assets are held in a Target Date Fund with stock exposure declining with age following the common rule $\omega_t^s = (100 - Age)/100$.[6] This is a Qualified Default Investment Alternative (QDIA) as per Department of Labor regulations (US DOL 2006).

Wealth dynamics during retirement. The worker can retire and claim social security benefits between age 62 and 70. After retirement at the endogenous age K, the individual has the opportunity to save outside the tax-qualified retirement plan in stocks and bonds:

$$X_t = C_t + S_t + B_t \qquad (6)$$

His cash on hand for the next period evolves as follows:

$$X_{t+1} = S_t R_{t+1} + B_t R_f + Y_{t+1}(1 - h_t) + W_t - Tax_{t+1}. \qquad (7)$$

Old age retirement benefits provided by Social Security are determined by the worker's Primary Insurance Amount (PIA), which depends on his 35 best years of earnings.[7] Social Security payments (Y_{t+1}) in retirement $(t \geq K)$ are given by:

$$Y_{t+1} = PIA_K \cdot \lambda_K \cdot \varepsilon_{t+1}. \qquad (8)$$

Here, λ_K is the adjustment factor for claiming before or after the normal retirement age, which is equal to age 66.[8] The variable ε_t is a transitory shock $\varepsilon_t \sim \mathrm{LN}(-0.5\sigma_\varepsilon^2, \sigma_\varepsilon^2)$, which reflects out-of-pocket medical and other expenditure shocks in retirement as in Love (2010). During retirement, benefits payments from Social Security are partially taxed[9] by the individual federal income tax rate as well as the 1.45 percent Medicare and 4 percent city and state taxes.

We model the 401(k) plan payouts as follows:

$$F_{t+1}^{401(k)} = \omega_t^s \left(F_t^{401(k)} - W_t \right) R_{t+1} + (1 - \omega_t^s) \left(F_t^{401(k)} - W_t \right) R_f, \textit{for } t < K \quad (9)$$

Under US law, plan participants must take retirement account payouts from age 70 onwards, according to the Required Minimum Distribution rules (m) specified by the Internal Revenue Service (2012). Accordingly, withdrawals from the retirement account must take into account the following constraints: $F_t^{401(k)} m \leq W_t < F_t^{401(k)}$.

Baseline Results in a 'Normal' Interest Rate Environment

Next we evaluate, in a 'normal' interest rate world, how people would optimally choose their consumption, work effort, the claiming age for social security benefits, investments in as well as withdrawals from tax-qualified 401(k) plans, and investments in stocks and bonds. We posit that households maximize the value function (1) under budget restrictions. This optimization problem cannot be solved analytically, so it requires a numerical procedure

using dynamic stochastic programming. To generate optimal policy func-
tions, in each period t we discretize the space in four dimensions $30(X) \times 20$
$(F^{401(k)}) \times 8(P) \times 9(K)$, with X being cash on hand, $F^{401(k)}$ assets held in the
401(k) retirement plan, P permanent income, and K the claiming age. Next,
we simulate 100,000 independent life cycles based on optimal feedback
controls for each of the six population subgroups of interest (male/female
with <HS, HS, and Coll+). We then aggregate the subgroups to obtain
national mean values using weights from the National Center on Education
Statistics (2012). Specifically, the weights are 50.7 percent female (and
62 percent with Coll+, 30 percent with HS, and 8 percent with <HS), and
49.3 percent male (and 60 percent with Coll+, 30 percent HS and 10 percent
<HS).

Figure 8.1 reports results for our baseline calibration assuming a risk-free
interest rate of 1 percent, and an expected return on stocks of 5 percent with
a volatility of 18 percent. The life cycle graphs appear in the upper panels,
while social security benefit claiming behavior appears in the lower panels.
Moreover, results for men appear on the left, and for women on the right.

Panels A and B of Figure 8.1 demonstrate that, during working life, labor
income substantially exceeds consumption. This is partly due to the fact that
we show pre-tax income, so after income taxes, net labor income tracks
consumption more closely. During the worker's first decade in the job
market, he saves only a small amount due to the fact that he is liquidity-
constrained when young. (The worker also cannot increase consumption
by borrowing against future labor income). From age 35 onward, savings
rise, especially in the 401(k) plan retirement plan to peak around age 59.
Thereafter, he systematically draws down assets from the plan, since after
age 59.5, he need no longer pay the 10 percent penalty tax for early
withdrawals. In retirement, between age 62 and 70, his social security
income falls below average consumption, with the difference financed by
retirement plan withdrawals.

For women, though their labor income is lower than for males, they still
accumulate almost the same amount of retirement plan assets. This can be
explained by the fact that the average life expectancy for women is substantially higher than for men, so women must save more to maintain desired
consumption levels over a longer period. For example, at age 25 (the
starting point of our life cycle model), the life expectancy of females is
age 81, or about 4.5 years more than for males. Both women's and men's
consumption drops slightly during the retirement period, which is in line
with both empirical evidence and theoretical life cycle literature (Battistin
et al. 2009; Chai et al. 2011). This can be explained by the sharp increase
in leisure time after people claim social security benefits.[10]

Panels C and D of Figure 8.1 reveal that the social security claiming
patterns generated by our model align closely with empirical claiming

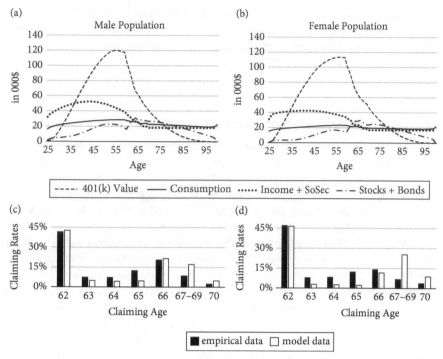

Figure 8.1. Life cycle behavior and social security claiming patterns for males and females

Note: The top two panels show expected life cycle patterns for males and females (consumption, income, assets in 401(k) tax-qualified plans, and bonds/stocks). The lower two panels present claiming rates generated by our life cycle models versus empirical claiming rates as reported by the US Social Security Administration for the year 2014. Expected values are calculated from 100,000 simulated lifecycles based on optimal feedback controls. Results for the entire female (male) population are computed using income profile for three education levels: 62% +Coll; 30% HS; 8% <HS (60% +Coll; 30% HS; 10%<HS). Parameters used for the baseline calibration are as follows: risk aversion $\rho = 5$; time preference $\beta = 0.96$; leisure preference $\alpha = 0.9$ (female) $\alpha = 1.1$ (male); endogenous retirement age 62–70. Social Security benefits are based on average permanent income and the bend points in place in 2013; minimum required withdrawals from 401(k) plans are based on life expectancy using the IRS-Uniform Lifetime Table in 2013; tax rules for 401(k) plans are as described in Horneff et al. (2015). The risk premium for stocks returns is 4% and return volatility 18%; the risk-free rate in the baseline case is 1%.

Source: Authors' calculations.

rates reported by the US Social Security Administration.[11] That is, our model generates a large peak at the earliest claiming age at 62, whereas in the data, about 45 percent of workers claim their benefits at this point. Additionally, and also in line with the evidence, our baseline results show a smaller second peak at the (system-defined) FRA of 66; here about

15 percent of workers claim benefits for the first time. Overall, the results of our baseline calibration confirm that our model produces realistic results that agree with observed work, saving, and claiming age behavior of US households.

Understanding the Impact of Interest Rates

Having provided the baseline 'normal' environment results, we next evaluate the changes in a different interest rate environment. To this end we examine two experiments. First, we reduce the (real) risk-free interest from 1 percent to 0 percent, and second, we increase the real interest rate to 2 percent. (In both cases we keep the equity risk premium at 4 percent). Table 8.1 reports results for men and women, separately.

In Table 8.1, we report the rates at which people claim their social security benefits by age, as well as the overall claiming age. One key finding is that the lower the risk-free interest rate, the higher the claiming age. In other words, when the long-term interest rate falls to zero, women claim about 0.4 years later, and men almost a full year later. Another point to note is that claiming at the earliest possible age of 62 declines quite notably, more so for men but also for women. We explain this by noting that, when expected returns are high, the worker can claim early social security benefits without needing to withdraw as much from his retirement assets, which continue to earn higher returns for a while longer. But when the real interest rate is low, a worker can delay claiming social security in exchange for higher lifelong benefits, and the cost of taking more from his retirement count to support consumption is lower. This is in line with Shoven and Slavov (2014) who argued that, by delaying claiming, people can maximize the actuarial net present value of their lifetime social security benefits in times of low returns.

TABLE 8.1 Social security claiming ages for females and males

	Claiming rates (%) by age									Average Claiming Age
	62	63	64	65	66	67	68	69	70	
Panel A: Female										
0% Interest Rate	46.1	2.1	2.2	3.1	7.2	5.5	9.8	10.7	13.3	65.1
1% Interest Rate	46.6	2.8	2.6	2.3	11.6	7.4	10.0	7.9	8.8	64.8
2% Interest Rate	47.6	2.5	2.4	2.4	13.1	9.9	9.6	5.4	6.9	64.7
Panel B: Male										
0% Interest Rate	39.9	3.5	4.7	4.6	16.3	13.1	7.2	5.2	5.5	64.8
1% Interest Rate	42.7	4.9	4.3	4.7	21.6	11.3	3.4	2.4	4.8	64.5
2% Interest Rate	49.6	5.6	4.5	6.2	24.7	4.0	1.5	1.4	2.6	63.9

By contrast, when returns are higher, the net present value of benefits is maximized by claiming early. Evidence from Shoven and Slavov (2012) and Cahill et al. (2015) also suggests that low (high) interest rates result in later (earlier) claiming ages. Accordingly, our results are in line with empirical evidence.

Table 8.2 shows how wealth accumulation changes under the two interest rate regimes, both inside and outside the 401(k) plan. In the low return environment, workers build up less wealth in their retirement plans. For instance, when the safe yield is 0 percent, middle aged women (aged 55–64) optimally accumulate an average of about $88,200 in their 401(k) plans, while in the 2 percent yield scenario, they average one-third more, or $117,700, at the same point in their life cycle. Middle-aged men accumulate $83,200 in the zero-rate environment, and 45 percent more ($120,600) in the 2 percent interest rate scenario. Interestingly, the opposite pattern applies to assets held outside the tax-qualified retirement plans. That is, women age 45–54 hold $16,600 in liquid stocks and bonds when the interest rate is zero, but only $9,800 in the 2 percent interest rate scenario. The same effect also applies to males.

The divergent impact of low versus high interest rates on asset holdings inside versus outside tax-qualified retirement plans can be explained as follows. When the interest rate is low, people work fewer hours per week

TABLE 8.2 Life cycle asset accumulation patterns for females and males

	Female			Male		
	0% Interest Rate	1% Interest Rate	2% Interest Rate	0% Interest Rate	1% Interest Rate	2% Interest Rate
Panel A: 401(k) assets in $000						
Age 25–34	16.8	18.1	21.1	9.9	13.6	14.9
Age 35–44	57.9	70.0	80.2	48.6	65.0	70.3
Age 45–54	92.4	105.0	124.4	91.4	109.2	122.7
Age 55–64	88.2	99.5	117.7	83.2	101.6	120.6
Age 65–74	33.5	48.4	64.4	27.4	43.6	63.1
Age 75–84	10.8	19.5	30.8	8.5	16.0	26.4
Age 85–94	1.6	4.0	7.9	1.2	2.7	5.8
Panel B: Non-qualified assets in $000						
Age 25–34	2.7	3.0	2.6	6.4	4.5	4.3
Age 35–44	11.1	5.8	4.9	18.3	10.8	10.8
Age 45–54	16.6	14.0	9.8	25.6	21.1	18.6
Age 55–64	16.5	19.3	16.0	24.7	22.6	18.3
Age 65–74	25.3	25.9	25.3	28.4	27.2	25.3
Age 75–84	19.7	21.2	21.8	21.1	22.2	23.3
Age 85–94	11.5	13.0	14.1	12.5	13.9	14.3

early in life, compared to workers in the higher interest environment. For example, women work two hours per week less between ages 25 and 60 than they do in the 2 percent interest rate scenario.[12] The reason is that, in the higher return scenario, it is more attractive to build up savings early in life as these can grow at the higher rate. More work effort then generates higher labor income, and because of the progressive tax system, this results in larger allocations to the tax-exempt retirement accounts. In addition, returns earned on assets held inside the 401(k) plan are tax-free. This second advantage is, of course, smaller in a zero-return environment. Accordingly, when interest rates are low (high), workers devote more (less) of their savings to non-retirement accounts.

Conclusions

Financial writers have noted with concern that the long-term impact of very low interest rates has been to drive some investors to 'hunt for yield,' taking on riskier investments (Bryan 2016). Yet little academic research has focused on how persistent low returns would optimally shape workers' and retirees' decision making regarding accumulation and retirement patterns. Our life cycle model integrates realistic tax, social security, and minimum distribution rules, as well as uncertain income, stock returns, and mortality. The baseline calibration generates a large peak at the earliest claiming age at 62, in line with the evidence. Additionally, baseline results produce a smaller second peak at the (system-defined) FRA of 66. Overall, the results of the baseline calibration confirm that our model produces realistic results that agree with observed work, saving, and claiming age behavior of American households.

The results of alternative interest rate regimes are also quite informative. One sensible result is that people are predicted to save less during periods of low returns. Second, people finance consumption relatively early in retirement by drawing down their 401(k) assets sooner. Third, low rates also change *where* people save. During low-return periods, workers save less in tax-qualified accounts and more outside tax-qualified plans, until retirement. The reason is that the tax advantages of saving in 401(k) plans are relatively less attractive, inasmuch as the gain from saving in pre-tax plans is lower, and because the return on assets in the retirement account are lower in a low-return environment. And fourth, we find that low interest rates drive workers to claim social security benefits later, so they can take advantage of the relatively high payoff to deferring retirement under current rules. In this way, we confirm that tax and social security claiming rules have a powerful effect on how households are able to adjust to financial market fluctuations.

Notes

1. We also provide a theoretical backing for the empirical claiming age patterns identified by Shoven and Slavov (2012, 2014).
2. Dollar values are given in 2013 terms.
3. Details are given in Horneff et al. (2016).
4. This approach to retirement benefit taxation is therefore similar to how regular DB and DC plan payments are handled under US tax law. We abstract here from Roth 401(k)s.
5. For details, see Horneff et al. (2016).
6. This was suggested by Malkiel (1996), for instance.
7. The benefit formula is a piece-wise linear function of the Average Indexed Monthly Earnings providing (as of 2013) a replacement rate of 90 percent up to a first bend point ($791), 32 percent between the first and the second bend point ($4768), and 15 percent above that. See US SSA (2017).
8. The factors we use are 0.75 (claiming age 62), 0.8 (claiming age 63), 0.867 (claiming age 64), 0.933 (claiming age 65), 1.00 (claiming age 66), 1.08 (claiming age 67), 1.16 (claiming age 68), 1.24 (claiming age 69), and 1.32 (claiming age 70). See US SSA (2017).
9. For tax rules for social security see US Social Security Administration (2017). Based on the combined income up to 85 percent of social security can be taxed for households with high income additional to social security benefits. Yet because of quite generous exemptions, most households receive their social security benefits tax-free (see Horneff et al. 2016).
10. This pattern conforms to evidence on expenditure drops after retirement found by Aguiar and Hurst (2005).
11. For instance, see the US Social Security Administration (2015), Table 6.B5. We adjust their data to omit disability conversions at age 65 and scale the other age brackets so they sum to 100 percent.
12. These numbers are not reported in Tables 8.1 and 8.2; computations available on request.

References

Aguiar, M., and E. Hurst (2005). 'Consumption vs. Expenditure.' *Journal of Political Economy* 113(5): 919–48.

Arias, E. (2010). 'United States Life Tables, 2005.' *National Vital Statistics Reports* 58(10): 1–132.

Battistin, E., A. Brugiavini, E. Rettore, and G. Weber (2009). 'The Retirement Consumption Puzzle: Evidence from a Regression Discontinuity Approach.' *American Economic Review* 99(5): 2209–26.

Bernanke, B. (2015). 'Why Are Interest Rates So Low?' *Brookings Institution Report.* March 30. https://www.brookings.edu/blog/ben-bernanke/2015/03/30/why-are-interest-rates-so-low/.

Bryan, B. (2016). 'Central Bankers are Doing Something That Hasn't Happened in 5,000 years and Drastically Changing the World Economy.' *BusinessInsider.com.* August 19. http://www.businessinsider.com/record-low-interest-rate-impact-2016-8.

Cahill, K., M. Giandrea, and J. Quinn (2015). 'Evolving Patterns of Work and Retirement,' in L. George and K. Ferraro (eds.), *The Handbook of Aging and the Social Sciences.* London, UK: Academic Press, pp. 271–91.

Chai, J., W. Horneff, R. Maurer, and O. S. Mitchell (2011). 'Optimal Portfolio Choice over the Life Cycle with Flexible Work, Endogenous Retirement, and Lifetime Payouts.' *Review of Financ,* 15(4): 875–907.

Cocco, J., F. Gomes, and P. Maenhout (2005). 'Consumption and Portfolio Choice over the Life Cycle.' *Review of Financial Studies* 18(2): 491–533.

Gomes, F., and A. Michaelides (2005). 'Optimal Life-Cycle Asset Allocation: Understanding the Empirical Evidence.' *Journal of Finance* 60(2): 869–904.

Horneff, V., R. Maurer, O. S. Mitchell, and R. Rogalla (2015). 'Optimal Life Cycle Portfolio Choice with Variable Annuities Offering Liquidity and Investment Downside Protection.' *Insurance: Mathematics and Economics* 63(1): 91–107.

Horneff, V., R. Maurer, and O. S. Mitchell (2016). 'Putting the Pension Back in 401(k) Plans: Optimal versus Default Longevity Income Annuities.' NBER Working Paper 22717. Cambridge, MA: National Bureau of Economic Research.

Hubener, A., R. Maurer, and O. S. Mitchell (2016). 'How Family Status and Social Security Claiming Options Shape Optimal Life Cycle Portfolios.' *Review of Financial Studies* 29(4): 937–78.

Internal Revenue Service (2012). *Retirement Plan and IRA Required Minimum Distributions FAQs.* Washington, DC: IRS. https://www.irs.gov/Retirement-Plans/Retirement-Plans-FAQs-regarding-Required-Minimum-Distributions.

Lewin, J. (2016). 'Swiss Bond Yields Now Negative Out to 50 Years.' *FT.com.* July 5. https://www.ft.com/content/2ae4237a-2d3e-33dd-b9e0-120c4a93a29c.

Love, D. A. (2010). 'The Effects of Marital Status and Children on Savings and Portfolio Choice.' *Review of Financial Studies* 23(1): 385–432.

Malkiel, B. G. (1996). *A Random Walk Down Wall Street: Including a Life–Cycle Guide to Personal Investing.* 6th edn., New York: Norton.

National Center of Educational Statistics (2012). 'Historical Summary of Faculty, Students, Degrees, and Finances in Degree-granting Institutions: Selected Years, 1869–70 through 2005–06.' https://nces.ed.gov.

Shoven, J. B., and S. N. Slavov (2012). 'The Decision to Delay Social Security Benefits: Theory and Evidence.' NBER Working Paper 17866. Cambridge, MA: National Bureau of Economic Research.

Shoven, J. B., and S. N. Slavov (2014). Does it Pay to Delay Social Security? *Journal of Pension Economics and Finance* 13(2): 121–44.

US Department of Labor (US DOL) (2006). *Fact Sheet: Default Investment Alternatives under Participant-Directed Individual Account Plans.* Washington, DC: DOL. https://www.dol.gov/ebsa/newsroom/fsdefaultoptionproposalrevision.html.

US Social Security Administration (2015). *Annual Statistical Supplement to the Social Security Bulletin, 2015*. Washington, DC: SSA.

US Social Security Administration (2017). *Fact Sheet: Benefit Formula Bend Points*. Washington, DC: SSA. https://www.ssa.gov/oact/cola/bendpoints.html.

Zeng, M. (2017). 'US 10-Year Note Yield Hits Low for the Month.' *WallStreetJournal. com*. March 31. https://www.wsj.com/articles/u-s-bonds-rebound-from-earlier-losses-1490108750?tesla=y.

Chapter 9

Retirement Saving and Decumulation in a Persistent Low-Return Environment

Jason J. Fichtner and Jason S. Seligman

The effects of the 2007–2008 financial collapse and related Great Recession continue to impact the retirement well-being of millions of people. The Federal Reserve has kept its benchmark short-term interest rate at or near zero for several years in an effort to stimulate the economy. Although low interest rates can financially benefit those borrowing money to buy a house, a car, or to fund a new business, such low rates can directly weaken the financial well-being of retirees who are living off their life savings, while also making it more difficult for pension plans to accumulate assets necessary to pay future benefits without taking on additional risk by over-investing in stocks.

Low interest rates also translate into lower yields on fixed-income assets, meaning the interest (coupon) payments that seniors rely on in retirement will generally be lower than anticipated. This lack of income could lead to hardship, reduced consumption, and an inability to pay bills. A continued low interest rate environment affects the value of both defined benefit (DB) and defined contribution (DC) plans. To the extent that the difference between returns on stocks and bonds (the equity premium) is larger, or smaller, the low interest rate environment's impact is more, or less, limited to fixed-income assets. That has further implications for the impacts of different asset allocations in a low interest rate environment.

Several other chapters in this volume address how saving and retirement may be affected in a persistent period of low returns and/or low interest rates. For example, Blanchett et al. and Wallick et al. discuss optimal retirement savings in a period of low returns, while Ilmanen and Rauseo consider how to achieve greater returns and income in a low yield environment. The chapter by Horneff et al. takes a classic holistic approach to the life cycle planning problem, and confronts the low interest rate dilemma in that context.

Here we argue some grounds for skepticism that what we observe can be formalized as an objective 'strategy.' This is because so much of what we see has been a function of asset prices over the 2008–2014 period, and results will be conditional on initial levels of wealth over this period. And, while other chapters take a normative frame, addressing what can, or what ought to be done, this chapter offers a more empirical frame, focusing on what households have actually done.

Over the low interest rate period we analyze two notable and generally positive trends. First, high wealth households have benefitted from strong equity returns. Second, home equity has served in a protective role for lower wealth households who own homes. But these successes are nuanced, since the bottom 90 percent of the 2014 wealth distribution experienced large losses in 2008, and it had not yet recovered by 2014. Moreover, the protective role of home equity has become limited. In particular, older persons in the bottom quarter of the wealth distribution, who are on average 18 or fewer years into retirement, have exhausted all their household wealth.

Of course, all groups took large and meaningful losses during the financial crisis, but in the low yield environment, those below the 90th percentile have not recovered, and those below the 25th percentile have consumed all their wealth. This does not mean that these households have no income: instead, Social Security income is a very important protective asset for these lower wealth households. We do not focus on households' use of Social Security wealth, because this wealth cannot change very much for individuals who have already claimed benefits. Yet, we acknowledge that those not yet in retirement might gain further income protection from delaying claiming Social Security retirement benefits (Reilly and Byrne in this volume).

While Social Security is an important program for low- and middle-wealth households, the finances of Social Security have also been challenged by the low interest rate environment. Low interest rates negatively impact Social Security's broader finances because Social Security Trust Funds depend in part on the interest earned on investments in US Treasury bonds. By law, Social Security must invest any surpluses in Treasury bonds and cannot buy or hold other financial assets such as stocks, mutual funds, or corporate bonds. Allocation-based strategies for contending with the low interest rate environment are not thus in the Social Security Administration's (SSA's) purview.

Revenue generated from interest payments to the Trust Funds has been declining since 2009 (US Social Security Administration 2016b). Although the Federal Reserve's policy of low interest rates is designed to stimulate economic growth, which is good for employment and wage growth on which the Trust Fund's financial position also depends, not all growth is equal in terms of its benefit to the Trust Funds.[1] In particular, declines in labor force participation over much of the recovery mean that there has been less employment and wage growth on which social security payroll taxes are levied.

Coupled with low interest rates, this lack of payroll tax revenue growth hastens the depletion of the combined Social Security Trust Funds, currently projected for 2034. Continued low interest rates, slow economic growth, and increases in the percentage of the US population in retirement all contribute to a quicker depletion of the Social Security Trust Funds. This threatens the financial security of retirees as they face a risk of greater Social Security benefit cuts much sooner as a result of accelerated Trust Fund depletion.

One way to help current older workers focuses on delayed claiming strategies. In fact, we do see some evidence of delayed retirement and workforce re-entry among recent Health and Retirement Study (HRS) birth cohorts. For seniors who can delay claiming social security, there is an opportunity to increase their use of an inflation-protected annuity (US Social Security Administration 2017b). Further, the marginal cost of this strategy for individuals can be appealing. While private companies that sell annuities in the private sector generally adjust their payouts and make them less generous when life spans increase or when interest rates decrease, social security's age adjustments are fixed by law. Further, the Delayed Retirement Credit (DRC) has increased for those reaching age 65 since the turn of the century, making the returns for this strategy better than they were for most of the program's history.[2] For someone whose full retirement age is 66, each year of delayed claiming returns approximately 8 percent. Delaying claiming until age 70 thus results in a 32 percent higher monthly benefit, which can be appealing.

Further, given the continued trend away from employer-sponsored DB pensions, individuals are bearing more longevity risk. Longevity risk is driven by accumulation and allocation risks, as well as by decisions to draw down assets in retirement. A persistent low-interest rate environment makes the challenges of saving for retirement and spending in retirement more difficult, as it is difficult to make up for lost yields.

In what follows, we investigate impacts of the low interest rates over the 2008–2014 period in the HRS on savings, wealth, and asset allocation both before and in retirement. Following this, we consider alternative portfolio and wealth management strategies and their potential to add value in a persistent low return environment. First, however, we review the related prior literature.

Related Prior Literature

The financial crisis of 2007–2008 resulted in a great and unanticipated loss of wealth for millions of Americans. The US stock market, measured by the S&P 500 index, fell 56.7 percent over a little less than a year and a half.[3] Housing prices plummeted and the unemployment rate quickly rose into the double-digits. General confidence in the financial system was shaken. Financial wealth declined by 15 percent for the median household as a result of the 2008 financial crisis (Shapiro 2010). These economic conditions dramatically changed the retirement landscape for millions of Americans and likely influenced retirement behavior as well.

This period was also remarkable for the speed at which the decline in financial markets, housing, and employment occurred, and, according to the HRS,[4] about 28 percent of older households reported that they had been affected 'a lot' by the financial crisis, 46 percent responded they had been affected 'a little', and only 26 percent said they were not affected (Hurd and Rohwedder 2010). Those already in retirement fared better than those not yet retired (Wells Fargo Securities 2012), suggesting that many households will face significant barriers to reaching their pre-recession retirement goals and will likely need to save more or work longer than originally planned.

A sudden and unplanned drop in wealth and income can have significant effects on retirement behavior. Younger or middle-aged workers have more than a decade before retirement, and so they still have time to recover financial losses. A financial shock that includes steep drops in the value of stock prices, investment portfolios, and housing assets might cause a delay in retirement plans[5] with workers remaining in the workforce longer so as to rebuild retirement savings (Bosworth and Burtless 2011). Those near or post-retirement are more limited in their ability to attain or maintain a secure retirement. For those near retirement, a financial crisis might change the timing of retirement.[6] For current retirees, sudden declines in wealth from housing assets and financial portfolios might force immediate changes in consumption.

The HRS data also provide evidence of the financial crisis on the timing of retirement.[7] Hurd and Rohwedder (2010) analyzed respondents who were working in 2008, and they found that the percentage of workers intending to work past age 62 increased 3.5 percentage points over the 58.2 percent proportion reported one year earlier.[8] The number of respondents reporting that they planned to work past age 65 increased even more: 7.8 percentage points above the 38.6 percent who responded they planned to work past age 65 in 2008 (Hurd and Rohwedder 2010). More recent survey research has confirmed that more seniors are working after the recession than before (Wells Fargo Securities 2012). The number of people indicating they plan to work past the age of 65, or work for some pay in retirement, has also risen (Coronado 2014).

Taken together, these facts suggest that many are planning on working longer and retiring later as a result of the financial crisis. Hurd and Rohwedder (2010:11) conclude that 'the economic crisis has caused households in and near retirement to suffer sizeable losses in assets. These households responded in several ways: they reduced spending and as a result, increased saving, they reported an intent to work longer, and anticipate bequeathing less' (Hurd and Rohwedder 2010: 14). Since the financial crisis, the annual personal saving rate has also trended upward, from around 1 percent to near 6 percent (Glick and Lansing 2011). All else equal, a reduction in wealth from a negative financial shock appears to have resulted in workers near retirement increasing income and saving, by remaining in the workforce longer and reducing consumption.[9]

Of course, given gains in longevity, working longer may not reduce the total number of years spent in retirement. According to the Social Security Administration, a man reaching age 65 today can expect to live to age 84, on average, while a woman reaching age 65 can expect to live to almost 87 years old (US Social Security Administration 2017a). People retiring at age 65 should therefore plan to financially support themselves for at least 20 years, based on average longevity. Yet roughly one out of every four people age 65 today will live to age 90, while one out of every ten will live past age 95 (US Social Security Administration 2017a). Longer retirement periods therefore require more savings. A continued low-interest rate environment not only exacerbates challenges in saving for retirement during the accumulation phase, but it also greatly increases the risk of outliving retirement savings during the decumulation phase.

The loss of a job can also affect retirement behavior. As Bosworth and Burtless (2011: 24) noted, 'at ages past 60 and especially past 65 . . . reduced employment levels caused by a weak job market very quickly translate into reduced labor force participation rates' (Bosworth and Burtless 2011: 14). An employment shock, such as a sudden loss of a job and a labor market with high unemployment might hasten the decision on when to retire. The unemployment rate for workers aged 55 to 64 more than doubled during the Great Recession (US Bureau of Labor Statistics 2010a). Also, older workers who lost their jobs during this period were more likely to have longer durations of unemployment compared to younger workers. According to data from the US Bureau of Labor Statistics, 49 percent of unemployed workers aged 55 or older had been unemployed for 27 weeks or longer, compared with 28 percent of unemployed workers age 16 to 24, and 41 percent of unemployed workers age 25 to 54 (US Bureau of Labor Statistics 2010b). A Congressional Research Service study found that older workers who became unemployed have a higher incidence of withdrawing from the labor market (Congressional Research Service 2007). When they did so, they replaced earnings with other sources of income such as pensions and social security benefits. Unemployment among older workers contributes significantly to the probability of retirement (Bosworth and Burtless 2011).

Researchers have long recognized the role social security benefits play in a secure retirement.[10] Social security retirement benefits provide income security for millions of Americans, with 61 percent relying on social security for 50 percent or more of their income, and 33 percent relying on social security for 90 percent or more of their income.[11] While those with a greater dependency on social security income are generally regarded as more economically vulnerable, the financial crisis has affected the income of these retirees less (Hurd and Rohwedder 2010). Thus, there is less to say about the impact of low interest rates on this population, as their exposure to financial market assets was limited.

For others, low interest rates are making it more difficult to achieve pre-set wealth targets. To achieve these targets, people can spend less and save more now, take on additional risk in the pursuit of higher yielding assets, work longer, and/or plan to spend less in retirement. None of these options are without costs, so a persistently low interest rate environment exacerbates challenges. According to one analysis, the likelihood of exhausting retirement assets increases from 21 percent to 54 percent in an extended period of low interest rates (Prudential Insurance Company of America 2013). In fact, our work with HRS data is consistent with the conclusion that the low interest rate period has contributed to a large increase in the risk of asset exhaustion.

Though the broad equity and housing markets are now recovering, those who sold their equity holdings, and who sold, or lost their homes, have not benefitted from the recovery. While there is conflicting evidence on whether retirees are falling short of adequate resources for retirement, the preponderance of evidence suggests that future retirees will be less financially prepared than in past decades (Fichtner 2014; Munnell et al. 2014).

Effects of the Low Interest Rate Environment on Saving, Wealth, and Asset Allocation

Our work with the HRS provides additional support for these conclusions.[12] The 1992–2014 HRS panel we employ contains self-reports at two-year intervals, affording the opportunity to examine the wealth of elderly households, observe allocations across financial assets, and look at income. After offering a descriptive look at the cohort comparisons, we decide how long-term trends have played out across various age groups ahead of, and throughout, the low interest rate period. The HRS age groups are obtained by segmenting the panel into five-year birth cohorts; those born between 1931 and 1935, 1936 and 1940, and so on, through 1956–1960. While we include this last birth cohort cluster, its age and relative short duration in the panel offer less information on savings and asset trajectories. Following this investigation of cohort dynamics, we then consider differences in experience across the wealth distribution.

Cohort-Based Descriptive Analyses. A first observation is that the value of bonds held outside of mutual funds has increased over time, but from-and-to low average levels. Figure 9.1 shows that there appears to be a general

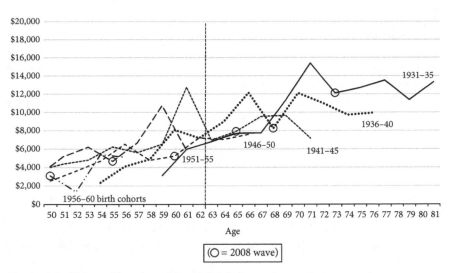

Figure 9.1. Value of bonds and bond funds for various cohorts over time

Source: Authors' calculations from RAND HRS Version P panel data 1992–2014. Excludes bonds held inside mutual funds.

attenuation of growth in accumulations over the last two to three waves of HRS data (2010–2014). When viewing this figure, it is useful to keep in mind that interest rates were still declining in 2014. Other patterns are consistent with the idea that the lower interest rates since the Great Recession (i.e., past the circles marking the 2008 wave data for each cohort-group path) have continued to mute allocations in this type of investment.

Bonds have historically played a protective role for seniors' income, especially absent inflation risks. Accordingly, one might posit that risk sensitivity is an important predictor of bond allocations. Therefore we construct a four-point Arrow Pratt risk aversion scale from survey responses in the HRS and look at these groups separately in Figure 9.2 to investigate this intuition. Results show that 63 percent of the sample falls within the most risk averse category.

Targeting the least risk-averse 13 percent of the sample, we still find lower reliance on bond portfolios. There are some notable exceptions, however, especially among the oldest and youngest in our sample. Indeed, bond portfolios have generally done better than expected over this period as rates have not only been generally low but also declined over the period studied. Inflation has been quite low as well; thus it is possible that some among the least risk averse increased their investments in bonds, essentially making a bet, on appreciation related to declining interest rates (perhaps as a result of chasing past returns). Yet we are hesitant to make too much of

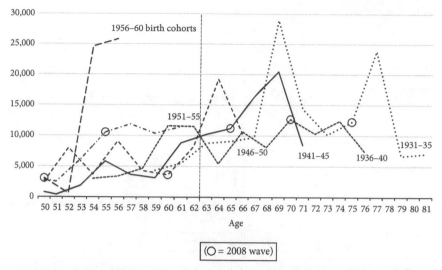

Figure 9.2. Value of bonds and bond funds for various cohorts over time in 2015 US dollars: those reporting as least risk averse via Arrow-Pratt measure HRS data 1992–2014

Source: Authors' calculations from RAND HRS Version P panel data 1992–2014. Excludes bonds held inside mutual funds.

this because of small sample sizes and low overall reported balances in the data. Overall, even among the least risk averse, there was evidence of attenuation in bond accumulations in the period since the Great Recession.

Another historically protective asset has been the home. HRS data include information on home and mortgage values, allowing us to construct measures of home equity and the ratio of loan-to-value (LTV). We begin by charting the evolution of the value of households' primary residence. As of 2014, estimated values of primary residences had not fully recovered to the peak levels reached in 2008, but notably, the general patterns of declines were relatively uniform. Recent cohorts do not appear to have suffered from outsized home value depreciation over the period since the Great Recession. Generally, then, even after the financial crisis, homeowners have not suffered a major decline in this key retirement asset.[13] And reassuringly, homeowners have continued to pay down their mortgages, so the ratio of home loan to home value, LTV, has generally continued to decline. This shores up home values that might otherwise be at risk (see Figure 9.3).

In fact, though LTV has generally been higher for the more recent cohorts, since the youngest HRS cohorts have even accelerated their mortgage pay-downs relative to those that came before them. This is seen in the crossing of cohort-series at the top left of the graph in Figure 9.4. This could

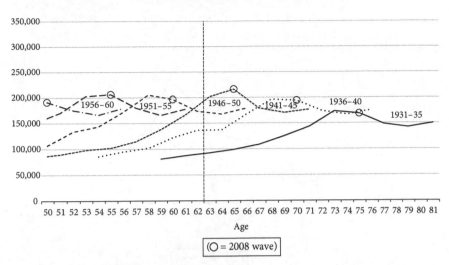

Figure 9.3. Value of primary residence for various cohorts over time in 2015 US dollars, HRS data 1992–2014

Source: Authors' calculations from RAND HRS Version P panel data 1992–2014.

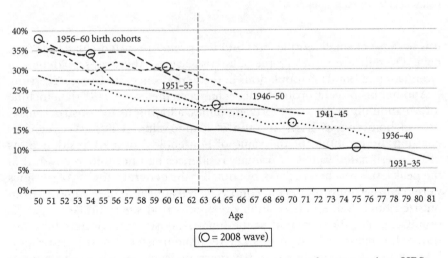

Figure 9.4. Loan to value: primary residence for various cohorts over time, HRS data 1992–2014

Source: Authors' calculations from RAND HRS Version P panel data 1992–2014.

be the result of the stricter rules governing mortgage issuance which would tend to reduce refinancing and home-equity-based lines of credit. Yet, rather than being lender driven (and thus based on the supply of credit), the decline could also be demand driven. That is, borrowers might be more reluctant to borrow as much in the aftermath of the financial crisis. Finally, the pattern could be due to relative prices and opportunity costs—an impact of the low interest rate environment. For example, lower interest rates generate lower interest payments, reducing the realized value of mortgage interest deductions for tax purposes. It is certainly possible that each of these three factors plays a role in explaining the data.

Another real-estate-related asset category, 'other property,' might arguably be of value to aging households in a low interest rate environment, because (1) although these properties require ongoing maintenance, such holdings can pay a stream of rental income; and further because (2) they may appreciate in value. In fact, Figures 9.5 and 9.6 show a notable break in the real estate holding habits of cohorts based on risk preferences. For the most risk averse, one observes increasing holdings, even following the Great Recession (Figure 9.5). Yet for the least risk averse, accumulation patterns generally flatten or decline from the peak in 2008 (Figure 9.6). The mountain-like profile representing holdings for the 1951–55 cohort is distinct and perhaps has to do with more speculative real estate activity before and after the US housing bubble burst in 2007–2008 among these birth cohorts.[14]

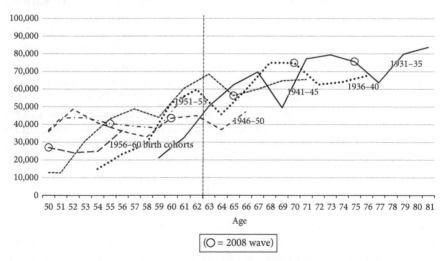

Figure 9.5. Net value of other real estate for various cohorts over time in 2015 US dollars: those reporting as most risk averse via Arrow-Pratt HRS data 1992–2014

Source: Authors' calculations from RAND HRS Version P panel data 1992–2014.

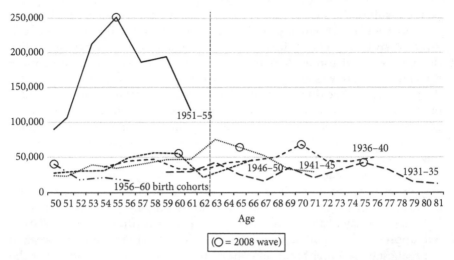

Figure 9.6. Net value of other real estate for various cohorts over time in 2015 US dollars: those reporting as least risk averse via Arrow-Pratt HRS data 1992–2014

Source: Authors' calculations from RAND HRS Version P panel data 1992–2014.

Moving from consideration of assets that pay a stream of income or services (i.e. bonds, homes and rental properties) we next look at trends in income. Here the evidence suggests that younger cohorts are earning higher incomes for longer, but there is no general evidence of a compensating increase in income following the asset markdowns during in the Great Recession. That is, older households do not appear to have delayed exit or re-entered the labor market to any marked degree. (See Figure 9.7).

Interestingly, the general patterns for income tapering across cohorts are consistent with the evolution of mortgages illustrated in Figure 9.5. Younger cohorts have more income and hold higher mortgage balances at similar ages. A look at more liquid assets and short-term debt shows that cohorts have behaved very similarly over time. As a rule, they all generally hold liquid balances between $10,000 and $20,000 and manage their finances such that other debt tapers to the $4,000–$6,000 range by age 62–63.

In sum, focusing on balances for traditional retirement investments provides mixed results in terms of risk-return characteristics and both cash and asset management strategies. Observed patterns suggest delayed income tapering may be aligned with delayed mortgage payoff, and that investments in bonds may be muted in the low interest rate environment since the Great Recession. By comparison, the value of stocks (equity and mutual fund holdings) has grown for most cohorts following the negative shocks related to the financial crisis (Figure 9.8).

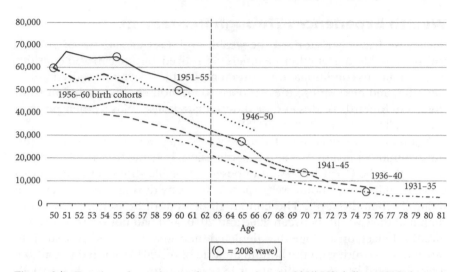

Figure 9.7. Earnings for various cohorts over time in 2015 US dollars, HRS data 1992–2014

Source: Authors' calculations from RAND HRS Version P panel data 1992–2014.

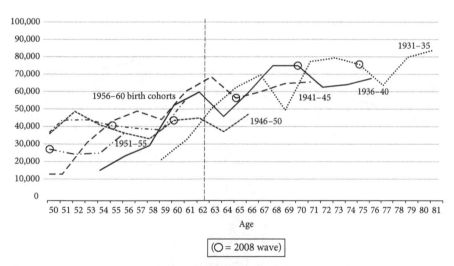

Figure 9.8. Net value of equities and mutual fund holdings for various cohorts over time in 2015 US dollars, HRS data 1992–2014

Source: Authors' calculation from RAND HRS Version P panel data 1992–2014.

Wealth Experiences Through Retirement

So far, we have characterized the wealth and asset allocations of cohorts without considering whether members are retired, but we can also consider asset evolutions conditional on retirement. People self-report retirement in the HRS, and next we use these reports to tag households' evolution from this event forward. To this end we differentiate households by their place in the overall wealth distribution in 2014.

Again we compare cohorts based on where they were in 2008 to compare the evolution of wealth pre- and post-recession. Looking first at total wealth, we see that the Great Recession imposed a notable shock on assets across every wealth group: none were spared. Patterns during the recovery are quite different, however. The bottom 10 percent of households lost more than half their wealth between 2008 and 2010, and had not yet recovered as of 2014. In fact, on average they depleted their wealth around 16 years into retirement. Focusing on the bottom quartile of the 2014 wealth distribution, it too depleted its assets within about 18 years of retirement (see Figure 9.9). This is notable inasmuch as it is less than the 20-or-so years that financial advisors might use for longevity. By 18 years into retirement, the bottom 50 percent of all HRS households averaged only about $50,000 in net financial assets, and the 75th percentile of the distribution had just over twice that amount.[15]

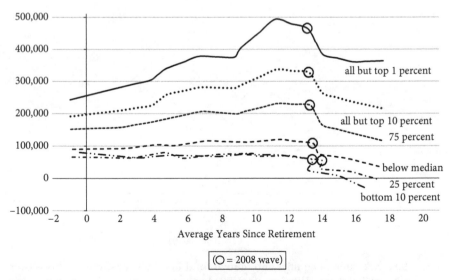

Figure 9.9. Average total assets in 2015 US dollars before and after retirement

Source. Authors' calculation from RAND HRS Version P panel data 1992–2014.

By contrast, the top 10 percent, who generally were older and had been retired longer at the time of the Great Recession, saw strong increases in their total assets, more than recovering their losses. Figure 9.10 makes it clear that the wealthiest 10 percent started with more assets before the Great Recession, but that does not explain why total wealth for this group grew afterwards. Specifically, this subgroup held higher allocations to stock and mutual funds, and it has increased its proportional allocations over time (see Figure 9.11). The same is true for allocations to bonds, though the proportions of these allocations are lower (Figure 9.12).[16]

One asset class where groups behaved more uniformly is with respect to allocations to very short-term debt investments, where all groups reduced allocations since the Great Recession. In 2008, these comprised from 1 to 4.4 percent of financial wealth, but since 2008, all groups curtailed their holdings between 1.2 and 2.4 percentage points.

There is also an interesting bit of evidence on liquidity, as seen in Figure 9.13. Early in our data, liquid asset positions were relatively uniform. But as groups moved toward 2014, cash increasingly made up a greater proportion of assets for those lower in the wealth distribution, until there was a collapse (correlated with insolvency).

While the cause of this trend remains unclear, there are two hypotheses worth considering. First, the increase in cash can be related to expenses rising relative to assets. Second, insolvency may in part be driven by

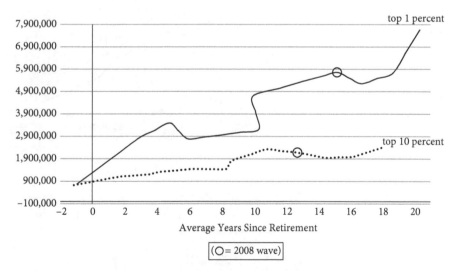

Figure 9.10. Average total assets before and after retirement in 2015 US dollars: for HRS households with a retired person

Source: Authors' calculations from RAND HRS Version P panel data 1992–2014.

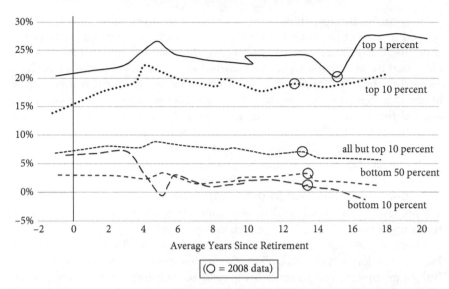

Figure 9.11. Proportion of stocks to total assets for HRS households with a retired person

Source. Authors' calculations from RAND HRS Version P panel data 1992–2014.

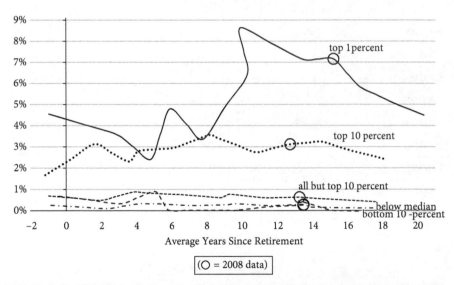

Figure 9.12. Proportion of bonds to total assets for HRS households with a retired person (excludes bonds held through mutual funds)

Source. Authors' calculations from RAND HRS Version P panel data 1992–2014.

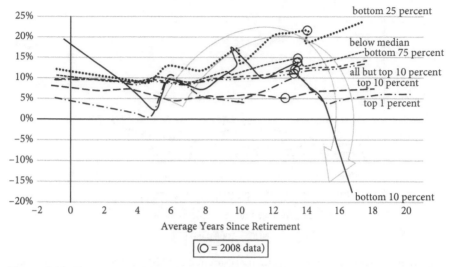

Figure 9.13. Proportion of liquid to total assets for HRS households with a retired person

Source: Authors' calculations from RAND HRS Version P panel data 1992–2014.

preferences to hold non-performing assets such as homes. Increases in liquid asset positions among the lower half of the 2014 wealth distribution emerged well ahead of the Great Recession, in support of the second hypothesis.

Moving to home values, conditional on owning a home, the lowest 25 percent of the asset distribution in 2014 appear to have relied on home equity to finance their retirement, to various degrees. For the bottom 10 percent of the wealth distribution, home equity drawdowns were nearly complete, as seen in Figure 9.14. This also confirms some degree of allocative response to changes in interest rates.

Multivariate Regression Analysis and Results

Next we employ the HRS data in order to explore potential factors contributing to total asset positions, controlling for household characteristics. We use multivariate regression and investigate bond and liquid allocations, in keeping with the idea that these assets, generally thought of as safe for elders, will be vulnerable in a low interest rate environment.

Our dataset includes household-level information that helps us to control for many important factors driving wealth and portfolio allocations. (See Table 9A.1, in the Appendix). To account for differential household mortality

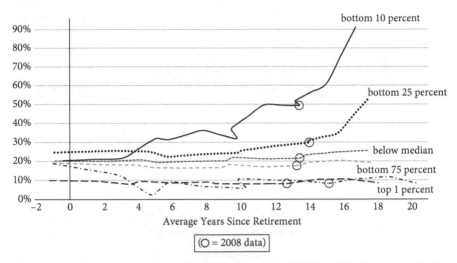

Figure 9.14. Loan to value for primary residence for HRS households with retired person

Source: Authors' calculations from RAND HRS Version P panel data 1992–2014.

and associated changes in household size, we include both household members separately, and we control on marital status, sex, and a marriage-gender interaction term. We use panel regressions for work and Tobit regressions for proportions or ratios.

Variables of interest. We target two types of dependent variables, the first being measures of total household wealth, and the second being measures of portfolio allocation. Household wealth is skewed, especially in the aftermath of the Great Recession, as we observed above. In regressions with the full sample, we employ two binary variables targeting the top and bottom 10 percent of the wealth distribution. We also run panel data Tobit regressions on portfolio allocations and on the home LTV dependent variable.

The explanatory variable of main interest is the low interest rate indicator, coded to equal 1 for all interviews following December 2008, which was the month the Federal Reserve dropped the Federal Funds Rate to a target range of 0–25 basis points. Because this key rate drives global interest rates for fixed income products, and because it stayed in the same near-zero target window well past the last 2014 interview date, this binary variable captures the low interest rate environment rather parsimoniously.

We also control on whether the respondent was retired and the number of years retired, tagging retirement as of the first interview announcement. The number of years retired is measured as the difference from retirement year and the interview date. Age and the square of age use the oldest living spouse (in married households). Household education is similarly reported from the maximum education status using the HRS 5-point scale. As an additional measure for education, we calculate any spousal difference in household educational attainment. This education-spread in the household attenuates the return to the education variable. We also control for risk tolerance, employing a scaled Arrow Pratt measure derived in the RAND HRS dataset.

Finally, we include household level controls for race and ethnicity, marital status, sex, and cohort indicators, as well as whether they are in the top or bottom 10 percent of the wealth distribution.

Results. We first ran panel regressions to determine the impact of the low interest rate era on households' total asset position. In the sample of roughly 10,400 households, people experienced an average wealth shock of $84,000–$85,000 over the low interest period of 2009–2014. We note that this is controlling for retirement, labor force participation (ahead of and after initial retirement, and including part-time work), employer retirement plan, social security program participation, race, sex, marital status, age, cohort, and being in the top or bottom 10 percent of the wealth distribution. Our results are quite stable both in terms of economic and statistical significance (details appear in Table 9A.2). Additionally, among the lower portion of the wealth distribution, we found that the low interest rate period was again associated with very large declines in wealth.

Therefore, of course, protective factors that can be identified, for instance, the married and the better educated fared better. It also appears that some households re-engaged in market work when confronted with lower asset balances, as labor force participation is correlated with lower asset balances. This relationship flips, however, in the lowest 25 percent of the distribution (see Table 9A.3). We suspect that this has to do with a general paucity of assets for retirees in this group.

Turning to bond allocations, using the panel Tobit estimator, we observe estimated declines of roughly 0.1 to 0.2 percentage points for bond allocations during the low interest rate period. This represents a fairly large attenuation effect given the low proportions of bonds reported above. The attenuation is much larger for the top 10 percent of the wealth distribution, where bond holdings were greater earlier in retirement. These findings survive several robustness checks, remaining statistically significant at or above the 5 percent confidence level (see Table 9A.4).

We next explore how stock and mutual fund allocations evolved in the panel Tobit framework. Again, the low interest rate period was associated with declines in equity and mutual fund allocations of 1.4–1.5 percentage points, but for the top and bottom 10 percent of the wealth distribution, effects differed. The bottom 10 percent allocated away from this asset class, by roughly an additional percentage point, while the top 10 percent increased its allocation by roughly 9 percentage points (see Table 9A.5).

Finally, we examine home LTV dynamics, where the estimates imply interest rate environment is a 2 percentage point increase in LTV. Again, however, the experiences of the top and bottom 10 percent were quite different. For the lowest 10 percent of the wealth distribution, there was a much larger 27 percentage point increase in LTV, while the LTV declined 11 percentage points among the top 10 percent. Thus, a 38 percentage point difference in the evolution of LTVs across these groups should give pause as to the financial security and overall stability of less well-off retirees, including the more fortunate among those who own homes (see Table 9A.6).

Conclusions

The Great Recession of 2007–2009 and the subsequent low interest rate environment deepened the challenges facing older Americans as they manage assets into and through retirement. Our analyses of traditional retirement holding yielded mixed results. For instance, most households took significant losses from which they have not fully recovered, yet results are heterogeneous. The wealthiest 10 percent saw marked improvements in its wealth since the Great Recession but around a quarter of retired households reported negative net asset positions by 2014. Those in the bottom quartile who own homes have extracted equity from their homes to finance their retirement.

While financial security in retirement may still be feasible, it surely will become challenging. Many will need to save more on their own and work longer, either retiring later or working part time in retirement. Additionally, older persons will need to consider the merits of delaying when they claim Social Security retirement benefits, to maximize the inflation-protected annuity this will produce.

Acknowledgments

The authors wish to thank Peter Brady, Julia Coronado, Sarah Holden, Emily Kessler, Anne Lester, Olivia S. Mitchell, David Richardson, Nikolai Roussanov, John Sabelhaus, Steve Utkis, and other PRC participants for many helpful comments and suggestions, along with Andrew Granato and Rebecca Landau for their excellent work as research assistants.

Appendix: Data and Regression Tables

TABLE 9A.1 Summary statistics

Variable	Obs	Mean	Std. Dev.	Min	Max
Dependent variables					
total assets ($2015)	226,564	356,349.30	990,892.60	−4,383,000.00	90,600,000.00
allocations and housing equity use					
equities & mutual funds	216,706	0.06	0.32	−40.00	80.00
bonds	216,706	0.01	0.05	−6.67	2.25
safe assets	216,706	0.03	0.26	−19.00	70.50
liquid assets	216,706	0.11	0.56	−110.00	43.50
loan to value for primary residence	174,537	0.19	0.29	0.00	1.50
Other variables					
low interest rate era {0, 1}	226,564	0.27	0.44	0.00	1.00
household labor force participation {0, 1}	182,814	0.47	0.48	0.00	1.00
household reports retirement {0, 1}	286,376	0.63	0.48	0.00	1.00
number of years retired	230,834	8.33	11.70	−22.00	78.92
household holds a DB pension {0, 1}	449,940	0.08	0.27	0.00	1.00
household holds a DC account {0, 1}	449,940	0.09	0.28	0.00	1.00
household has OASI income {0, 1}	226,564	0.59	0.49	0.00	1.00
household has SSI or DI income {0, 1}	226,564	0.09	0.29	0.00	1.00
home ownership {0, 1}	223,879	0.78	0.41	0.00	1.00
risk {, . . ., 4} least to most risk averse	230,772	3.28	1.08	1.00	4.00
education {max: respondent, spouse}[a]	449,916	3.34	1.40	1.00	5.00
education {max—min: respondent, spouse}	449,916	0.68	0.95	0.00	4.00
household white {0, 0.5, 1}	449,007	0.75	0.43	0.00	1.00

(continued)

TABLE 9A.1 Continued

Variable	Obs	Mean	Std. Dev.	Min	Max
household hispanic {0, 0.5, 1}	447,189	0.11	0.31	0.00	1.00
respondent is female	449,940	0.56	0.50	0.00	1.00
respondent is married	226,564	0.67	0.47	0.00	1.00
married & female	226,564	0.33	0.47	0.00	1.00
age {max: respondent, spouse}	226,562	68.33	10.72	24.67	109.67
age squared	226,562	4,784.27	1,513.78	608.44	12,026.78
person born 1931–35 {0, 1}	449,940	0.12	0.32	0.00	1.00
person born 1936–40 {0, 1}	449,940	0.13	0.34	0.00	1.00
person born 1941–45 {0, 1}	449,940	0.09	0.29	0.00	1.00
person born 1946–50 {0, 1}	449,940	0.10	0.29	0.00	1.00
person born 1951–55 {0, 1}	449,940	0.11	0.31	0.00	1.00
person born 1956–60 {0, 1}	449,940	0.10	0.30	0.00	1.00
2014 wealth in top 10 percent {0, 1}	226,564	0.07	0.26	0.00	1.00
2014 wealth in bottom 10 percent {0, 1}	224,976	0.07	0.26	0.00	1.00

Notes:

[a] Education codes: {1: less than high school (HS), 2: GED, 3: HS, 4: some college, 5: college & above}

Source: Authors' computations.

TABLE 9A.2 Panel regression analysis of total assets, full sample

Total Assets ($2015)	coefficient	z-stat	coefficient	z-stat	coefficient	z-stat	coefficient	z-stat
low interest rate era {0,1}	-$84,351	-10.56	-$84,516	-10.58	-$83,610	-10.52	-$83,777	-10.57
household labor force participation {0, 1}	-$3,662	-0.28	-$11,749	-1.17	-$11,666	-1.16	-$11,711	-1.17
household reports retirement {0, 1}	$11,881	0.93						
number of years retired	$2,096	2.94	$2,194	3.11	$2,225	3.16	$2,206	3.14
household holds a DB pension {0, 1}	-$49,583	-5.99	-$49,883	-6.03	-$49,513	-6.00	-$49,501	-6.00
household holds a DC account {0, 1}	-$44,682	-5.70	-$44,775	-5.71	-$45,075	-5.77	-$45,097	-5.77
household has OASI income {0, 1}	$9,412	1.00	$10,641	1.14	$10,940	1.18	$10,885	1.18
household has SSI or DI income {0, 1}	-$28,723	-2.15	-$27,261	-2.06	-$27,589	-2.09	-$27,576	-2.09
home ownership {0, 1}	$136,572	12.55	$136,548	12.55	$137,251	12.68	$137,199	12.68
risk {, . . ., 4} least to most risk averse	-$6,033	-1.00	-$6,007	-1.00	-$6,562	-1.09	-$6,558	-1.09
education {max: respondent, spouse}[a]	$90,266	15.05	$90,251	15.04	$91,403	15.75	$91,384	15.75
education {max—min: respondent, spouse}	-$62,852	-8.72	-$62,757	-8.70	-$63,962	-8.89	-$63,913	-8.88
household white {0, 0.5, 1}	$63,024	3.68	$62,947	3.68	$59,813	3.50	$59,923	3.50
household hispanic {0, 0.5, 1}	-$9,327	-0.40	-$9,465	-0.40				
respondent is female	-$32,306	-1.54	-$31,972	-1.52	-$33,565	-1.60	-$28,294	-2.11
respondent is married	$57,473	3.25	$57,879	3.28	$58,282	3.34	$62,980	6.33
married & female	$6,374	0.31	$5,967	0.29	$6,719	0.33		
age {max: respondent, spouse}	$42,322	9.09	$42,882	9.30	$43,065	9.40	$43,044	9.40
age squared	-$212	-6.21	-$216	-6.39	-$218	-6.48	-$217	-6.47
person born 1936–40 {0, 1}	$78,544	4.18	$78,779	4.19	$75,871	4.03	$76,060	4.04
person born 1941–45 {0, 1}	$92,446	4.47	$92,898	4.49	$89,878	4.34	$90,198	4.36
person born 1946–50 {0, 1}	$138,146	6.40	$138,614	6.42	$138,180	6.41	$138,554	6.43
person born 1951–55 {0, 1}	$224,741	9.20	$225,043	9.21	$219,837	9.03	$220,338	9.07
person born 1956–60 {0, 1}	$150,886	3.60	$151,310	3.61	$149,181	3.56	$149,924	3.59
2014 wealth in bottom 10 percent {0, 1}	-$105,526	-3.39	-$105,387	-3.39	-$104,515	-3.36	-$104,569	-3.36

(continued)

TABLE 9A.2 Continued

Total Assets ($2015)	coefficient	z-stat	coefficient	z-stat	coefficient	z-stat	coefficient	z-stat
2014 wealth in top 10 percent {0, 1}	$1,230,160	60.53	$1,230,057	60.51	$1,236,205	60.78	$1,236,274	60.78
constant	−$2,092,375	−12.91	−$2,102,129	−13.01	−$2,105,273	−13.13	−$2,109,482	−13.20
observations	87,381		87,415		87,832		87,832	
number of groups	10,408		10,408		10,426		10,426	
R-squared between	34.6%		34.6%		34.7%		34.7%	
R-squared overall	21.0%		21.0%		21.0%		21.0%	

Notes:
[a] Education codes: {1: less than high school (HS), 2: GED, 3: HS, 4: some college, 5: college & above}

Source: Authors' computations.

TABLE 9A.3 Panel regression analysis of total assets, subsamples of the wealth distribution

Panel Regression—Dependent Variable:	Full Sample		Bottom 90 percent		Bottom 75 percent		Bottom 50 percent		Bottom 25 percent		Bottom 10 percent	
Total Assets ($2015)	coefficient	z-stat	coefficient	z-stat	coefficient	z-stat	coefficient	z-stat	coefficient	z-stat	coefficient	z-stat
low interest rate era {0, 1}	-$84,351	-10.56	-$78,081	-22.83	-$68,913	-21.15	-$45,828	-18.23	-$30,208	-7.51	-$71,325	-9.83
household labor force participation {0, 1}	-$3,662	-0.28	-$7,183	-1.26	-$10,552	-1.99	-$3,852	-0.97	$6,635	1.02	$12,773	1.10
household reports retirement {0, 1}	$11,881	0.93	$5,469	0.99	$2,376	0.46	-$242	-0.06	$3,463	0.52	$3,239	0.28
number of years retired	$2,096	2.94	$1,231	3.83	$566	1.99	$223	1.04	-$94	-0.30	$437	0.62
household holds a DB pension {0, 1}	-$49,583	-5.99	-$35,642	-9.96	-$19,027	-5.48	-$9,590	-3.36	-$14,671	-2.88	-$9,471	-1.12
household holds a DC account {0, 1}	-$44,682	-5.70	-$29,404	-8.68	-$17,749	-5.41	-$6,871	-2.60	$3,741	0.80	-$13,718	-1.77
household has OASI income {0, 1}	$9,412	1.00	-$2,018	-0.50	-$1,858	-0.49	$479	0.16	$2,478	0.53	$1,245	0.15
household has SSI or DI income {0, 1}	-$28,723	-2.15	-$26,283	-4.77	-$24,649	-5.04	-$15,919	-4.72	-$12,018	-2.46	-$11,650	-1.17
home ownership {0, 1}	$136,572	12.55	$120,605	26.74	$101,817	25.82	$81,806	30.93	$83,179	21.50	$75,407	10.08
risk {1, . . ., 4} least to most risk averse	-$6,033	-1.00	-$2,039	-0.74	-$1,099	-0.45	-$1,344	-0.73	$2,151	0.87	$3,414	0.61
education {max: respondent, spouse}[a]	$90,266	15.05	$74,087	27.76	$42,964	18.41	$23,381	13.23	$18,404	7.46	$24,933	4.34
education {max–min: respondent, spouse}	-$62,852	-8.72	-$43,574	-13.28	-$24,724	-8.55	-$14,172	-6.32	-$12,117	-3.71	-$18,998	-2.54
household white {0, 0.5, 1}	$63,024	3.68	$72,653	9.76	$42,597	6.88	$9,277	2.13	$3,046	0.52	-$19,298	-1.43
household hispanic {0, 0.5, 1}	-$9,327	-0.40	-$25,903	-2.55	-$20,494	-2.44	-$12,299	-2.10	-$3,100	-0.40	$31,686	1.57
respondent is female	-$32,306	-1.54	-$10,704	-1.17	-$5,043	-0.63	-$1,657	-0.29	$3,617	0.46	$10,520	0.58
respondent is married	$57,473	3.25	$43,980	5.82	$27,978	4.07	$17,382	3.50	$15,421	2.12	$34,517	2.21
married & female	$6,374	0.31	-$1,436	-0.16	$8,638	1.08	$3,298	0.57	$5,528	0.65	-$3,207	-0.18
age {max: respondent, spouse}	$42,322	9.09	$27,411	13.83	$15,279	8.13	$6,490	4.51	$4,599	2.07	$3,264	0.76
age squared	-$212	-6.21	-$152	-10.49	-$84	-6.11	-$38	-3.60	-$27	-1.63	-$12	-0.36
person born 1936–40 {0, 1}	$78,544	4.18	$31,076	3.62	$13,732	1.83	-$13,984	-2.39	-$18,302	-2.18	$14,679	0.66
person born 1941-45 {0, 1}	$92,446	4.47	$32,410	3.41	$7,039	0.84	-$11,429	-1.76	-$18,114	-1.95	$10,675	0.48
person born 1946-50 {0, 1}	$138,146	6.40	$59,654	6.10	$17,598	2.03	-$7,047	-1.06	-$11,452	-1.22	$39,793	1.86
person born 1951-55 {0, 1}	$224,741	9.20	$79,884	7.25	$37,292	3.84	$11,114	1.52	-$15,952	-1.55	$19,227	0.85
person born 1956-60 {0, 1}	$150,886	3.60	$61,404	3.25	$16,155	0.99	-$16,236	-1.37	-$29,070	-1.85	-$3,721	-0.11

(continued)

TABLE 9A.3 Continued

Panel Regression—Dependent Variable:	Full Sample		Bottom 90 percent		Bottom 75 percent		Bottom 50 percent		Bottom 25 percent		Bottom 10 percent	
Total Assets ($2015)	coefficient	z-stat	coefficient	z-stat	coefficient	z-stat	coefficient	z-stat	coefficient	z-stat	coefficient	z-stat
2014 wealth in bottom 10 percent {0, 1}	−$105,526	−3.39	−$117,588	−8.85	−$63,855	−6.10	−$14,897	−2.37	−$3,700	−0.57	–	–
2014 wealth in top 10 percent {0, 1}	$1,230,160	60.53	–		–		–		–		–	
constant	−$2,092,375	−12.91	−$1,276,248	−18.45	−$695,406	−10.68	−$274,813	−5.57	−$215,142	−2.85	−$234,398	−1.65
observations	87,381		75,907		59,509		33,621		13,966		3,534	
number of groups	10,408		9,091		7,230		4,276		1,898		500	
R-squared between	34.6%		19.1%		14.7%		15.4%		13.3%		15.7%	
R-squared overall	21.0%		12.4%		8.7%		10.0%		9.0%		13.0%	

Notes:
[a] Education codes: {1: less than high school (HS), 2: GED, 3: HS, 4: some college, 5: college & above}.

Source: Authors' computations.

TABLE 9A.4 Tobit regression analysis of bond allocations

Panel Tobit—Dependent Variable

Bond Allocations	Coefficient (%)	z-stat	Coefficient (%)	z-stat	Coefficient (%)	z-stat	Coefficient (%)	z-stat
low interest rate era {0, 1}	-0.1	-2.49	-0.1	-2.51	-0.2	-6.58	-0.2	-5.50
household labor force participation {0, 1}	-0.1	-2.07	-0.2	-3.61	-0.1	-2.99	-0.1	-3.07
household reports retirement {0, 1}	0.1	0.98						
number of years retired	0.0	2.85	0.0	3.05	0.0	3.49	0.0	3.01
household holds a DB pension {0, 1}	0.0	-0.13	0.0	-0.16	0.0	-0.28	0.0	-0.43
household holds a DC account {0, 1}	0.1	1.32	0.1	1.31	0.0	0.44	0.0	0.20
household has OASI income {0, 1}	-0.1	-2.18	-0.1	-2.04	-0.1	-2.13	-0.1	-1.75
household has SSI or DI income {0, 1}	-0.2	-2.47	-0.2	-2.37	-0.1	-2.71	-0.1	-2.01
home ownership {0, 1}	-0.2	-3.47	-0.2	-3.47	-0.2	-4.50		
alt regressor—loan to value							-0.1	-1.83
risk {, . . . , 4} least to most risk averse	0.0	0.35	0.0	0.36				
education {max: respondent, spouse}[a]	0.2	11.17	0.2	11.16	0.2	13.28	0.2	12.65
education {max—min: respondent, spouse}	-0.2	-6.35	-0.2	-6.33	-0.2	-7.38	-0.2	-7.48
household white {0, 0.5, 1}	0.3	4.13	0.3	4.13	0.2	4.78	0.2	4.18
household hispanic {0, 0.5, 1}	-0.1	-1.61	-0.1	-1.62	-0.1	-0.96	-0.1	-1.13
respondent is female	-0.1	-1.71	-0.1	-1.69	-0.2	-3.37	-0.2	-2.13
respondent is married	-0.1	-1.67	-0.1	-1.64	-0.2	-3.02	-0.2	-2.14
married & female	0.2	1.82	0.2	1.79	0.3	3.25	0.2	2.17
age {max: respondent, spouse}	0.1	2.22	0.1	2.36	0.0	1.97	0.1	2.51
age squared	0.0	-2.15	0.0	-2.29	0.0	-1.31	0.0	-2.07
person born 1936–40 {0, 1}	-0.3	-4.12	-0.3	-4.10	-0.3	-4.55	-0.3	-4.36
person born 1941–45 {0, 1}	-0.4	-5.69	-0.4	-5.65	-0.4	-5.65	-0.4	-5.22
person born 1946–50 {0, 1}	-0.5	-6.07	-0.5	-6.03	-0.4	-5.66	-0.4	-5.66
person born 1951–55 {0, 1}	-0.5	-5.59	-0.5	-5.57	-0.4	-5.11	-0.4	-5.00
person born 1956–60 {0, 1}	-0.6	-3.67	-0.6	-3.65	-0.2	-2.41	-0.3	-2.85
2014 wealth in bottom 10 percent {0, 1}	-0.2	-2.04	-0.2	-2.03	-0.2	-2.66	-0.1	-0.93
2014 wealth in top 10 percent {0, 1}	1.5	21.92	1.5	21.92	1.6	25.98	1.5	23.39
constant	-1.7	-2.08	-1.7	-2.15	-1.4	-2.09	-2.0	-2.74

Notes:

[a] Homeownership and LTV must be substituted in regression specifications.

Source: Authors' computations.

TABLE 9A.5 Tobit regression analysis of equity and mutual fund allocations

Panel Tobit—Dependent Variable

Equity and Mutual Fund Allocations	Coefficient (%)	z-stat	Coefficient (%)	z-stat	Coefficient (%)	z-stat	Coefficient (%)	z-stat
low interest rate era {0, 1}	-1.4	-3.67	-1.4	-3.68	-1.9	-6.91	-1.5	-8.11
household labor force participation {0, 1}	-2.0	-3.22	-2.1	-4.76	-2.0	-5.53	-2.0	-7.62
household reports retirement (0, 1)	0.2	0.38	0.0	-1.03	0.0	-1.02	0.0	0.19
number of years retired	0.0	-1.08	0.6	1.59	0.2	0.74	0.0	0.04
household holds a DB pension {0, 1}	0.6	1.59	0.7	1.82	0.6	2.03	0.6	3.24
household holds a DC account {0, 1}	0.7	1.82	-0.4	-0.96	-0.8	-2.13	-0.3	-1.33
household has OASI income {0, 1}	-0.5	-1.01	-1.8	-3.09	-1.9	-4.18	-2.1	-6.09
household has SSI or DI income {0, 1}	-1.8	-3.09	-1.7	-3.82	-1.5	-4.60		
home ownership {0, 1}	-1.7	-3.83						
alt regressor—loan to value[b]							0.7	2.61
risk {,..., 4} least to most risk averse	0.0	-0.26	0.0	-0.26				
education {max: respondent, spouse}[a]	2.1	14.52	2.1	14.53	2.0	17.07	1.7	17.66
education {max—min: respondent, spouse}	-1.2	-7.18	-1.2	-7.17	-1.1	-8.15	-0.9	-7.77
household white {0, 0.5, 1}	2.6	6.13	2.6	6.13	2.5	7.86	2.3	8.39
household hispanic {0, 0.5, 1}	-1.8	-3.09	-1.8	-3.09	-1.4	-3.26	-1.5	-4.06
respondent is female	-0.7	-1.07	-0.7	-1.06	-0.3	-0.64	-0.6	-1.36
respondent is married	-0.4	-0.68	-0.4	-0.67	-0.1	-0.27	-0.5	-1.17
married & female	0.9	1.23	0.9	1.22	0.3	0.54	0.6	1.25
age {max: respondent, spouse}	-0.4	-2.01	-0.4	-1.98	-0.6	-3.66	-0.3	-2.89
age squared	0.0	2.20	0.0	2.17	0.0	4.38	0.0	3.19
person born 1936–40 {0, 1}	-0.7	-1.49	-0.7	-1.48	-0.6	-1.54	-0.9	-2.80
person born 1941–45 {0, 1}	-0.7	-1.40	-0.7	-1.39	-0.2	-0.58	-1.0	-2.84
person born 1946–50 {0, 1}	-1.4	-2.34	-1.4	-2.33	-0.8	-1.80	-1.1	-2.88
person born 1951–55 {0, 1}	-2.7	-3.78	-2.6	-3.78	-1.5	-2.95	-1.9	-4.67
person born 1956–60 {0, 1}	-2.8	-2.48	-2.8	-2.48	-1.4	-2.31	-1.8	-3.69
2014 wealth in bottom 10 percent {0, 1}	-2.4	-3.09	-2.4	-3.09	-2.5	-4.40	-2.4	-4.32
2014 wealth in top 10 percent {0, 1}	8.7	18.42	8.7	18.42	8.9	22.49	9.0	28.24
constant	15.0	1.96	14.8	1.94	18.0	3.23	11.2	2.75

Notes:

[a] Education codes: {1: less than high school (HS), 2: GED, 3: HS, 4: some college, 5: college & above}.

[b] Homeownership and LTV must be substituted in regression specifications.

Source: Authors' computations.

TABLE 9A.6 Tobit regression analysis of LTV ratios among homeowners

Panel Tobit—Dependent Variable

Loan to Value | Home Ownership	Coefficient (%)	z-stat	Coefficient (%)	z-stat	Coefficient (%)	z-stat	Coefficient (T)	z-stat
low interest rate era {0, 1}	2.0	8.33	2.0	8.33	2.0	8.46	2.0	8.47
household labor force participation {0, 1}	2.1	5.33	2.1	5.33	2.1	5.34	2.1	5.30
household reports retirement {0, 1}	-1.6	-4.32	-1.6	-4.32	-1.6	-4.30	-1.6	-4.19
number of years retired	-0.2	-7.20	-0.2	-7.21	-0.2	-7.11	-0.2	-7.08
household holds a DB pension {0, 1}	0.6	2.51	0.6	2.51	0.6	2.50	0.6	2.49
household holds a DC account {0, 1}	0.7	2.93	0.7	2.93	0.7	2.94	0.7	2.93
household has OASI income {0, 1}	0.6	2.21	0.6	2.21	0.6	2.22	0.6	2.04
household has SSI or DI income {0, 1}	0.6	1.34	0.6	1.34	0.6	1.32		
added regressor—equities allocation	2.0	5.35	2.0	5.35	2.0	5.35	2.0	5.34
risk {1, . . . , 4} least to most risk averse	-0.7	-3.33	-0.7	-3.33	-0.7	-3.39	-0.7	-3.40
education {max: respondent, spouse}[a]	2.8	13.24	2.8	13.24	2.9	13.32	2.8	13.27
education {max—min: respondent, spouse}	-0.5	-2.10	-0.5	-2.10	-0.5%	-2.10	-0.5	-2.08
household white {0, 0.5, 1}	-3.3	-5.15	-3.3	-5.15	-3.2%	-5.15	-3.3	-5.18
household hispanic {0, 0.5, 1}	-1.6	-1.80	-1.6	-1.80	-1.5%	-1.77	-1.5	-1.77
respondent is female	0.0	-0.02						
respondent is married	3.1	5.14	3.1	7.07	2.7%	8.25	2.7	8.36
married & female	-0.6	-0.89	-0.6	-1.42				
age {max: respondent, spouse}	-1.8	-12.56	-1.8	-12.56	-1.8	-12.56	-1.8	-12.50
age squared	0.0	9.91	0.0	9.91	0.0	9.88	0.0	9.81
person born 1936–40 {0, 1}	3.1	4.74	3.1	4.74	3.1	4.69	3.1	4.69
person born 1941–45 {0, 1}	5.4	7.59	5.4	7.59	5.4	7.50	5.4	7.51
person born 1946–50 {0, 1}	8.4	11.26	8.4	11.26	8.4	11.18	8.4	11.21
person born 1951–55 {0, 1}	8.6	10.06	8.6	10.06	8.5	9.98	8.5	9.99
person born 1956–60 {0, 1}	10.4	7.03	10.4	7.04	10.2	6.92	10.2	6.93
2014 wealth in bottom 10 percent {0, 1}	27.2	21.99	27.2	21.99	27.1	21.98	27.2	21.99
2014 wealth in top 10 percent {0, 1}	-11.0	-15.97	-11.0	-15.97	-11.0	-15.96	-11.0	-15.98
constant	84.4	16.74	84.4	16.83	84.6	16.87	84.3	16.84

Notes:

[a] Education codes: {1: less than high school (HS), 2: GED, 3: HS, 4: some college, 5: college & above}.

Source: Authors' computations.

Notes

1. It is possible that the low interest rate environment will be around for a shorter period than some have projected.
2. For example, while the annual rate of increase for those born in 1933 or 1934 is 5.5 percent, for those born ten or more years later, the DRC is 8 percent per year.
3. The S&P 500 index value at market close on October 10, 2007 was 1562.47, and on March 9, 2009 it was 676.53. The National Bureau of Economic Research, the arbiter of the start and end dates of a recession, determined that the recession that began in December 2007 ended in June 2009, roughly coinciding with the peak and trough dates of the S&P 500 index.
4. The HRS is a longitudinal survey of health, retirement, and aging that has been conducted every two years since 1992 and interviews more than 22,000 Americans over the age of 50.
5. In this context, 'retirement plans' refer to peoples' goals, strategies and behaviors, not to DC or DB retirement plans.
6. The timing of retirement can be affected by more than age, including accumulated savings, the availability of an employer-provided pension, the willingness or ability to continue working part-time in retirement, personal health, access to health coverage, and general economic conditions.
7. The authors used data from the 2006 and 2008 core surveys, as well as data from two supplemental surveys, the Consumption and Activities Mail Survey (CAMS) and the HRS Internet Study. Although the time between the 2008 HRS interview and a subsequent 2009 HRS Internet survey was insufficient to observe actual behavior, the data nonetheless can be used to shed light on retirement expectations (Hurd et al. 2005).
8. What is described here are the expectations of working past either age 62 or age 65. Hurd et al. (2005) have found that these retirement expectations are predictive of actual retirement.
9. For a theoretical model of this behavior see Chai et al. (2012).
10. For a summary of research work on this area see Burkhauser et al. (2009).
11. These percentages are reported for aged units receiving benefits. An aged unit is defined by the Social Security Administration as 'a married couple living together or a nonmarried person, which also includes persons who are separated or married but not living together.' All figures in this sentence reported from: US Social Security Administration (2016a).
12. RAND version P include HRS data through the 2014 wave, all figures adjusted to 2015 dollars (Health and Retirement Study 2006).
13. This is consistent with Federal Reserve G20 Financial Accounts of US data, which show that as of Q3 2016 household owners' equity in real estate was 96.8 percent of the pre-recession peak, from Q1, 2006. Two years earlier, in Q3 2014 the recovery in these data was 77.9 percent—much less complete (Glick and Lansing 2011).

14. This cohort's wealth may evolve in ways that are interesting to other researchers in the future.
15. When considering these asset numbers recall that, as well as assets, the vast majority of those we are looking at here receive Social Security income. Asset depletion thus does not necessarily mean that 10–25 percent of households do not have resources on which to rely.
16. Because bonds can be held in mutual funds, we reason that the HRS data represent an under-reporting of bonds and over-reporting of equities, as a proportion of overall portfolios.

References

Blanchett, D., M. Fink, and W. Pfau (2018). "Low Returns and Optimal Retirement Savings," in R. Clark, R. Maurer, and O. S. Mitchell (eds.), *How Persistent Low Returns Will Shape Saving and Retirement*. Oxford, UK: Oxford University Press, pp. 26–43.

Bosworth, G., and G. Burtless (2011). 'Recessions, Wealth Destruction, and the Timing of Retirement.' CRR Working Paper No. 2010–22. Chestnut Hill, MA: Center for Retirement Research at Boston College.

Burkhauser, R., A. Gustman, J. Laitner, O. S. Mitchell, and A. Sonnega (2009). 'Social Security Research at the Michigan Retirement Research Center.' *Social Security Bulletin* 69(4): 51–65.

Chai, J., R. Maurer, O. S. Mitchell, and R. Rogalla (2012). 'Life Cycle Impacts of the Financial Crisis on Optimal Consumption – Portfolio Choices and Labor Supply,' in R. Maurer, O. S. Mitchell, and M. J. Warshawsky (eds.), *Reshaping Retirement Security: Lessons from the Global Financial Crisis*. Oxford, UK: Oxford University Press, pp. 120–50.

Congressional Research Service (2007). CRS Report for Congress, *Unemployment and Older Workers*. Washington, DC.

Coronado, J. (2014). 'The Changing Nature of Retirement.' PRC Working Paper No. WP2014-07. Philadelphia, PA: Pension Research Council.

Fichtner, J. J. (2014). 'Addressing the Real "Retirement Crisis" Through Sustainable Social Security Reform.' Testimony before the United States Senate, Committee on Finance, Subcommittee on Social Security, Pensions, and Family Policy, May 21.

Glick, R., and K. J. Lansing (2011). 'Consumers and the Economy, Part I: Household Credit and Personal Saving.' *FRBSF Economic Letter No. 2011–01*. San Francisco, CA: Federal Reserve Board of San Francisco.

Health and Retirement Study (2006). Produced and Distributed by the University of Michigan with Funding from the National Institute on Aging (grant number NIA U01AG009740) [Public Use Dataset]. Ann Arbor, MI: University of Michigan.

Horneff, V., R. Maurer, and O. S. Mitchell (2018). "How Persistent Low Expected Returns Alter Optimal Life Cycle Saving, Investment, and Retirement Behavior," in R. Clark, R. Maurer, and O. S. Mitchell (eds.), *How Persistent Low Returns Will Shape Saving and Retirement*. Oxford, UK: Oxford University Press, pp. 119–31.

Hurd, M., M. Renti, and S. Rohwedder (2005). 'The Effect of Large Capital Gains or Losses on Retirement,' in D. A. Wise (ed.), *Developments in the Economics of Aging.* Chicago, IL: University of Chicago Press.

Hurd, M. D., and S. Rohwedder (2010). 'The Effects of the Economic Crisis on the Older Population.' MRRC Working Paper No. 2010–231. Ann Arbor, MI: Michigan Retirement Research Center.

Ilmanen, A., and M. Rauseo (2018). "Intelligent Risk Taking: How to Secure Retirement in a Low Expected Return World." in R. Clark, R. Maurer, and O. S. Mitchell (eds.), *How Persistent Low Returns Will Shape Saving and Retirement.* Oxford, UK: Oxford University Press, pp. 81–98.

Munnell, A., M. Rudledge, and A. Webb (2014). 'Are Retirees Falling Short? Reconciling the Conflicting Evidence.' PRC Working Paper No. 2014–05. Philadelphia, PA: Pension Research Council.

Prudential Insurance Company of America (2013). *Planning for Retirement: The Impact of Interest Rates on Retirement Income.* Newark, NJ: Prudential Insurance Company of America. http://research.prudential.com/view/page/rp/32291

Reilly, C., and A. Byrne (2018). "Investing for Retirement in a Low Returns Environment: Making the Right Decisions to Make the Money Last," in R. Clark, R. Maurer, and O. S. Mitchell (eds.), *How Persistent Low Returns Will Shape Saving and Retirement.* Oxford, UK: Oxford University Press, pp. 61–80.

Shapiro, M. D. (2010). 'The Effects of the Financial Crisis on the Well-Being of Older Americans: Evidence from the Cognitive Economics Study.' MRRC Working Paper No. 228. Ann Arbor, MI: Michigan Retirement Research Center.

US Bureau of Labor Statistics (2010a). *Issues in Labor Statistics, Summary 10–04.* Washington, DC: Bureau of Labor Statistics. www.bls.gov/opub/ils//summary_10_04/older_workers.htm

US Bureau of Labor Statistics (2010b). *Labor Force Statistics from the Current Population Survey.* Washington, DC: Bureau of Labor Statistics. www.bls.gov/data/#unemployment

US Social Security Administration (2016a). 'Fast Facts & Figures.' Washington, DC: SSA. https://www.ssa.gov/policy/docs/chartbooks/fast_facts/2016/fast_facts16.html#page5

US Social Security Administration (2016b). 'Trust Fund Data.' Washington, DC: SSA. https://www.ssa.gov/OACT/STATS/table4a3.html

United States Social Security Administration (2017a). *Calculators: Life Expectancy.* Washington, DC: SSA. https://www.ssa.gov/planners/lifeexpectancy.html

United States Social Security Administration (2017b). *When to Start Receiving Retirement Benefits.* Washington, DC: SSA. https://www.ssa.gov/pubs/EN-05-10147.pdf

Wallick, D. W., D. B. Berkowitz, A. S. Clarke, K. J. DiCurcio, and K. A. Stockton (2018). "Getting More from Less in Defined Benefit Plans: Three Levers for a Low-Return World," in R. Clark, R. Maurer, and O. S. Mitchell (eds.), *How Persistent Low Returns Will Shape Saving and Retirement.* Oxford, UK: Oxford University Press, pp. 44–60.

Wells Fargo Securities (2012). 'Retirement in America: Extending the Finish Line.' Wells Fargo Special Commentary. San Francisco, CA: Wells Fargo.

Part III

New Designs for Pension Plan Sponsors

Chapter 10

Helping Employers Become Age-ready

Yvonne Sonsino

After years of concerted effort, employers in the developed world have designed and implemented numerous processes to reduce racial, ethnic, and sex discrimination in the workplace. Yet age is the last remaining frontier that employers must tackle, in terms of adjusting to an increasingly diverse workforce. By 2050, almost one quarter of the world's population will be over the age of 60, almost three times the mid-20th century figure. Longer lives require additional financing, and many older people will still need to work to finance these longer lives. In addition, as people see pension tax incentives decline, state retirement ages rise, and returns on pension investments fall, they are beginning to realize that early exodus from the workplace may not be feasible.

Of course, some firms recognize that older workers are productive and well aligned with customer demographics, yet others have not yet perceived opportunities accompanying the aging workplace. This chapter therefore focuses on how employers can prepare to embrace the growing number of older employees in the workplace.

Key Elements of an Age-ready Workplace

A recent UK population survey suggested that old age may actually be less relevant than we might believe for individuals. Over 80 percent of those surveyed in a UK analysis (aged 18–99) said they wished to keep active as long as possible, learn new things, and mix with those of different ages and generations (AONR 2016). In other words, employers would do well to heed the report's conclusion, namely that *age does not define us.*

To this end, firms will need to consider several key factors when designing a more age-friendly workforce. In particular, we focus on the role of employers in helping workers attain health and financial wellness; building their motivation/commitment, as well as new skills; and focusing on workplace design alongside succession planning. We take up each in turn.

Health and Financial Wellness

The term 'wellness' has come to connote more than just physical and mental health. Indeed, today it refers to methods helping employees to make healthy lifestyle changes while addressing emotional and mental health issues.

Health and Aging. A good place to start this discussion is to recognize that there is little evidence that chronological age is a determinant of good health, cognitive and physical ability, sickness absence, work-related injuries, or workplace productivity (Yeomans 2013). Instead, workers over age 50 have been proven to have similar physical ability to younger workers, in terms of physical strength and stamina. While muscle strength and aerobic capacity does decline between the ages of 30 and 65, most age-related declines in physical capacity do not normally affect job performance, as physical capacity varies more across individuals than by age. Moreover, today few jobs require sustained strength over a long period of time, and labor-saving machinery and devices are often used to supplement brute force. It is also worth noting that other aspects of job performance, such as good timekeeping, helping colleagues, better anger management and people skills, do improve with age.

In addition, workers under the age of 35 have proven to exhibit higher sickness absence rates (2.6 percent) than their older counterparts (2.4 percent for those age 50+); in the UK the sickness absence cost to employers amounts to an annual £16 billion (Xpert HR 2015). Lost productivity due to absenteeism and presenteeism has been estimated at 7.85 percent of payroll (Lambert 2015) Of course, one can reduce this with targeted and proactive prevention strategies targeted at all age groups.

While some health conditions do rise with age, including stress, musculo-skeletal disorders, and cardiovascular disease, it may not be workers' ages but rather workplace-specific conditions driving the results. And though eyesight and hearing also deteriorate with age, these can usually be compensated with spectacles or hearing aids, and by environmental adaptations such as better lighting and sound proofing. Regarding mental health, it is commonly found that cognitive performance remains relatively stable until the age of 70, and that cognitive skills such as intelligence, knowledge, language, and complex problem solving are resistant to age-related declines, and can continue to improve with age until 60 (Yeomans 2013). Yet the aging of the workforce will imply that dementia will become an increasing problem. As a consequence, regular annual physicals will likely need to include cognitive well-being assessments along with early detection and intervention. Such cognitive tests have not yet been adopted widely, though employers will likely need to implement these for workers of all ages.

Health-related insurance costs will also rise as the workforce ages. In the UK, it has been estimated that a workforce ten years older than average will cost 56 percent more than the baseline, and 98 percent more if the workforce is 15 years older (Mercer 2015a). In countries lacking state-sponsored healthcare, such as the United States, employer benefit costs may rise more. Given persistently low investment returns, political turmoil, and growth and trade challenges, such a rise in benefit costs will present a growing challenge. One way to address this would be to do more to prevent disease and chronic conditions. The Oxford Health Alliance (2017) indicated that curtailing three risk factors (tobacco use, poor diet, and lack of physical exercise) will protect against the four major chronic diseases (diabetes, heart disease, lung diseases, and some cancers). Models that use health data captured from individuals through wearable devices can also be useful in containing costs as good health behavior will be treated favorably for underwriting purposes.

Financial wellness. Paying for each extra year of life can be expensive, and one response to this is to delay and indeed, redefine, retirement. In the United States, the 'freelance' or 'gig' workforce is predicted to grow from 53 million workers in 2016 to over 100 million by 2020 (Rashid 2016); many of these will be older individuals. Short-term temporary assignments and part-time work also can supplement pension income and help people balance work–life tensions.

It will be increasingly important for employers to help younger as well as older workers understand retirement needs and opportunities. For instance, plan sponsors will need to enhance access to programs that help people forecast their longevity and retirement needs, as well as software programs to help them plan and save for later life. Employers can help fill retirement income gaps by offering regular and personalized reminders to nudge people to save more. Short personalized videos and other visual methods make this information more likely to encourage pension saving (Mercer 2017). Increasingly, advice will be offered via digital or robo-advice platforms, which are online services that provide automated, algorithm-based portfolio management advice without the intervention of human financial planners.

Despite these clear needs, a recent UK survey found that only 26 percent of UK employers gave employees access to helpful financial planning (Mercer 2015a, b); by contrast, over two-thirds of US firms offered employees financial advice. It is also worth noting women may be the most vulnerable and needing of such advice, since in most countries, women live longer than men, often have career gaps for childbirth and caring, and tend to earn less over their lifetimes with an average pension gap of 40 percent in Europe (Sonsino 2015; Mercer 2017). A related question arises as to whether the products made available will be age-friendly (Financial Conduct Authority 2016). In particular, more evidence is needed to explain how to provide financial advice to older versus younger people, some of whom may be cognitively impaired. Looking ahead, as employees work longer, they may confront age limits for work-related employee benefits and, in the United States, requirements to withdraw from their retirement accounts.

Motivation and commitment. In the past, life cycle earnings profiles have traced out an inverted U-shape, with pay levels declining after age 50. As yet, however, there is little evidence on how future pay profiles may change as people remain employed for longer. Today's five-year olds, who could live to 120, could have a working life of 80+ years. Figuring out how employees can remain motivated and committed in the same job for 80 years defies belief. If firms are to accommodate such long careers, these should be linked to productivity measures ensuring success. There is already evidence suggesting that even those who are very happy in their jobs are considering leaving, and even more so among the younger generations (Mercer 2015b). Moreover, money will no longer be the only or even the main motivator. Learning opportunities, job and working time flexibility, the quality of one's colleagues, and even a greater sense of purpose will need to be examined as alternative motivators.

Training and skills. A related concern is that almost two-thirds of current primary-school children will take jobs as adults that do not even exist today (WEF 2016). Moreover, close to one-third of job-related skills will change by 2020, meaning employers will require bigger training budgets and recruitment efforts unparalleled in the past. Office and administration workers will be replaced by automation, along with many manufacturing and production jobs as well as many posts in construction and extraction, and even the professions. Positions that are likely to increase will be for data scientists in business, financial, and operational activities, driven by rising processing power and the possibility of mining big data pools. Information security analysts will also be in greater demand as more cyber-crime occurs and corresponding prevention strategies are devised. It is also expected that there will be a greater need for educators to support reskilling needs, and carers, to support the aging population (Frey and Osbourne 2013; OECD 2016; McKinsey Global Institute 2017).

The fact that this Fourth Industrial Revolution (Schwab 2016) is coinciding with large demographic shifts presents new challenges for those seeking to attract, hire, train, and keep employees. Employers must be not only age-ready, but they must also prepare for changes in the future of work as well. Already, annual spending rates for training are growing at over 10 percent of compound annual growth rate (ReportsnReports 2016), and ensuring readiness for older workers will be a component of the larger need to reskill.

Workplace design. Workplace ergonomics impact peoples' bodies and mental states, so these too will become more salient to employers as their workforces age. Evidence shows that BMW enhanced older workers' productivity by 7 percent by making many small and inexpensive changes, including better seats, adjustable workbenches, and wooden flooring providing better cushioning and insulation (Champion 2009). Other job sites, such as those for utility workers, water/drainage engineers, road/ construction workers, and others working outdoors, may not be able to offer similar improvements. Nevertheless, some employers are using older field engineers as trainers of the next generation, or using them as consultants and trouble-shooters.

Flexible working is also growing more common in this increasingly diverse workforce. In the UK, for instance, a recent survey showed that over half of all workers would prefer a flexible work schedule over a 5 percent salary boost, and some 45 percent of those would sacrifice pay rises of 10 percent to have flexible working arrangements (My Family Care and Hydrogen 2016). Additionally, over 80 percent of people seeking work stated they would rather have flexible working than any other employee benefit. Yet there is, thus far, no standardized definition of flexible working. It can include the possibility of working remotely (where), working non-standard hours (when), freelance contracting (how), and multiple jobs (what), 'shift-stacking' (where people may work for several employers at a time and arrange shift patterns to fill their availability during the workweek). Human resources managers will need to devise a framework to help define jobs' flexibility quotients and to review how flexible jobs influence other workers. Moreover, there may be obstacles to such practices embedded in labor law and social protection systems, such as overtime, sick, and holiday pay requirements, which will make it difficult for people to offer their time on a freelance or flexible basis.

Succession planning. Firms need to engage in predictive labor-force analysis so as to do a better job recruiting from the outside and moving people internally. As many nations have outlawed mandatory retirement, human resource teams now face additional uncertainty about when jobs will become vacant. Moreover, some employers believe that older workers 'take work away' from younger ones, leading them to conclude that they should bring in fresh talent and move older workers out. Additionally, some employers believe that older workers cost more than younger incumbents, suggesting that costs could be cut by additional turnover.

At a macroeconomic level, of course, the so-called 'lump of labor' belief has been widely refuted based on empirical evidence: in particular, the labor market does not offer a fixed number of jobs. Instead, offering generous early retirement programs tends to damage younger workers' prospects

(Gruber and Wise 2009). Accordingly, in the UK, Andy Briggs, CEO of Aviva UK Life, has spearheaded a campaign called One Million More (BITC 2017). The aim of this program is to boost older workers' labor force participation in the UK to the same levels as persons aged 35–49 by 2022, or about one million additional workers. It is estimated that this would increase GDP by 5.5 percent. Inasmuch as the UK is slated to experience a significant labor shortage in the coming years, keeping older people employed can help make up the difference (Mercer 2017).

Regarding how relatively expensive older workers may be, Mercer's UK pay survey data show that, in many jobs, pay actually climbs steeply for the young and then plateaus at a relatively early age. For example, in lower-level and unskilled jobs, 25-year-olds earn similar pay as 55-year-olds; for more skilled professional and middle managers, 35-year-olds earn about the same as 60-year-olds. Across all pay levels, pay declines by 0.1 to 7.4 percent per annum after age 50. In other words, older workers may not necessarily be more costly, contrary to many employers' beliefs. This may be partly due to the large cohort effect of this generational group, which in some studies has been shown to depress wages (Sapozhnikov and Triest 2007). Other studies, however, show wages are increasing for older workers due to a higher educational attainment relative to younger age groups than in the past (Burtless 2013). This bodes well for economies with both a growing and an educated older population.

In the workplace of the future it will also be important for firms to consider workers' ages as a standard diversity and inclusion metric. Currently in the UK, over 90 percent of employment agencies do not determine whether clients are discriminating on the basis of age, and very few firms check to see whether managers hire workers older than themselves (Mercer 2015a). Though age bias in recruitment and promotion is illegal, it still occurs and will need to be tackled head on.

Potential Roles for Other Stakeholders

Prior to the first Industrial Revolution in the 1700s, individuals and their households bore most of the financial risks due to unemployment, exclusion, sickness, disability, and old-age. Thereafter responsibility for managing risk moved toward state- and employer-sponsored social protection plans. Yet now, risk management is devolving once again to individuals, posing new challenges to manage sickness, disability, unemployment, and longevity (Sonsino & Veitch 2017).

Employers will need to reconfigure their future workforce decisions against this complex backdrop of social and cultural expectations. For instance, a recent UK study found that over 70 percent of workers expected their employers to do more to prepare them for the future (Mercer 2015a, b). As we have argued above, this conflict of expectations will surely become increasingly political in the future. Moreover, state retirement and health systems around the world are urging their employees to do more with less, as people live longer and medical care becomes ever more sophisticated and expensive. Individuals and their families will also be challenged to take a more active role.

Conclusions

The so-called Silver Economy is already the third largest 'economy' in the world (European Commission 2015). Becoming an age-ready employer in this context has a compelling business rationale. As well, becoming more age-ready also requires firms to optimize physical and mental wellness for workers of all ages, including providing training and skill upgrades. At the same time, thoughtful workplace changes can increase worker motivation, engagement, and productivity, and these developments are likely to engage all generations over careers that could last for 80+ years.

References

Age of No Retirement (AONR) (2016). *Age Does Not Define Us.* London, UK: AONR. https://www.ageofnoretirement.org/uploads/1c1588b37c4d5591646849 5ef1f648d3.pdf

Business in the Community (BITC) (2017). 'Business Champion for Older Workers calls for a million more older people in work by 2022.' Business in the Community Press Release, February 6. London, UK: BITC. http://age.bitc.org.uk/news-opinion/news/press-release-business-champion-older-workers-calls-million-more-older-people-work

Burtless, G. (2013). 'The Impact of Population Ageing and Delayed Retirement on Workforce Productivity.' Washington, DC: Brookings Institute, May 31. https://www.brookings.edu/research/the-impact-of-population-aging-and-delayed-retirement-on-workforce-productivity/

Champion, D. (2009). 'How BMW is Planning for an Aging Workforce.' *Harvard Business Review,* March 11. https://hbr.org/2009/03/bmw-and-the-older-worker

European Commission (2015). *Growing the European Silver Economy.* Brussels: European Commission. https://ec.europa.eu/eip/ageing/library/growing-silver-economy_en

Financial Conduct Authority (2016). 'Aging Population: Update from the FCA.' London, UK: FCA. https://www.fca.org.uk/news/news-stories/ageing-population-update-fca

Frey, C. B., and M. A. Osbourne (2013). *The Future of Employment: How Suscpetible are Jobs to Computerisation?* Oxford, UK: Oxford Martin School.

Gruber, J., and D. A. Wise (2009). *Social Security Programs and Retirement around the World: The Relationship to Youth Employment.* Cambridge, MA: National Bureau of Economic Research.

Lambert, V. (2015). 'Britain's Healthiest Company 2015.' *The Telegraph Online,* September 4. http://www.telegraph.co.uk/sponsored/business/britains-healthiest-company/

McKinsey Global Institute (2017). *Harnessing Automation for a Future that Works.* Washington, DC: McKinsey & Company. http://www.mckinsey.com/global-themes/digital-disruption/harnessing-automation-for-a-future-that-works

Mercer (2015a). *Ageing Workforce: Employee Health and Benefits.* London, UK: Mercer. https://www.uk.mercer.com/our-thinking/ageing-workforce/ageing-workforce-video-employee-health.html

Mercer (2015b). *Age-Friendly Employer Research,* London, UK: Mercer. https://info.mercer.com/rs/521-DEV-513/images/Age-Friendly%20Employer%20Research%20Mercer%20.pdf?mkt_tok=3RkMMJWWfF9wsRohvavLeu%2FhmjTEU5z16usvXK%2B1g5t41El3fuXBP2XqjvpVQcdhNb3GRw8FHZNpywVWM8TIKdIRt9F4PQznCWg%3D

Mercer (2017). *The Emerging British Workforce Crisis.* London, UK: Mercer. https://www.uk.mercer.com/our-thinking/brexit-emerging-british-workforce-crisis.html

My Family Care and Hydrogen (2016). 'Flexible and Family Friendly Working,' http://flexibleworkingreport.com

OECD (2016). *Automation and Independent Work in a Digital Economy: Policy Brief on the Future of Work.* Paris, France: OECD Publishing.

The Oxford Health Alliance (2017). OxHA Summit 2014. http://www.oxha.org/

Rashid, B. (2016). 'Rise of the Freelancer.' *Forbes Magazine,* January 26. https://www.forbes.com/sites/brianrashid/2016/01/26/the-rise-of-the-freelancer-economy/#76d06cda3bdf

ReportsnReports (2016). *Global Corporate Training Markets 2016–2020.* http://www.reportsnreports.com/reports/749286-global-corporate-training-market-2016-2020.html

Sapozhnikov, M., and R. K. Triest (2007). 'Population Aging, Labor Demand, and the Structure of Wages.' Working Paper No. 07–8. Boston, MA: Federal Bank of Boston.

Schwab, K. (2016). *The Fourth Industrial Revolution.* New York: Dover Books.

Sonsino, Y. (2015). *The New Rules of Living Longer: How to Survive your Longer Life.* London, UK: MSL Publishing.

Sonsino, Y. S., and I. Veitch (2017). *The Global Risks Report 2017, 12th Edition.* Geneva, Switzerland: World Economic Forum.

World Economic Forum (WEF) (2016). *The Future of Jobs.* Geneva, Switzerland: WEF. http://www3.weforum.org/docs/WEF_Future_of_Jobs.pdf

XPertHR (2015). 'Absence Rates and Costs: XpertHR Survey 2015.' London, UK: XPertHR. http://www.xperthr.co.uk/survey-analysis/absence-rates-and-costs-xperthr-survey-2015/156086/

Yeomans, L. (2013). *An Update of the Literature on Age and Employment.* London, UK: Health and Safety Executive. http://www.hse.gov.uk/research/rrpdf/rr832.pdf

Chapter 11

State-sponsored Retirement Savings Plans: New Approaches to Boost Retirement Plan Coverage

William G. Gale and David C. John

Many workers need help in building retirement security to supplement their social security benefits. The share of the workforce covered by a retirement saving plan has remained relatively flat in recent decades (Copeland 2014). The current low-return investment environment also makes it more difficult for people to accumulate a target of wealth in retirement, especially if the onset of retirement saving is delayed. As a result, bringing people into the retirement system and having them initiate contributions to retirement accounts as early as possible remains an important priority (see Reilly and Byrne's chapter in this volume).

Recent federal policy has not had a significant effect on coverage rates. The US Pension Protection Act of 2006 encouraged automatic enrollment in defined contribution (DC) plans. While the policy raised participation rates among those workers who were already offered a plan, it did little to expand coverage rates. In 2014, an Obama administration executive order established the MyRA, which is available nationally as a starter retirement saving account, but it has generated only very limited participation and was since cancelled under the Trump administration. Federal legislation creating an automatic Individual Retirement Account (IRA) and open multiple employer plans (MEPs) has been introduced but not enacted.[1]

In the wake of stagnant coverage trends and lacking comprehensive federal legislation, several states have acted on their own. Five states (California, Connecticut, Illinois, Maryland, and Oregon) have enacted Secure Choice plans based on the Automatic IRA (AARP 2017). In these plans, states sponsor a simple, low-cost payroll deduction plan managed by private-sector providers. The structure is similar to Section 529 college savings plans. With some exceptions, employers are required to participate in the plan if they do not offer workers another type of retirement plan. Eligible workers are automatically enrolled. In addition, two states (Washington and New Jersey) are developing retirement savings marketplaces, state-sponsored websites that enable small businesses to find retirement plans that are pre-screened to meet certain criteria. Many other states are considering Secure Choice plans, marketplaces, or other options, such as Vermont's decision to start an open MEP. The best plan for a particular state will depend on its economic needs, political constraints, and other factors.

Although federal legislative action has been lacking, federal regulations by the Department of Labor in 2016 temporarily eased the implementation of state actions, by confirming conditions under which state-sponsored retirement savings plans are exempt from federal pension regulation (81 F.R. § 92639).[2] Yet in 2017, Congress used the Congressional Review Act to overturn the relevant regulations and to prohibit agencies from issuing similar rulings in the future without advance congressional approval. While reversing these regulations will hamper state-sponsored plans, it will not necessarily end them.[3]

This chapter evaluates models and features used in state-sponsored retirement saving plans. These plans have the potential to raise the number of Americans with access to payroll-deduction retirement saving plans, and thus to reduce the number of retirees with few financial resources other than social security benefits. They could also improve the sponsoring states' fiscal outlooks, by reducing the extent to which future retirees depend on taxpayer-financed government services.[4]

Our main conclusion is that, regardless of which approach—Secure Choice, open MEP, marketplace, or other—is taken, plans that boost coverage most will feature two characteristics: required provision of retirement savings plan by firms, and automatic enrollment of eligible workers. Yet we also note that, under current legal and regulatory conditions, Secure Choice is the only model that enables states to require that employers provide a plan.

This chapter provides background on workers' access to retirement saving plans, describes options that states have taken to date and other actions they could pursue, and evaluates the importance of coverage mandates on firms and automatic enrollment of workers.

Workers' Access to Retirement Savings Plans

The proportion of US private sector workers with access to an employer-sponsored payroll deduction retirement savings plan or pension has remained stagnant for several decades. Figure 11.1 shows the share of private sector workers covered by a retirement savings or pension plan between 1987 and 2013.[5] Both coverage rates and plan participation have remained relatively constant over the 26-year period. Despite a slight uptick in the late 1990s, coverage in 2013 was the same as it was in the 1980s (as shown in Figure 11.1).

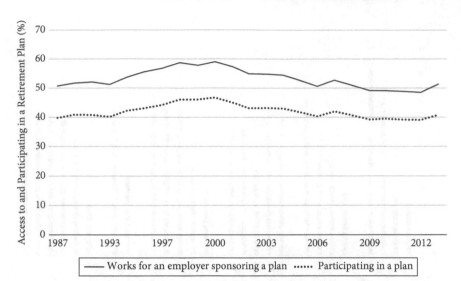

Figure 11.1. Access to and participation in US private sector employer-sponsored retirement plans, 1987 to 2013 (workers aged 21–64)

Source: Copeland (2014).

Access to a retirement plan varies by workers' demographic characteristics and firm size, as shown in Figure 11.2. Coverage rates in 2012:[6]

- are higher for higher paid employees, from 23 percent in the lowest quartile to 81 percent in the highest quartile;
- are higher for the better educated. Only 27 percent of workers with less than a high school degree were covered, compared to 69 percent of those with a bachelor's degree or more education;
- are fairly constant with respect to age, after workers reach age 25. Coverage rates vary from 54 to 64 percent for workers aged 25 to 64;
- are higher for full-time than for part-time workers;
- are higher for whites than for other groups;
- and rise with firm size. Among firms with 50 or fewer workers, only 28 percent of workers have access to a retirement savings plan. Among firms with 1,000+ employees, 70 percent have access to a plan.

Participation rates, given coverage, are fairly high, as shown in Figure 11.3. Conditional participation rates exceed 72 percent for all worker characteristics and firm sizes, except for three categories—workers aged 18–24, workers in the lowest earnings quartile, or high school dropouts. Even in those categories, conditional participation rates exceed 50 percent. Likewise, Figure 11.3 shows that conditional participation rates have been

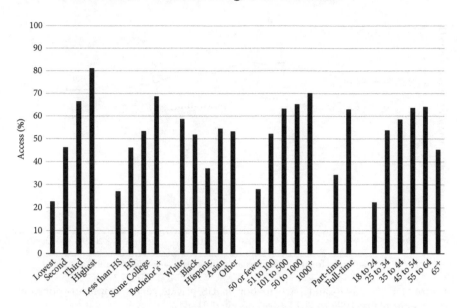

Figure 11.2. US private sector retirement plan access by selected demographics

Note: Access is defined as working for an employer who offers a retirement plan and being eligible for that plan.

Source: GAO (2015) analysis of 2012 SIPP data.

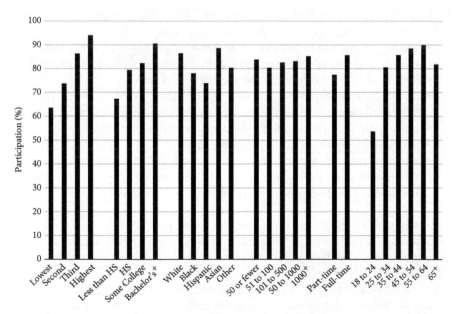

Figure 11.3. Participation in a US private sector retirement plan conditional on access

Source: GAO (2015) analysis of 2012 SIPP data.

high and relatively steady—between 79 percent and 81 percent—since 1987. These facts suggest that expanding coverage will expand participation as well.

Lack of access to workplace pensions matters because it impedes the accumulation of retirement wealth. About 61 percent of employees with access to an employer-sponsored plan held more than $25,000 in overall (non-defined-benefit) saving balances, and 35 percent held $100,000 or more. By contrast, among those without access to a plan, 87 percent held less than $25,000 and only 5 percent held $100,000 or more (Helman et al. 2016).[7]

Designing State-sponsored Plans to Meet the Needs of Small Business Employees

Two principal models for state-approved plans have been used to date, though others may be considered in the future. Table 11.1 describes each of the major approaches and Table 11.2 summarizes several advantages and disadvantages of each option. A successful plan will be practical for small businesses and the state to implement, and will meet the needs of affected employees.

TABLE 11.1 Comparison of state retirement plan structures

	Auto IRA	Open MEP	Marketplace	MyRA
Account Structure	Payroll deduction IRA (Traditional or Roth)	401(k) or other DC plan	Varies. May include SIMPLE IRAs, Auto IRAs, Roth IRAs, 401(k), MyRA	Roth IRA
Employer Participation Requirement	Yes	No	No	No
Employer Contribution	No	Allowed	Allowed	No
Contribution Limits	$5,500 annually ($6,500 if over 50)	Same as for a 401(k): $18,000 annually ($24,000 if over 50)	Depends on account type	$5,500 annually ($6,500 if over 50). After $15,000 must roll over into private Roth IRA
ERISA Coverage?	No	Yes	Marketplace itself is not covered but individual plans may be	No

Source: Derived from Pew Charitable Trusts (2017).

TABLE 11.2 Advantages and disadvantages to retirement plan types

	Secure Choice (Auto-IRA)	Open MEP	Marketplace	MyRA
Advantages	• Simple and low cost • Employers have virtually no regulatory burden or fiduciary responsibility • Easy to change contribution amounts • Employees do not need to take action to participate and maintain complete control over their account	• Allows employer contributions • Higher contribution limits • ERISA protection • More likely to have additional investment and financing options • Lower regulatory burden for employers • Streamlined compliance at the state level • Can use auto-enrollment	• Allows the state to pre-screen retirement plans to ensure they meet certain standards • Can provide high quality information about retirement alternatives • Employers can choose their level of involvement • State does not have any involvement with ERISA	• Good way for new savers to get in the habit of saving • Simple and easy to understand • Limited to no risk of loss • No fees • National program is available to everyone
Disadvantages	• Low contribution limits • No employer matches • Strength of employee protections depends on state law • Plans in different states may have different rules	• May impose higher costs and more responsibilities on employers than IRAs • Employer must ensure fiduciary responsibilities are handled by provider	• No direct incentive for employers to adopt a retirement savings plan (will do little to raise coverage). • Does nothing to simplify retirement saving or reduce regulatory burdens for small employers • Needs an enforcement mechanism to ensure that plans continue to be adequate	• Low maximum size • No real potential for contributions to grow • No mechanism to roll over account to a private provider once maximum size is reached • Uncertain political future

Secure choice (Auto IRA). Five states (California, Connecticut, Illinois, Maryland, and Oregon) have enacted Secure Choice programs based on the Automatic IRA (see Table 11.3; Iwry and John 2009; AARP 2017). Under these plans, states sponsor a simple and low-cost plan using a payroll-deduction IRA. The programs apply to employers who offer no other retirement saving or pension plan. Employers face few regulatory burdens, no fiduciary responsibility, and no contribution responsibilities. Most employers already use either an outside payroll provider or payroll processing software, so the cost of setting up the deduction and forwarding contributions would be minimal. Employees are enrolled automatically and can opt out or adjust their contribution levels. Contributions are invested into a Target Date Fund or similar vehicle, unless employees choose to allocate funds to one of a few other basic investment options. Investment management and record keeping are contracted to a private provider. States handle fiduciary responsibilities and consumer protections.

Secure Choice plans were developed to meet the needs of small businesses and their employees. One criticism of using a payroll deduction IRA is that contribution limits are significantly lower than for 401(k) plans. In 2017, workers under 50 could contribute up to $18,000 annually to 401(k) plans, but only $5,500 to an IRA. Small business employees, however, are likely to have lower median earnings than those of larger firms, suggesting lower optimal targets for wealth accumulation.[8] In addition, the significant gap in contribution limits between IRAs and 401(k)s can reduce the extent to which the program might encourage firms to drop their existing 401(k)s in favor of a Secure Choice plan. Secure Choice plans are not covered by the Employee Retirement Income Security Act (ERISA), the major federal law regulating employee benefits. Thus the strength of employee protections in Secure Choice plans depends on state laws and may differ from the extensive protections guaranteed under ERISA.

The Illinois Secure Choice Savings Program was enacted in January 2015 and went into effect in 2018. The plan applies to all employers with at least 25 employees, who have been in business for at least two years, and who do not currently provide a qualifying savings plan. Smaller employers can voluntarily participate (Illinois State Treasurer 2016). Employees will be automatically enrolled in a Roth IRA with a 3 percent default contribution rate.

The Oregon Saves program, enacted in 2015, went into effect in 2018. The plan requires all Oregon employers either to join the state Oregon Saves plan or offer their own qualified retirement plan (State of Oregon 2017). Employees are to be automatically enrolled in a Roth IRA with a 5 percent default contribution rate.

California's Secure Choice program was enacted in September 2016 and will soon phase in. The program will require employers who have five or

Table 11.3 Comparison of state retirement plan actions

	California	Illinois	Oregon	Maryland	Connecticut	Washington	New Jersey
Date Enacted	September 29, 2016	January 5, 2015	June 25, 2015	May 10, 2016	May 27, 2016	May 18, 2015	January 19, 2016
Date Implemented	Bill effective January 1, 2017. Implementation in 2018 or later.	Effective June 1, 2017. Participants must be able to enroll within two years and employers have 9 months after that to set up automatic payroll deposits. Phased enrollment	Individuals were able to begin contributions from July 1, 2017	July 1, 2016	January 1, 2018	January 1, 2017	Not specified
Plan Type	Auto IRA	Roth IRA	Roth IRA	At least one payroll deposit IRA	Roth IRA	Marketplace containing selection of: SIMPLE IRAs, myRAs, Auto IRAs, and/or 'life insurance plans for retirement purposes'	Marketplace containing selection of: SIMPLE IRAs, myRAs, Auto IRAs, and/or 'life insurance plans for retirement purposes'
Automatic Enrollment	Yes	Yes	Yes	Yes	Yes	Not required	Not required
Default Contribution Rate	3% (Board can adjust from 2% to 5%), option for auto-escalation at no more than 1% per year until rate reaches 8%.	3%	5% standard rate, 1% minimum and no maximum	Not specified	3%	None Specified	None Specified

Source: Derived from Pew Charitable Trusts (2017).

more employees and who do not otherwise offer a retirement plan to automatically enroll their employees in a state-sponsored IRA overseen by the Secure Choice Retirement Savings Investment Board. The default contribution rate will begin at 3 percent of workers' payroll, with the option for the Board to implement an automatic escalation policy (automatically increasing contributions by 1 percent per year, capped at a rate of 8 percent). Funds will initially be invested in low-risk securities such as Treasury bonds, after which more investment options will be made available (California State Treasury 2017). While the low-risk investments will reduce the chance of loss, they will also make it harder for California savers to build significant retirement balances.

The Connecticut Retirement Security Program, enacted in 2016, is also now in place. The plan requires employers with five or more employees and who do not provide a retirement savings option to join the state plan. Employees will be automatically enrolled in a Roth IRA with an initial 3 percent default contribution rate (Act Creating the Connecticut Retirement Security Program 2016). A public-private oversight board, the Connecticut Retirement Security Authority, was established to oversee the implementation of the program.

The Maryland Small Business Retirement Savings Program and Trust started in 2017. The plan requires private employers who do not currently offer a retirement savings plan and who have been in business for the last two years to enroll their employees in an Auto IRA. The program is required if an employer uses an outside payroll provider or a payroll software program. Businesses that comply with the law will receive a waiver on an annual $300 business report filing fee (Maryland General Assembly 2016). A Small Business Retirement Savings Board, which oversees the program, selects Auto-IRA plans and contribution rates.

Marketplaces. Two states (Washington and New Jersey) are implementing retirement savings marketplaces (see Table 11.3). A marketplace is a state-sponsored website that enables small businesses to find retirement savings or pension plans. The marketplace will display a diverse array of plans—including payroll deduction IRAs, SIMPLE IRAs, open MEPs, MyRA, and perhaps even 401(k) plans and defined benefit (DB) plans—offered by several different providers. The state pre-screens retirement plans, ensuring that the options presented to employers meet certain standards (regarding, for example, fees) and provide unbiased information about retirement plan options. Because the marketplace merely lists plan options, a state has no potential ERISA liability and does not take on any of the employer's legal responsibilities. The marketplace design enables employers to determine which type of plan best meets their and their employees' needs, including whether they prefer an ERISA-covered plan. A marketplace could be coupled with a requirement that employers provide coverage, as discussed in the next section. But, by itself, a marketplace does nothing to simplify retirement saving or to reduce the regulatory burdens and fiduciary responsibilities that would be placed on smaller employers.

Washington's Small Business Retirement Marketplace, enacted in 2015, became fully operational in 2017. Employers with fewer than 100 employees are eligible to participate but are not required to do so. The law permits the government to provide incentives for employers to do so. The marketplace is to contain a variety of low-cost savings options provided by financial services firms (SIMPLE IRAs and payroll deduction IRAs, for example) and investment choices, as well as access to the federal MyRA.

New Jersey enacted a marketplace plan in 2016 based on Washington's model, available to companies with fewer than 100 employees; participation is voluntary. The marketplace must offer a similar variety of low-cost savings options, at least two investment choices and access to MyRA (Bernard 2016).

Open MEPs. Beyond Secure Choice plans and marketplaces, states can also choose to operate an open MEP.[9] In 2017, Vermont approved legislation establishing an MEP, and the New York City Comptroller's office proposed a variant of an open MEP in 2016 as part of a larger retirement savings plan (Office of the New York City Comptroller 2016). Philadelphia is also considering an open MEP for that city's small businesses (City of Philadelphia Office of the Comptroller 2017). Federal regulations require employers participating in private sector MEPs to have a common bond (such as being in the same industry). By contrast, state-sponsored MEPs do not face this restriction; they may cover workers from firms without a common bond. Under an 'open MEP,' several small businesses may join together to offer a common type of account to each employer's workforce. The common plan structure reduces the compliance burden and places most fiduciary responsibilities on the plan administrator. State-sponsored open MEPs could be open to any small business in the state that wants to offer its employees a retirement plan. As with the Secure Choice model, these open MEPs would use services that are contracted out to private sector providers.

Wealth accumulation can be higher in an MEP because the plans contain higher contribution limits and employers can make contributions. MEPs are also more likely to offer loan provisions and more diverse investment choices. Both MEPs and Secure Choice plans reduce administrative costs for small employers, compared to offering a comparable retirement plan on their own. But MEPs may impose higher administrative costs and greater responsibilities on employers than IRA-based plans, since MEPs would typically offer more services and employers must meet certain fiduciary and regulatory responsibilities under ERISA. As discussed below, participation in a state-sponsored MEP would be voluntary, as states are not allowed to require employers to offer ERISA-regulated plans.

MyRA. Another option states could pursue would be to encourage workers to sign up for MyRA accounts, though this is now unlikely with the cancellation of the MyRA product.

Other state and local actions. Over the past few years, legislation has been introduced in more than half of the remaining states (beyond those listed above) to either establish state-sponsored retirement programs, or to create a commission to study them (Georgetown University Center for Retirement Initiatives 2017). In 2017 alone, legislators in over ten states proposed legislation to enact state-sponsored retirement savings plans or create a feasibility study. In 2012, Massachusetts enacted the Connecting Organizations to Retirement Program (CORE), a voluntary 401(k) plan for non-profit firms having fewer than 20 employees, where the state controls administrative costs. States are also experimenting with different plan features. For example, West Virginia and Utah have proposed Auto IRA plans without a mandate that employers participate.

In addition, cities such as New York City, Seattle, and Philadelphia have expressed interest in creating retirement plans for local private-sector workers. New York City proposed creating a voluntary marketplace to access easy-to-use 401(k) plans, including a newly created publicly funded Empire City 401(k) MEP, SEP-IRAs, and SIMPLE IRAs. Employers who do not offer a plan on their own or through the marketplace would be mandated to enroll employees in a new NYC Roth IRA in which the first $15,000 is invested in a MyRA account and anything above that would be put in more conventional investment vehicles (Office of the New York City Comptroller 2016). The overturning of Department of Labor (DOL) regulations that would have enabled cities to establish Auto IRAs complicates the implementation of much of this plan. Philadelphia created a working group to develop a plan, as well as a series of outreach efforts with the local community (City of Philadelphia Office of the Controller 2016). As mentioned, these efforts resulted in the recommendation that the city establish an open MEP (City of Philadelphia Office of the Controller 2017).

Small business needs. A key factor in designing a successful state-sponsored plan is understanding why small businesses currently do not offer plans and what reform features they support. In order for these plans to attract sufficient political support, it is imperative to have small businesses believe that a state proposal is feasible and designed to meet the needs of their workers. At the same time, each state must understand how small businesses will react to the proposal, and what proportion of employers required to offer a plan will use the state plan.

The expense and complexity of small business retirement plans are major reasons why employers fail to offer them. On an asset-weighted basis, the smallest existing private sector retirement savings plans can cost up to four

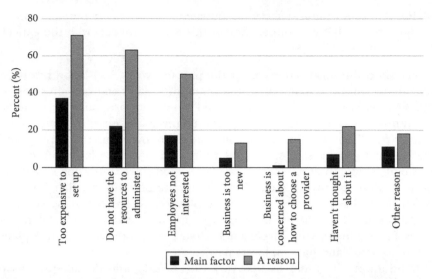

Figure 11.4. Reasons small and medium-sized businesses do not offer retirement plans

Note: Survey data is directly from source attributed below. The study authors surveyed owners of small and medium-sized business without retirement plans in place about their views on implementing such a plan.

Source: Pew Charitable Trusts (2017, Figure 1).

times as much as larger plans (Steverman 2017). In a recent survey, 37 percent of small businesses that did not offer plans said that the main reason was because they were too expensive to set up. About 71 percent cited it as one of the factors contributing to their decision, as shown in Figure 11.4. Another 22 percent said the main reason was that the company did not have the resources to administer a retirement plan, with a total of 63 percent mentioning this as a reason. The focus on cost was reinforced later in the survey when small- and medium-sized business owners were asked what would motivate them to offer a retirement plan, and the answer that drew the largest support was an increase in profits, followed by the provision of a business tax credit for starting a plan (Pew Charitable Trusts 2017: 3). Interestingly, the survey found that the creation of a retirement plan with reduced administrative requirements and the availability of easy-to-understand information would have almost no effect on plan offerings, with over half of those responding saying that those factors would make them no more likely to offer a plan.

By contrast, small businesses responded positively in the survey to a mandatory retirement savings plan with features like those found in the Auto IRA, as shown below in Table 11.4. About 92 percent of small- to

TABLE 11.4 Individual features of an Auto IRA that business owners support

	'Somewhat Support' or 'Strongly Support' (%)[a]
Businesses' only responsibility would be to withhold money from participating employees' paychecks and send it to the retirement account on their behalf.	79
Businesses would not be required to contribute to the plan.	83
Businesses would not have any legal responsibility for their employees' retirement accounts.	86
Employees who don't have access to a retirement savings plan at their work would be offered the chance to participate in one.	92
By default, workers would contribute to the retirement savings account unless they took action to opt out of the program.	72
Employees could stop or change their contributions at any time.	92
As a starting point, participating employees would contribute a set amount of 3 percent of their paychecks to the retirement account.	79
As a starting point, participating employees would contribute a set amount of 6 percent of their paychecks to the retirement account.	69
Employees could withdraw their own contributions to the account at any point without a penalty.	82

[a] The study authors surveyed owners of small and medium sized business without retirement plans in place about their views on implementing such a plan. For this question, employers were asked to indicate their support for features of a hypothetical retirement plan similar to an Auto IRA that would be sponsored by an outside organization and not a business like theirs.

Source: Survey data from Pew Charitable Trusts (2017).

medium-sized employers expressed some level of support for enabling employees who lacked a workplace retirement plan to participate. Further, 79 percent supported the idea that employers would only have the responsibility to withhold money from an employee's pay and send it to the retirement account, and 83 percent supported employers not being required to contribute. Overall, 86 percent of surveyed employers expressed some level of support for an Auto IRA-based program. Yet that support was less than enthusiastic, with 59 percent 'somewhat' supporting, as shown in Figure 11.5.

Features of an open MEP are also popular with small- to medium-sized employers, with 88 percent of employers supporting allowing both employers and employees to contribute, and 84 percent favoring the reduced legal liability found in an open MEP (see Table 11.5).[10] Employers also supported a marketplace, with almost 86 percent saying that it would be helpful to improve retirement savings. Yet, this contrasted with earlier answers stating

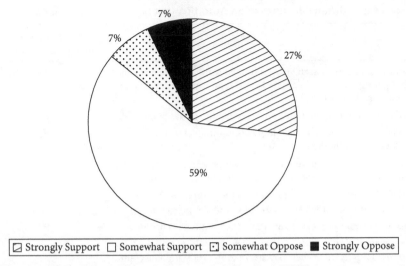

Figure 11.5. Employer attitudes toward Auto IRA plans: US firms

Note: Survey data is directly from source attributed below. The study authors surveyed owners of small- and medium-sized business without retirement plans in place about their views on implementing such a plan.

Source: Pew Charitable Trusts (2017, Figure 3).

TABLE 11.5 Individual features of a multiple employer plan (MEP) that business owners support

	'Somewhat Support' or 'Strongly Support'(%)[a]
Several businesses could adopt a group retirement savings plan run by their state treasurer's office	55
Both employers and employees could make contributions	88
Employers and employees have some choice in how to invest their contributions	92
The state would handle record keeping, financial reporting, and communication for the plan	57
Employers would have reduced legal liability compared with operating their own plan	85

Notes:
[a] The study authors surveyed owners of small- and medium-sized business without retirement plans in place about their views on implementing such a plan. For this question, employers were asked to indicate their support for features of a hypothetical retirement plan similar to an MEP that would be sponsored by an outside organization and not a business like theirs.

Source: Survey data from Pew Charitable Trusts (2017).

that easy-to-understand information and a plan with reduced administrative requirements would make employers no more likely to start a plan.

Evaluating State-sponsored Plans

The two features essential to the success of state-sponsored retirement savings plans are, first, requiring an employer to offer a retirement saving option, and, second, automatic enrollment of workers into that plan.

An effective state-sponsored plan will generate several results. In addition to raising coverage and generating high participation rates among the newly covered workers, it should also induce significant contributions, provide safe and rewarding investments, impose low fees, and induce responsible withdrawal patterns. Notably, the states that have enacted Secure Choice plans have already included provisions that address fees and initial investment choices. Several of them recognize the need for an appropriate level of contributions and have taken steps in that direction. Others have discussed responsible withdrawal options, but have recognized that this discussion must come after the plan is established.

State-sponsored plans may also reduce the amount that states and the federal government must spend in the future to support retirees with inadequate resources (Trostel 2017). For states, these savings would predominantly be due to reductions in Medicaid costs and certain housing programs. The amount of saving per state would depend on the size of the low-income population and the scope of assistance provided through public programs. Federal savings would come from reductions in demand for other means-tested programs (such as Supplemental Security Income [SSI]), as well as from the federal share of Medicaid funding.[11] It is also possible that state-sponsored retirement savings programs will increase state revenues. If states tax retirement income, then any increased retirement savings will eventually lead to higher revenue. In addition, higher retirement income may lead retirees to spend more money, which can result in higher sales and corporate tax revenue.

Boosting coverage through mandatory provision. Requiring employers to offer a plan would be the most effective way to increase coverage.[12] Most mandatory provision rules require that all companies offer some type of retirement savings or pension plan to their workers. Firms that offer 401(k)s or DB pension plans already meet this requirement. Those who do not would have to either establish such a plan or offer their employees access to a state-sponsored retirement savings plan. Under federal law, required coverage can only apply to an IRA-based retirement plan; states are forbidden from requiring employers to establish an ERISA-regulated retirement plan.

There is some evidence that a state-sponsored plan without mandatory provision is unlikely to significantly increase coverage rates. For example, at the end of 2016, only about 20,000 people had enrolled in the nationwide MyRA program (Lobosco 2016). Even with much more promotion, a voluntary program is unlikely to encourage employers who are mainly concerned with running a business to open a retirement plan for their employees.

Small businesses do have concerns about state government involvement in retirement saving, expressing much stronger support for a plan sponsored and administered by a private sector provider, such as an insurance company or mutual fund, than for a plan administered by the federal or state government. As a result, employers are split almost 50–50 between those who would participate in the state-sponsored plan and those who would start their own retirement plan (Pew Charitable Trusts 2017: 8).

Nevertheless, it may be counterproductive for states to require small-to-medium businesses to offer a payroll deduction IRA or their own plan and then to leave it to the private sector to provide the plans from its usual offerings.[13] Such plans would initially have high prices, undermining support for the program early on, although the entry of competition in the later years could reduce prices to some extent. Therefore, pairing a low-cost state-sponsored payroll deduction plan with a mandatory provision requirement is most likely to both increase coverage and provide employees with low-cost savings vehicles.

Boosting participation rates through automatic enrollment. In a traditional DC plan or IRA, individuals must specifically sign up to participate, designate a contribution level, and allocate contributions to investment vehicles before they can begin saving. Under automatic enrollment, eligible workers are placed in the plan and save a pre-determined amount in a pre-set investment option unless he or she decides otherwise. Savers always have complete control and can choose at any point to opt out or change their contribution levels or investment allocations. Automatic enrollment is key to boost participation among newly covered employees. While studies in the United States and other countries show the value of automatic enrollment, adoption of the feature is currently voluntary for employers, and it is predominantly offered by larger companies.[14] A new United Kingdom retirement savings program offers evidence on the potential effects of a universal automatic enrollment system.[15] Under the UK reforms, all employers will eventually be required to offer a retirement plan that automatically enrolls workers and meets minimum contribution levels. These reforms are being phased in over several years ending in 2019, and experience with them will be valuable for understanding the potential effects of state-sponsored retirement plans. Specifically, an early evaluation of these reforms shows a substantial increase in both retirement plan coverage and participation at all incomes, ages, genders, employer sizes, and among both full-time and part-time workers (Department for Work and Pensions 2016). Almost seven million UK workers have been automatically enrolled in retirement plans, at almost 300,000 different employers. Some 265,000 employees who opted out the first time have been re-enrolled. Participation has been very high in the UK plan, but it varies by age, working hours, and employer size (James 2017). Opt-out rates range from about 8 percent at the largest employers, to roughly 11 percent at firms with 50–99 employees; the proportion climbs to 17 percent for the smallest firms having 19 employees or fewer. About 90 percent of full-time employees participate, compared with the average of 82 percent for part-time workers. About 93 percent of employees under age 30 participate, compared to 91 percent of those aged 30–49, and only 77 percent of workers over age 50. Controlling for other factors, automatic enrollment may be responsible for a 37-percentage-point increase in overall participation (Cribb and Emmerson 2016). Automatic enrollment has been especially effective in increasing participation among younger workers, with a 52-percentage-point increase in workers aged 22–29, and 37 percent in workers aged 30–39. It also has a major effect on low-to-moderate income workers, with an increase in participation of 54 percentage points among those with earnings in the lowest earnings quartile and 46 percentage points among those in the second quartile.

These findings, combined with surveys of automatically enrolled workers in the United States, imply wide support for the mechanism even among those who have opted out. This makes a compelling case for including the mechanism in state-sponsored retirement savings plans (Retirement Made Simpler 2009).

Conclusion

There is near universal agreement that pension coverage rates for American workers are lower than they could be, yet state-sponsored retirement savings plans are only just starting. Five states are implementing Secure Choice plans, one is starting an MEP, and two are implementing marketplaces, with the programs set to be fully phased in over the next few years. These numbers are expected to grow in the near future as other states consider establishing a state-sponsored plan. The most important determinants of the programs' ability to reach their full potential are straightforward: requiring firms to offer either the state plan or their own plan, and automatically enrolling workers. In principle, these two features matter more than whether the underlying account is an IRA or a 401(k). As a practical matter, however, federal regulations forbid states from requiring employers to offer

ERISA-regulated plans, making an IRA-based state program the only option consistent with mandatory provision.

Enabling all Americans to save for retirement from the day they begin work until the day they fully retire is an idea that has been discussed for decades. The new plans being implemented offer great potential to raise coverage, participation, and retirement wealth accumulation among a broad swath of the American workforce.

Notes

1. For example, the Obama administration included an Automatic IRA proposal in every proposed budget. The most recent Automatic IRA proposal by that administration would have required employers with more than ten employees in operation for over two years to enroll employees in a Roth IRA with a 3 percent default contribution rate. Employers with fewer than 100 employees who did so would receive a temporary tax credit of $1,000 for up to three years in addition to an annual credit of $25 per employee (up to $250) for six years (Office of Management and Budget 2017). Members of Congress also proposed bills mandating employers to offer an Automatic IRA in each of the preceding six years. More recently, the American Savings Account Act of 2017 would have automatically enrolled private sector workers lacking access to a retirement savings plan into a newly created American Savings Account, similar to the Thrift Savings Plan currently offered to federal government employees. During 2017, Members of Congress also proposed legislation to decrease barriers to Open MEPs in the private sector (Retirement Security for American Workers Act 2016; Retirement Security for American Workers Act 2017) and to authorize the creation of state-sponsored MEPs (State Retirement Savings Act 2016).

2. Additional Department of Labor (DOL) regulations gave certain cities similar powers. Seattle, Philadelphia, and New York City wrote letters of interest to the DOL asking whether their 2015 ruling that cleared the way for states to enact state-sponsored retirement plans also applied to cities. DOL responded by clarifying that a political subdivision qualifies if they meet three criteria: (1) state law gives them the authority to require employers' participation in payroll deduction savings programs; (2) the political subdivision has a population that is at least the size of the least populous state (currently Wyoming, with 600,000 residents); and (3) the state in which the subdivision is located cannot already have a statewide retirement program for private-sector employees. These additional regulations were final in January 2017, but were overturned by a Congressional Review Act resolution that was passed by Congress and signed by President Trump later that year.

3. The regulations clarify that if states offer an Auto IRA under certain conditions, the plans do not fall under the Employee Retirement Income Security Act (ERISA). Although states now working on such a plan believe that the regulations

are helpful in avoiding a legal challenge, they also believe that they have legal authority under earlier, less explicit laws and regulations.

4. A study by Segal Consulting estimated that if all states sponsored a retirement savings program, taxpayers would save $5 billion over the first decade in Medicaid costs and that these savings would continue to increase over time. Fifteen states have the potential to save over $100 million each over the first decade (Segal Consulting 2017).

5. The Current Population Survey measured coverage between 1987 and 2013. After 2013, the survey was redesigned and the accuracy of its later results has been questioned. For this reason, we do not include data after 2013.

6. Participation and coverage information presented in this section is adapted from a Government Accountability Office (GAO) (2015) analysis of data from the Census Bureau's Survey of Income and Program Participation (SIPP). We define retirement plan coverage (synonymous with access) as being an employee aged 18 or older who works for an employer who provides a retirement plan and is eligible for that plan. Since the GAO does not report trends in coverage, we use data from Copeland (2014). This Employee Benefit Research Institute (EBRI) report presents Current Population Survey data on retirement plan participation and coverage over time for workers aged 21 to 64.

7. EBRI defines 'having a retirement plan' as having an IRA, DB, or DC plan. The value of assets reported contains all investments except for the value of the respondent's primary residence and DB plan assets. Although workers without an employer-based plan can contribute to IRAs, very few do.

8. In California, research shows that employees without access to a retirement plan have a median income of $23,000 (Overture Financial 2016).

9. MEPs can be either open or closed. Under a closed MEP, all businesses that enter the plan must have some common interests (such as being in the same industry). An open MEP has greater flexibility in the types of business that it includes. All MEPs considered by the states are open MEPs because they allow any business that employs residents of that state to join.

10. While the employers like the ability to contribute if they so choose, they also do not want to be required to do so. This is reflected in the Auto IRA question.

11. These estimates assume that the retirement plans being examined increase the retirement income of low-income workers such that they would not qualify for public assistance programs. It also assumes that the individual does not need those supports before retirement and that retirement savings do not fall under the program's maximum allowed asset level. This last assumption is especially questionable as, under current federal law, the only program that completely exempts retirement assets from its asset test is the Supplemental Nutritional Assistance Program (SNAP).

12. Whether this requirement applies to all employers in the state or only to employers with more than a certain number of employers is a political decision.

13. Similarly, the United Kingdom found that relying on competition alone to reduce fees and create effective retirement products would not be effective as

many employers would not have enough information to choose a provider that offered good value. See Office of Fair Trading (2013).

14. See, for example, Madrian and Shea (2001) and Chetty et al. (2013).

15. A key difference is that the United Kingdom is phasing in the contribution level. Initially, employers and employees only contribute 1 percent of earnings each. This 2 percent total initial contribution is close to the usual 3 percent initial contribution in the United States. By April 2019, that will climb to a total of 8 percent of earnings. Also, the UK system exempts lowest income workers and does not collect contributions on the first £113 of weekly earnings.

References

AARP (2017). *State Retirement Savings Plans*. State Retirement Savings Resources Center. Washington, DC: AARP. http://www.aarp.org/ppi/state-retirement-plans/savings-plans/

Bernard, T. (2016). 'New Jersey Creates Retirement Savings Plan, Modified by Christie.' *The New York Times*, January 20: B2.

California State Treasury (2017). *California Secure Choice: Making Workplace Retirement Savings Possible for Millions of Californians*. Sacramento, CA: CA State Treasury. http://www.treasurer.ca.gov/scib/

Chetty, R., J. Friedman, S. Petersen, T. H. Nielsen, and T. Olsen (2013). 'Active vs. Passive Decisions and Crowd-Out in Retirement Savings Accounts: Evidence from Denmark.' *Quarterly Journal of Economics* 129(3): 1141–219.

City of Philadelphia Office of the Controller (2016). *Retirement Security in Philadelphia: An Analysis of Current Conditions and Paths to Better Outcomes*. Philadelphia, PA: Office of the Controller.

City of Philadelphia Office of the Controller (2017). *Retirement Security for All Philadelphians*. Philadelphia, PA: Office of the Controller.

Copeland, C. (2014). 'Employment-Based Retirement Plan Participation: Geographic Differences and Trends.' EBRI Issue Brief No. 45. Washington, DC: Employee Benefit Research Institute.

Cribb, J., and C. Emmerson (2016). 'What Happens when Employers are Obliged to Nudge? Automatic Enrolment and Pension Saving in the UK.' IFS Working Paper W16/19. London, UK: Institute for Fiscal Studies.

Department for Work and Pensions (2016). *Automatic Enrolment Evaluation Report 2016*. Ad hoc Research Report No. 45. London, UK: Department for Work and Pensions.

Georgetown University Center for Retirement Initiatives (2017). 'State Initiatives Transforming the Retirement Savings Landscape.' *Georgetown University Center for Retirement Initiatives*. March 7: http://cri.georgetown.edu/states/

Government Accountability Office (GAO) (2015). *Retirement Security: Federal Action Could Help State Efforts to Expand Private Sector Coverage*. GAO-15-556. Washington, DC: GPO.

Helman, R., Greenwald & Associates, C. Copeland, and J. VanDerhei (2016). 'The 2016 Retirement Confidence Survey: Worker Confidence Stable, Retiree Confidence Continues to Increase.' EBRI Issue Brief No. 422. Washington, DC: Employee Benefit Research Institute.

Illinois State Treasurer (2016). *Secure Choice.* Springfield, IL: State Treasurer. http:// illinoistreasurer.gov/Individuals/Secure_Choice

Iwry, J., and D. John (2009). 'Pursuing Universal Retirement Security Through Automatic IRAs.' Brookings Institution Working Paper. Washington, DC: Brookings Institution.

James, H. (2017). 'The Impact of Automatic Enrolment in the UK as at 2016.' Briefing Note Number 87. London, UK: Pension Policy Institute.

Lobosco, K. (2016). 'After One Year, 20,000 People are Saving for Retirement with Obama's MyRA.' *CNN Money,* December 16. http://money.cnn.com/2016/12/ 16/retirement/obama-myra-retirement-saving/index.html

Madrian, B., and D. Shea (2001). 'The Power of Suggestion: Inertia in 401(k) Participation and Savings Behavior.' *The Quarterly Journal of Economics* 116(4): 1149–87.

Maryland General Assembly (2016). 'Maryland Small Business Retirement Savings Program and Trust.' Fiscal and Policy Note SB 1007. Annapolis, MD: Maryland General Assembly.

Office of Fair Trading (2013). 'Defined Contribution Workplace Pension Market Study.' Office of Fair Trading OF1505: London, UK: Office of Fair Trading. http://webarchive.nationalarchives.gov.uk/20131101164215/http:/www.oft.gov.uk/ shared_oft/market-studies/oft1505

Office of Management and Budget (2017). *Analytical Perspectives: Budget of the US Government Fiscal Year 2017.* Washington, DC: Office of Management and Budget.

Office of the New York City Comptroller (2016). *The New York City Nest Egg: A Plan for Addressing Retirement Security in New York City.* New York: New York City Office of the Comptroller.

Overture Financial (2016). 'Final Report to the California Secure Choice Retirement Savings Investment Board.' RFP No. CSCRSIB03-14. Philadelphia, PA: Overture Financial.

Pew Charitable Trusts (2017). 'Small Business Views on Retirement Savings Plans.' Issue Brief. Washington, DC: Pew Charitable Trusts.

Reilly C., and A. Byrne (2018). "Investing for Retirement in a Low Returns Environment: Making the Right Decisions to Make the Money Last," in R. Clark, R. Maurer, and O. S. Mitchell (eds.), *How Persistent Low Returns Will Shape Saving and Retirement.* Oxford, UK: Oxford University Press, pp. 61–80.

Retirement Made Simpler (2009). 'Fact Sheet: 2009 Survey of Employee Sentiments on Saving for Retirement.' Washington, DC: Retirement Made Simpler.

Segal Consulting (2017). 'State Retirement Savings Initiatives Do More than Enhance Retirement Security for Private Sector Workers.' Data: Practical Research on Public Sector Benefits. Jenkintown, PA: Segal Consulting.

State of Oregon (2017). *Oregon Saves.* Salem, OR: State of Oregon. http://www. oregon.gov/retire/Pages/index.aspx

Steverman, B. (2017). 'Two-Thirds of Americans Aren't Putting Money in their 401 (k).' *Bloomberg,* February 21. https://www.bloomberg.com/news/articles/2017-02-21/two-thirds-of-americans-aren-t-putting-money-in-their-401-k

Trostel, P. (2017). 'The Fiscal Implications of Inadequate Retirement Savings in Maine' The University of Maine Working Paper. Orono, ME: The University of Maine.

Chapter 12

Global Developments in Employee Benefits

Natalia Garabato, Jonathan Gardner, and Steve Nyce

The last 25 years have seen defined benefit (DB) plans around the world increasingly replaced by defined contribution (DC) arrangements. While the pace and shape of this change varies across countries, it is increasingly evident that employers are moving away from providing retirement guarantees. In the last decade, we have witnessed occupational retirement pensions shifting to DC at an even faster pace in countries such as the United States and United Kingdom, while countries previously thought of as bastions of DB (such as the Netherlands) are starting to move to DC. Such a transition is now also being felt in the provision of health benefits, as more employers are looking to incorporate DC-type arrangements for funding health benefits.

It is clear that, despite the shift to DC, employers' commitment to benefits has not necessarily fallen. Indeed, employer costs have frequently grown due to legacy DB costs and rising healthcare costs. Employers are not turning away from benefits, but they are struggling in the face of rapidly increasing costs, a weak economy, constrained corporate budgets, and a more diverse workplace. Moreover, the DC model is itself under challenge. The assumption of engaged consumers that accompanied the birth of DC has been found wanting, with behavioral economics offering a number of heuristics and biases that raise concerns around employee engagement with retirement planning and savings decisions (Benartzi and Thaler 2007; Lusardi and Mitchell 2011). Given current savings levels, it is likely that many employees will reach old age with insufficient savings to be able to retire. Indeed, in some countries such as Chile, we are starting to see the first signs of discontent as retirement outcomes fail to meet employee expectations (The Guardian 2016).

There are also lingering questions whether, in a world of low growth, stagnating incomes, and increasingly diverse workforces, one-size-fits-all benefits plans can meet employee financial needs. Is it right that money should be saved into a retirement plan, when young workers at the start of their career are faced with student loan debt? Will employees be more engaged if they have the choice to redistribute benefit funding?

Faced with these issues, companies are questioning how they can get the best value for money from their benefit spend and are increasingly showing interest in moving to a new generation of benefits, characterized by greater flexibility and increased choice. This shift would encompass a broader range of employee financial needs and aim to improve employee engagement and well-being. Indeed a greater focus on employee well-being is fast becoming a centerpiece of employer benefits strategies. Today's emerging well-being programs reflect an evolution from the wellness programs that tended to focus in the past on the physical health of employees. Yesterday's wellness programs were often siloed, one-size-fits-all, and transactional, and they focused on a 'carrot and stick' approach to participation. The result has frequently been that employee engagement is abysmal and these programs have not delivered on their promises (Willis Towers Watson 2016a). By taking a broader view of well-being, including core components of physical, emotional, financial, and social health, employers are designing well-being programs to meet the needs of all employees and their complex sets of challenges, and they are reshaping the well-being and benefits programs of the future.

But this process also presents challenges, especially regarding how to help employees navigate a world that is becoming more flexible and tailorable. We argue that, with personalization and DIY approaches becoming a bigger part of the employee value proposition, employers are offering their workers more comprehensive packages. To make this work, employers need to better understand how they can use plan design and technology to guide and assist employees. Providing core security will remain a foundation of their benefit offerings. But with a much wider array of benefits available today, meaningful choice will also be key. Over the last decade as employers have watched their employees struggle with excess choice and fragmented benefits designs, they have learned that guardrails to 'bound' decisions and ensure the number of options are manageable are needed to help employees avoid costly financial mistakes.

New technology will be key to support decisions and provide suitable choice architecture, based on lessons from behavioral economics, to help employees overcome information overload. At the same time, employers will need to seek to ensure that individuals' health and financial security is not harmed. Furthermore, employers increasingly recognize that a key to successfully engaging employees around their benefits is by using one of their most valuable assets—the workplace itself—where peer effects and onsite support has proven for many organizations to be key to driving positive and sustainable changes in employee behaviors.

The chapter is organized as follows. First we overview the recent trends in employee benefits, highlighting the transition from DB to DC both in the pension and healthcare areas, as well as the influence and effect of the recent global financial crisis. Second, we analyze the main challenges and issues that have emerged along the growth of DC. Next, we present key trends that have consolidated and aligned to transform the shape of employee benefits. A final section discusses key takeaways on how employers are looking to leverage the recent changes in the benefit environment and develop their future benefits plans.

Overview of Recent Trends in Employee Benefits

From DB to DC retirement benefits. The first major development in employee benefits came with the emergence of DB pension plans. These plans granted workers a sense of retirement security, and as family-based retirement arrangements faded away, these programs provided a much-needed sense of security and fulfilled a societal goal (Hess 2013). DB plans started to grow more popular in the United States around the 1950s due to the combination of wage controls and tax incentives. In the UK, pension plans actually started as DC schemes, but the high inflation rates that followed World War II reduced their appeal, shifting workplace provision toward DB. Similarly, in a number of Western economies, employer provision of retirement plans started to grow in the 1950s and 60s.

The cost of DB plans was initially manageable, as the prospective retiree population was small and retiree life spans were short. But as workforces matured, life expectancy improved and the size of the promises increased. Moreover, the cost of providing traditional pension plans grew sharply. In addition, governments tightened regulation and changing reporting rules, moving toward more stringent market-based accounting, which led to a heavier regulatory burden. Regulation, especially tax rules, made it increasingly hard for sponsors to reap the upside potential of overfunding, driving sponsors to become increasingly vigilant on their contributions and making overfunding of DB systems unlikely.

At the same time, trends in the labor market, such as increased mobility of workers, a changing industry landscape, and the decline of unions, reduced the demand for DB pensions.

Overall, this increased regulatory burden, paired with the larger costs and affordability issues, and a lower demand for DB, raised the question of whether the effort of providing DB was actually worth it. The decline of DB had started, and with it began the second generation of retirement plans with the emergence and growth of DC plans.

New DC plans in the United States emerged in the early 1970s, encouraged by the Employee Retirement Income Security Act (ERISA) in 1974 and the Revenue Act of 1978, which established 401(k) plans and changed

Individual Retirement Account (IRA) rules. In 1981, the Internal Revenue Service (IRS) proposed regulations that made it clear that 401(k) contributions could be made from an employee's ordinary wages and salaries, ushering in the modern 401(k) plan. From this point, we have seen a gradual shift in provision from DB to DC within corporate America that quickened pace with the turn of the millennium.

The transition to DB has varied widely across countries. In Australia, the transition to DC was led by regulation that started with the 1986 superannuation award and was followed by the mandatory superannuation guarantee in 1992. In the UK, the move to DC was a little later, with the late 1980s marketing the reappearance of DC plans, but the change to DC was swifter. Over the decade from 2000 to 2010, the large majority of UK employers moved to offering only a DC plan to newly hired employees (Figure 12.1). Today, the UK's private-sector retirement landscape is almost entirely DC only for new hires (compared to around 70 percent of large private-sector employers in the United States).

For the UK, the recent introduction of mandatory automatic enrollment fuelled a rapid rise in DC membership. In 2012, just over 40 percent of private sector employees were contributing to an employer retirement plan; by 2016, this had risen to 60 percent. The global financial crisis of 2008–2009 accelerated and consolidated the trend to DC. Low interest rates and falling asset values paired with the ensuing deep economic recession. The uneven recovery and lower discount rates cut pension funding ratios and led to increased employer contributions at a time when many could least afford them (Towers Watson 2008). Additionally, lower interest rates magnify the

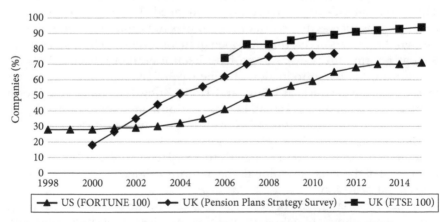

Figure 12.1. Percentage of companies offering only DC plans (1998–2015)

Source: Authors' computations using data from Willis Towers Watson.

adverse effect of increased longevity on liabilities, weakening solvency of DB plans and further eroding the economic basis for offering DB plans. Particularly, interest rates have a 'compounding' effect over longevity improvements as increments in longevity are more heavily felt when low interest rates prevail.

It seems that the global financial crisis, the looming risks of persistently low-interest rates that followed, and the impact these have had on the cost of DB pensions have provided the final excuse for employers to accelerate the move away from DB schemes. This DB decline is most evident in the United States and United Kingdom, where the incidence of pension freezes (ceasing future accrual for existing plan members) has risen significantly since 2008. Among the Fortune 500 companies that offered a DB plan in 1998, 21 percent of US plan sponsors froze their DB plans, and 21 percent had closed their primary DB plans to new entrants by 2009. Sponsors of US frozen plans outnumbered those with open primary plans for the first time in 2015; moreover, 39 percent sponsored frozen plans and 24 percent had closed their primary plans to new hires (Willis Towers Watson 2016b). In the UK, only 4 percent of the FTSE 100 had DB schemes which were closed to future accruals (frozen) in 2009, but by 2017, almost two-fifths of FTSE 100 companies had frozen their DB plans (Willis Towers Watson 2017). One in three of DB plans still open to accrual in 2015 is likely to be closed by 2020 (Towers Watson 2015a).

In emerging economies, the growth in DC has taken place over a shorter time frame, with DC emerging as a result of regulation encouraging or mandating private DC provision. For example, many Latin American countries introduced structural reforms for retirement savings and moved to funded DC plans during the 1980s and 1990s (Holzmann and Hinz 2005). The Latin American experience also influenced the reform processes in other regions such as the transition economies in Europe and Central Asia, though the process of reform developed quite differently in the two regions. Recent reform efforts in East Asia have been even more diverse, but it is noteworthy that the introduction of some type of DC component was a key factor in countries such as China and Hong Kong (Pai 2006; The World Bank 2016). What is clear is that, in these nations, one should probably talk more about the introduction of DC plans by governments instead of a shift to DC by employers. More recently, we have also seen moves toward DC arrangements in countries such as Germany, Japan, and the Netherlands, though all of these had traditionally been more wedded to the DB model of retirement provision.

In the Netherlands, the period 1995 to 2005 saw the majority of DB plans move from traditional final salary DB schemes to career average plans with conditional indexation where revaluation and uprating of benefits is determined by a pension plan's funding status. Such plans effectively limit the risks faced by employers, passing them to employees and retirees. In the period since the global financial crisis, we have seen plans move toward the collective DC model, where employer contributions are fixed. These plans are DC-like for employers, but they smooth investment returns and share risk among employees (especially across generations). Yet while such risk-sharing is frequently viewed as attractive by sponsors, it has not been well understood by employees. Periods in which indexation has been reduced or benefits cut to compensate for lower funding have been deeply unpopular, and there is increased disquiet as to whether younger generations are getting a fair deal from the current system.

As a result, several governments have proposed reforms that could mark a major shift in retirement provision. One option is to move to a system much closer to the individual DC account model, with employees having far greater flexibility and choice on how to use their pension contributions (Willis Towers Watson 2016c). Other countries have also evidenced some tentative moves to DC. In Germany, a recent draft law aims to expand the percentage of the workforce (particularly the lower-wage sector) covered by employer-provided retirement plans and individual retirement arrangements. The goal is to offer a combination of minor tax incentives and a new DC retirement plan option. Japan opened up the possibility of establishing corporate and individuals DC plans back in 2001. Since then, subsequent regulation has expanded eligibility criteria, and regulated the role of sponsors, fiduciaries, and investment rules (Willis Towers Watson 2016d). So, as Figure 12.2 shows, occupational retirement provision is increasingly concentrated on DC plans with DB provision increasingly rare.

Movement to DC health. The advent of DC in retirement plans is now moving to the healthcare area as well, particularly in the United States. Traditional DC healthcare plans, where the employer contributed a fixed-dollar amount toward the cost of an employee's health benefit each year and the employee paid the difference between that amount and the actual cost of the coverage elected, were popular during the heyday of flexible benefits plans in the 1980s and early 1990s. But these DC approaches lost their appeal when healthcare costs escalated in the late 1980s and employees' share of health plan costs consequently outpaced pay gains. Employers are now giving DC plans a second look for several reasons: a lower trajectory of cost increases over the last decade; the emergence of private exchanges designed around a DC funding model; and the desire to make the cost of coverage more transparent, which may encourage employees to buy a lower level of coverage.

A recent survey showed that more companies now use a DC health plan strategy than ever before: 25 percent in 2016, up from 20 percent in 2015. Moreover, the number of employers going DC is expected to nearly double

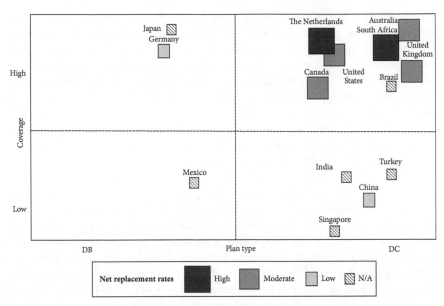

Figure 12.2. Stages of transition toward DC in occupational pension plans

Note: Prevalence and plan type are based on information for medium-sized and large private sector companies. Prevalence refers to the percentage of employers offering occupational plans.

Source: Authors' computations using data from Willis Towers Watson.

by 2018 (to 48 percent) based on those planning to or considering adopting the approach (Willis Towers Watson 2016e).

Whether the DC health plan approaches will spread will partly depend on the future of healthcare cost increases and whether private health exchanges can deliver on their value proposition. Additionally, many employers are designing these DC arrangements with guardrails and maintaining some degree of cost sharing within their programs. In fact, only 4 percent of employers have moved to a 'pure' DC strategy, with a flat dollar contribution amount that is the same for all employees regardless of plan type or tier. This is expected to increase to 16 percent by 2018 if companies follow through with their plans.

Rising costs. Despite these shifts to DC, employers' commitment to benefits has not declined. Instead, employer benefit costs have frequently risen due to legacy DB costs and rising healthcare costs.

In the United States, the cost of employee benefits as a percentage of pay has risen from 14.8 percent in 2001, to 18.3 percent in 2015. This increase is largely driven by increments in health costs that grew from 5.7 percent to 11.5 percent of pay over the same period (Figure 12.3). In short, healthcare

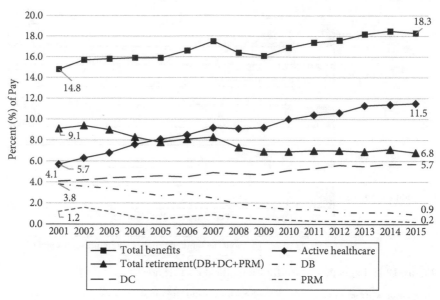

Figure 12.3. Total employer benefit values as a percentage of pay – United States

Note: Study focuses on employer spend as a percentage of average employee's pay toward: DB plans (hybrid and traditional DB plans), DC plans (401(k), 403(b), profit sharing, ESPP, etc.), Active Health Care and Post-Retirement Medical (PRM). Employer value for retirement benefits is based on information from the WTW Benefits Data Services (BDS) database, a comprehensive benefits data source on provisions to employees related to retirement, health and welfare, paid time off, lifestyle and flexible benefits. For retirement data prior to 2010, legacy data from Comparison (legacy Watson Wyatt system) and EBIC (legacy Towers Perrin system) were utilized. To ensure that spend as percentage of pay is comparable across all years 2001–2015 and legacy systems, multiplication factors were created and used to put values on a 2015 scale. Results shown for 2001–2015 use all companies in our valuation databases.

Source: Authors' computations using data from Willis Towers Watson.

costs are crowding out employee short-term term financial security through lower take-home pay and their long-term financial security through less generous retirement programs. This trend is expected to continue, with healthcare costs expected to increase at a faster pace than general inflation for the foreseeable future. In this prolonged period of relatively stagnant wage growth, employers are also becoming increasingly concerned about plan affordability. In fact, nearly 40 percent of employers are taking steps today to achieve more affordable health insurance premiums and point-of-care costs, while another 15 percent plan to take action over the next few years.

The trend towards higher healthcare costs is also evident outside the United States. In 2014, the global cost of private medical insurance benefits rose more than twice the rate of general inflation (Towers Watson 2014). Moreover, most insurers anticipate higher or significantly higher medical

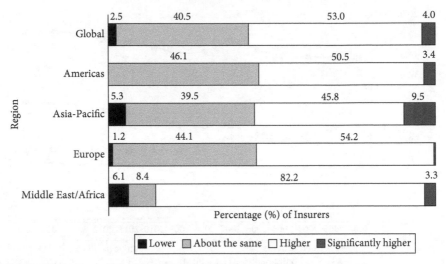

Figure 12.4. Expectations for future medical cost trends

Note: Figures present percentage of insurers answering the question 'How do you expect the medical trend in your overall book of business to change over the next three years compared to current rates?' in the Willis Towers Watson Global Medical Trends Survey. The Willis Towers Watson Global Medical Trends Survey was conducted in October and November 2015, and reflects responses from 174 leading medical insurers operating in 55 countries. Most participants have at least a 10 percent share of the group medical insurance market in their country.

Source: Willis Towers Watson (2016e).

trends over the next several years (Figure 12.4). Given the design of healthcare provision in most developed economies, the impact of medical inflation will be felt less directly by employees, though this does not mean the costs disappear. They are likely to be felt indirectly via taxation, national premiums, or even reduced public coverage in some areas or services.

As health takes a larger share of national resources, retirement and pay are suffering. In fact, probably the biggest threat to retirement security in the United States has been the rise of healthcare costs. In other countries, rising healthcare costs are increasingly weighing on government finances and squeezing other programs.

The drive towards flexibility and choice. With benefit costs rising, employers are working hard to counter their program costs and pass risk back to employees. Challenges facing employers today include the weak economy, constrained corporate budgets, and a more diverse workplace. Moreover, different generations have markedly different financial priorities, interests, and worries. For example, older workers (Baby Boomers) prioritize savings for retirement and health as they often own their homes and have little debt.

For Millennials, the focus is more short term; they have lived in a decade of little pay growth and limited career opportunities, and they find it hard to get on the housing ladder and pay back student loans (Willis Towers Watson 2016g).

When employees are asked how they would allocate a hypothetical benefits spend offered by their employer, more than half of the budget tends to be devoted to non-traditional benefits including insurance and income protection products (such as life and disability insurance and financial protection), as well as lifestyle benefits (including health and well-being products and employee discounts) (Figure 12.5).

Clearly the benefits packages of the future must accommodate these different priorities. In fact, more and more employers, especially in the United States, United Kingdom, and Canada, are offering ancillary benefits. Thus, exploring greater flexibility and choice through online platforms and exchanges and developing voluntary benefit programs is warranted.

Technology is also a key ingredient enabling transformation in the delivery of benefits. It has facilitated the move toward DC benefits by lowering the cost of individual account-based plans and increasing the use of flex programs,

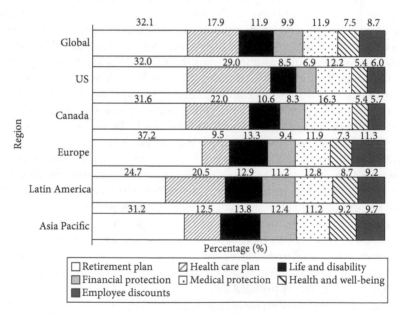

Figure 12.5. Employees' preferred allocation of benefits spend

Note. Figures present the percentage distribution of a hypothetical benefits spend. Sample includes all employees, except US and Canada where full-time employees only are considered.

Source: Willis Towers Watson (2016g).

enabling greater integration of many benefit programs. Not only is technology making the administration of choice easier for employers, it is also providing the tools to streamline the choices employees face (to avoid choice overload) and to provide a more engaging and user-friendly experience.

Other drivers of change: constraints on tax incentives and new approaches. Changes in tax incentives and policy reforms are also pushing companies to look at greater flexibility for employees. Faced with weakening government finances, many countries have sought to cap tax privileges through limits on the amount of contributions or the lifetime value of retirement savings that attract tax relief. For higher-earning employees, the caps mean that traditional retirement saving may not be tax efficient, so that greater flexibility offers an opportunity to better manage financial affairs.

It is also becoming increasingly evident that retirement savings cannot be looked at in isolation. In most countries, retirement savings have been overwhelmingly illiquid. For some especially sophisticated present-biased agents, this pre-commitment (illiquidity) is appealing (Beshears et al. 2015), but it is clearly sub-optimal for those facing high debt and simultaneously saving for retirement. There are a few cases such as the United States, where employees have long been able to borrow against their 401(k)s, or Singapore, where a portion of DC balances can be used to pay medical expenses, home purchases, or student loans. Yet in most countries, flexibility is extremely limited. Some countries allow for hardship withdrawals (e.g., Australia, New Zealand, and Peru) but the conditions for accessing savings and the limits on the amount that can be withdrawn are strict.

For better or worse, we are seeing signs of change, as countries begin to incorporate savings vehicles that tackle long-, medium-, and short-term needs, shifting toward a 'total savings' approach. In the UK for example, the introduction of the Lifetime Individual Savings Account (ISA) (launched in April 2017) provided fiscal incentives for savings for the under-40s that can be used to buy a first home or to build retirement savings. The Netherlands has proposed reforms to allow workers access to retirement savings before retirement for care or housing needs.

Together, these initiatives drive employers to ponder whether they should provide more flexibility in their benefits package to allow employees to better address their financial needs. From the employees' viewpoint, the possibility of using plan contributions as part of a broader wealth management strategy offers an opportunity to tackle pressing short-term financial issues (such as debt and housing). Nevertheless, the potential leakage eroding retirement savings is large.

Other drivers of change: A focus on well-being. Well-being is fast becoming a centerpiece of many employers' benefits strategies. Many organizations seek to differentiate their companies as a destination for talent. In part, employers seek to invest in their employees to offset workers' greater responsibilities in managing their benefits. New technologies that help personalize messages and advice are only a start.

Employers are taking these steps out of necessity, but they also recognize that a healthy and financially secure employee can be more productive. Surveys show that employees in good health and financially secure are 70 percent more productive than those with financial and health issues (Willis Towers Watson 2016g).

Today's emerging well-being programs reflect an evolution from the old-school wellness programs that tended to focus on employees' physical health. A recent survey showed that, in 2016, 30 percent of employers had already incorporated financial well-being as part of their organization's health and productivity strategy (Willis Towers Watson 2016a). The United States had a head start in this area with nearly half of employers incorporating personal financial well-being, yet other regions are also interested in broadening the spectrum of their benefits programs (Figure 12.6). In fact, we see growing interest in educating employees about ways to improve their financial well-being and to provide them with tools to help with budgeting and managing debts.

Other drivers of change: the globalization of benefits. Multinational businesses are increasingly managed more globally with the benefits marketplace moving in parallel. Workers are more transient, and pay and benefits are more transparent. Additionally, there is a movement towards the 'flattening' of designs across countries, with a more uniform and consistent set of benefits catering to an increasingly global workforce. Employers seek to

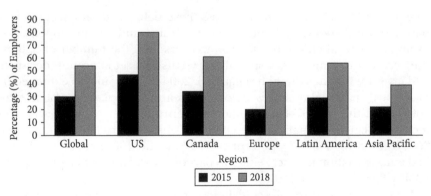

Figure 12.6. Adoption of a financial well-being strategy

Note: Figures present the percentage of employees in each region that had adopted a financial well-being strategy as part of their overall health and productivity strategy by 2015 and those planning to adopt one between 2016 and 2018.

Source: Willis Towers Watson (2016i).

avoid the administrative burden of many different benefit designs, seeking to provide a globally consistent but locally relevant total rewards package across key segments of their workforce. This is true not only in the United States and the United Kingdom, but in other territories as well. For example, Asian firms have recently moved to adopt flexible benefits in the region (Towers Watson 2015b).

Flexibility and personalization are instrumental to ensure that these globally coherent benefits packages are also locally relevant. Given enduring differences in cultures, regulations, and social insurance programs across countries, it is essential to retain adaptability, choice, and flexibility to make sure that global benefits packages cater to diverse workforce needs.

Issues Facing Flexibility and Choice

Firms are increasingly showing interest in a new generation of benefits, characterized by greater flexibility and increased choice. These will encompass a broader range of employee financial needs and improve employee engagement and well-being. But a lesson of the last two decades is that the engaged consumer model has not worked well in employee benefits. Behavioral economists have documented a number of heuristics and biases that hamper individual abilities to choose wisely (Benartzi and Thaler 2007). While workers recognize that it is their responsibility to make sure they have enough resources at retirement, the vast majority fail to engage in active retirement planning (Lusardi and Mitchell 2011).

The power of defaults. To try to bypass these behavioral biases, employers have been incorporating changes to plan design and default options. For example, to avoid choice overload, employers limit the number of options they present to employees, especially in terms of asset allocation decisions and investment funds (Sethi-Iyengar et al. 2004). Strong inertia exhibited by plan participants also makes automatic features appealing (Choi et al. 2006), and the use of pension automatic enrollment and auto escalation increase plan participation and contributions (Butrica and Karamcheva 2015). By 2015, some 31 percent of US Fortune 100 companies already had auto-escalation in place, either as part of the default or as a plan option (Willis Towers Watson 2016h).

These design features substantially ease employees' decision-making processes, but they can also come at a cost. Automation puts retirement, healthcare, and other choices on auto-pilot, making members unaware that they are choosing by not making a choice (OECD 2012). The issue with auto-piloting is that it is becoming increasingly evident that the default is not the starting point for an individual to make a decision, but rather it becomes the end point, with few employees deviating from the default.

For example, we know that automatic enrollment dramatically increases the probability that employees participate in a retirement plan, but at the same time a large majority of employees will stick to the default contribution rate. Frequently, this means employees fail to reap the maximum benefits from matching contributions, as the majority of plans set low auto-enrollment defaults (Madrian and Shea 2001; Choi et al. 2004).

Research from the UK suggests that when low contribution rates are set only around 26 percent of members contribute at the maximum. By contrast, when the maximum is the default, 77 percent of members select the maximum contribution rate. Where there is no default at all, some 64 percent select the maximum rate (Gardner 2013). The typical DC design of auto-enrolling employees into the minimum contribution rate therefore helps employees who would not have participated, but it reduces the contributions of those who would have joined anyway.

How can employers better manage choice and flexibility? As companies move to provide employees with a broader range of choices, one concern is whether employees are sufficiently equipped or engaged to cope with these options. Employees typically say more choice is desirable, but when they are left to their own decision making, they often make poor choices or do not make them at all (Sethi-Iyengar et al. 2004).

It seems undeniable that more financial education is needed, especially where employers offer a wide array of benefits. Yet it is also difficult to design and implement financial education programs that work well. There is evidence linking attendance at workplace seminars with administrative data showing that seminars at the workplace do not dramatically change employee behavior with respect to enrollment, increasing contributions, or changing asset allocation (Choi et al. 2004). Today, employers seek technology to reduce the barriers to choice: to use choice architecture to streamline the choices an employee faces; to use personalization and peer effects to increase employee engagement; and to use prompts and nudges to ensure employees review their situations on an ongoing basis.

The tension between flexibility and choice and retirement adequacy. With the global move to DC and the persistent low yield environment, workers and employers are increasingly concerned about the adequacy of retirement savings. For employees with DC plans, moderate reductions in yield have an outsized impact on replacement rates. Based on different return scenarios, savings rates that are needed to reach a replacement rate of 75 percent can be three times as much under current interest rates than they would be if returns tracked those of the last 40 years (see Ilmanen and

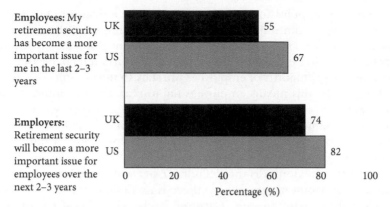

Figure 12.7. Expectation over importance of retirement security

Note. Figures present the percentage of employees and employers that agree or strongly agree with the statements: 'My retirement security has become a more important issue for me in the last two to three years' and 'Retirement security will become a more important issue for employees over the next two to three years' for employees and employers respectively.

Source: Authors' calculations using Willis Towers Watson.

Rauseo's chapter in this volume). For those with DB plans, the picture is not much better. As Blanchett et al. note in their chapter, lower-income workers will need to save about 50 percent more if low rates of return persist, and higher-income workers will need to save nearly twice as much in a low return environment compared to the optimal savings using historical returns. Given current low saving rates (see Reilly and Byrne, this volume), people will either have much lower standards of living in retirement or will need to work much later than prior generations. More than half of UK employees and around two-thirds of US employees report that retirement security has become a more salient concern, a concern also shared by employers. Both UK and US employers foresee this becoming an even more pressing issue in the near future (Figure 12.7). In the United States, there is emerging evidence that older Americans are exiting the workforce in a more flexible way and are willing to change employers, occupations, and work intensity late in life (see Quinn and Cahill's chapter in this volume).

Adequacy concerns are also prominent in the developing world. In Chile, for example, there have been massive protests against the national DC system as retirement outcomes fail to live up to expectations (The Guardian 2016). In response, the government is looking to enhance social security provision to compensate for weaknesses in the DC accounts (Comisión Asesora Sobre el Sistema de Pensiones 2015). Yet providing greater flexibility and allowing individuals to divert money previously allocated to retirement saving for other things may further jeopardize retirement security. 'Leakages' from retirement accounts can also lower savings if they are not repaid (Antolin and Stewart 2009). US research shows that about 1.5 percent of assets leak out of the 401(k)/IRA system each year, and so aggregate 401(k) and IRA retirement wealth is at least 20 percent lower than it would have been without current leakage rules (Munnell and Webb 2015).[1] Others estimate that for every dollar contributed to DC accounts in the population under age 55, 40 percent flows out of the system (without counting loans or rollovers) (Argento et al. 2015).

There is also evidence that early withdrawals increased during the global financial crisis (Argento et al. 2015). Nevertheless, it is unclear whether these withdrawals were sub-optimal from consumers' financial perspective. Where these funds alleviated severe financial distress and met pressing short-term needs, they could have been welfare enhancing. Committing funds in a long-term savings vehicle may not be optimal for many, especially for low- and moderate-income families without emergency savings or with too much debt. The possibility of withdrawals is an important determinant in the decision to join a retirement plan, and how much to contribute given participation (Munnell et al. 2001).

Against the backdrop of a decade of low pay growth around the world, employees are increasingly concerned about their short-term financial security as well as their retirement adequacy. This is reflected in how concerns around financial security have climbed to a top-of-mind issue for employees worldwide (Figure 12.8).

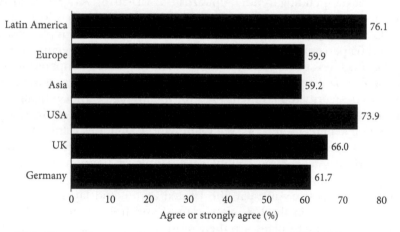

Figure 12.8. Financial security becoming a bigger issue over 2015–2016

Note: Figures present the percentage of employees that agree or strongly agree with the statements: 'My financial security has become a more important issue for me in the last two to three years.'

Source: Willis Towers Watson (2016g).

Why is this Time Different?

Many of these concepts are not new, since flexible benefits were first studied in the 1990s (Barber et al. 1992). The concept of employers moving from retirement plans to a broader concept of employee financial well-being has also been discussed frequently over the last decade. So why is this time different? Our view is that there are several trends aligning to transform and reshape the future of employee benefits.

Economic trends: a low growth world and the increased relevance of employee benefits. The last decade has seen a global economy drifting into one of the longest productivity slowdowns on record. Sluggish economic growth affects both developed and emerging economies. With few exceptions, the growth of labor productivity has been steadily declining since 2000, and the slowdown worsened between 2006 and 2015. Over this period, growth in GDP per capita averaged 0.6 percent in the United States and across the G7 as a whole (OECD 2017).

Slow economic growth and increased longevity also highlight the fragility of public safety nets. Governments have responded with reforms that cut the generosity and/or coverage of social security programs. Across the OECD (2016), various measures have been introduced to slow the growth in spending on retirement benefits, including raising the retirement age, tightening early retirement, and changing indexation and increments in pension payments. In the health area, real health spending has fallen and out-of-pocket spending trended upwards (OECD 2016). As a result, workers are becoming more pessimistic about the ability of social security programs to finance retirement. Over 70 percent of US and UK employees, and around 65 percent of employees globally, think that social security benefits will be much less generous when they reach retirement compared to today (Willis Towers Watson 2016g). This is not surprising considering that, in the US, Social Security replacement rates for the average earner retiring at age 65 are actually declining and expected to drop from 42 percent in 1985 to a projected 36 percent in 2030 (see Quinn and Cahill, this volume). As fears over safety nets have grown, so too has the relevance of private and employer benefit provision. For most employees, employer pension plans are the primary way they save for retirement. As Figure 12.9 shows, some four out of five employees in Australia, the United States, and Japan, and around three out of four in the UK, Netherlands, and Ireland, believe that their employer retirement plans are their most important source of retirement savings. Even in countries such as Germany and Canada that have rather generous social security arrangements, about 60 percent of employees see private retirement arrangements as their main retirement savings vehicle.

Low interest rates and economic uncertainty have also subjected legacy DB schemes and healthcare benefits to greater stress. With limited

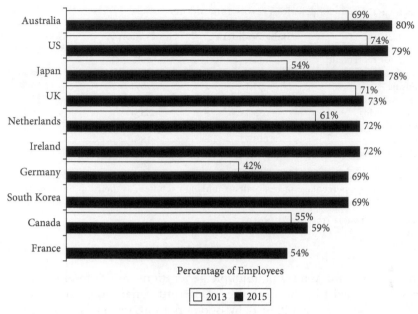

Figure 12.9. Relevance of employer retirement plans to finance retirement

Note: Figures present the percentage of employees that agree or strongly agree with the statement: 'My retirement plan is the primary way I save for retirement.' Sample: All employees, except US and Canada, where full-time employees only are included. No trend data available for Ireland, South Korea, or France.

Source: Willis Towers Watson (2016g).

productivity growth to be distributed, the small growth in worker compensation has been increasingly diverted to fund benefits rather than pay. Accordingly, employers and employees are increasingly looking to benefits to fulfill a broader range of need. With productivity growth stagnant, budgets are limited and companies are seeking to drive greater appreciation of their benefits within the same cost envelope. Here, greater choice and flexibility is a possible solution. Given meagre pay increases and economic growth, the possibility of allowing employees to use their benefit budgets to better meet their needs offers a means for employers to remain competitive and attract key talent.

Demographic trends: Changing workforce dynamics. In most Western countries, the workplace is facing two key demographic challenges. First, population aging and rising retirement ages are boosting the number of 'old' employees in the workforce. And second, large numbers of Millennials (the 'echo boom') are entering the workforce for the first time. Since 2017, Millennials (born between 1980 and 2000) have become the majority US

TABLE 12.1 Financial priorities across generations

Generation	Baby Boomers	Generation X	Generation Y
Saving for retirement	72%	56%	33%
Pay off debts	42%	47%	53%
Housing	34%	46%	55%
General costs	38%	42%	51%
General saving	33%	33%	36%
Other planned saving	22%	20%	29%
Leisure	19%	18%	20%
Children's expenses	16%	23%	10%
Medical expenses	22%	13%	8%

Note: Figures are percentage of respondents ranking each item as their top financial priority. Sample is US employees working full time.

Source: Willis Towers Watson (2016e).

adult population. As a result, multiple generations with different wants and needs will coexist in the workplace. Different generations have markedly different financial priorities: Baby Boomers think saving for retirement is their main financial goal, but for Generation X and Millennials (Generation Y), paying off debt and saving to buy a house are more pressing issues (see Table 12.1) (Willis Towers Watson 2016g).

Moreover, debt issues are very different today: 80 percent of Americans hold some form of debt such as mortgages, car loans, unpaid credit card balances, medical bills, student loans, or a combination of these (PEW Charitable Trust 2015). Older Americans are also carrying more debt into retirement than in previous decades (Georgetown University 2017). Eight in ten Baby Boomers have some form of debt, and about 47 percent are still paying off their homes. Two-thirds of all Millennials and 80 percent of college-educated Millennials have at least one source of outstanding long-term debt (Lusardi et al. 2014).

Many more workers now pursue a mobile or portfolio career. For older workers, retirement plans and even the concept of retirement is also changing. A generation ago, most workers retired before 65, but given the economic uncertainties, more employees plan to stay at work longer than before and work flexibly as they age. And the importance of making it easy for people to stay employed by providing incentives and training and reengineering job roles is becoming much more evident (see Reilly and Byrne, this volume). These changes are creating both opportunity and appetite for non-traditional benefits consistent with more flexible working.

Technology and consumer voice. Attempts to offer a broader range of benefit options in the past often floundered, as they proved to be too complex for both employers and employees. Employers struggled with the administrative burdens, and employees struggled with the complexity of the choices offered. Today, advances in technology are now overcoming these barriers. The cost and complexity of administering individual accounts and providing integration across different (vendor) solutions have fallen substantially and made offering choice a practical option for employers. Employees can now make choices between multiple benefits online, in real time, seamlessly, with online modellers and decision support.

In the United States, the private health insurance exchanges are an example of this move to online choice and flexibility. Exchanges accommodate employers' shift to the DC approach while creating an experience that more closely reflects online shopping (an 'Amazon'-like experience). Exchanges offer a much wider variety of benefit products and use decision support tools to help employees design their own tailored benefits package. In the process, these tools can be quite effective at pairing individuals with products that are a good fit for their personal or family situations. Employees respond strongly to the recommendations provided by those tools, and their confidence in the tools grows with repeated use. Early indications also suggest that the recommendations are not viewed as default options. Recent research shows that, when shopping for a medical plan option, 38 percent of employees bought the recommended plan while 31 percent bought a more expensive plan; just as many (31 percent) bought a less expensive plan option (Private Exchange Research Council 2016). Also, those that bought down tended to buy a much cheaper plan option ($2,735 less than the recommended plan) than those that bought up ($1,069 more expensive plan option). Employees are not simply accepting recommendations, but rather they are using the recommendations as a starting point to make independent decisions and shop around for plans that best meet their needs.

Decision support tools can strongly influence which types of benefits employees buy. For many employees, the new income protection and voluntary products their employers offer were previously unknown to them. As shown in Figure 12.10, employees are three to five times more likely to buy a product when recommended to do so than when not. Again, this evidence reinforces the power of recommendations and shows that they can strongly influence buying patterns (Private Exchange Research Council 2016).

The movement towards online interactions in other key fields, such as retail shopping, insurance, and banking is driving employees to expect a similar experience with their benefits offering. Benefits technology has already become more versatile and personalized through apps and tools, and it is enabling new ways of communicating with employees. Apps open up the possibility of reaching individuals just in time for key decisions and providing more interactive communication. At the same time, apps can provide useful data on employees which can be used to produce predictive

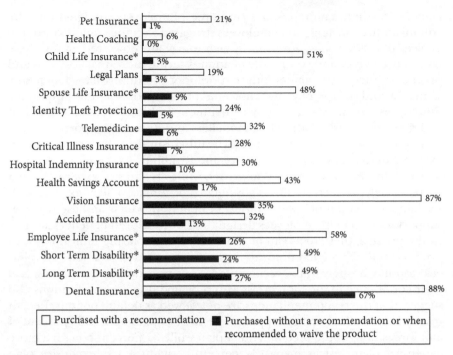

Figure 12.10. Impact of recommendation on buying decisions

Note: Figures are the percentage of employees buying each product with and without a recommendation through Liazon private exchanges. Sample: Data representative of all employees
in the study sample who bought a Medical plan. 'Purchased without a recommendation'
includes those choosing to get 'Advice' rather than getting a full recommendation (AKA those
using the 'Advice Path'). *Net employer-paid products.

Source: Private Exchange Research Council (2016).

analytics about the workforce and help design 'smart' defaults. These
technological advances are enabling employers to offer more meaningful
choices that can meet the complex and varying needs of today's workers.

Conclusion

The economic environment and changing workforce demographics are
offering new flexibility and choice, both within and across benefit plans.
This requires employers to see plans differently.

Core security and meaningful choice. Historically, companies have taken a
piecemeal approach to employee benefits, adding programs one-by-one.
Viewed in isolation, this might seem appropriate, but in aggregate this has

often resulted in an incoherent benefits offering. Also, as companies become more global, employers increasingly seek to build a consistent global framework based on the company's underlying principles and strategy, leaving room for local flexibility. At the same time, employers seek a core set of benefits offering essential health, retirement, and financial security. These can then be supplemented with options to purchase more generous provision, on top of the core, as well as the option to purchase additional voluntary benefits. Employees may choose to allocate money to benefits from a fund financed by the employer, or to buy products facilitated by the employer but paid for solely by the employee.

Decision support: segmentation and personalization. As companies add greater choice, they also add greater decision support to help their workforce make meaningful choices and use new technology to engage with employees. Employees expect the convenience of easy access to data and instant information on their plans (via the web or apps), and this is reflected in the tools employers provide in their benefits plans.

Well-being: an integrated technology-enabled approach. This broader approach to employee well-being includes core components of physical, emotional, financial, and social health. Benefit programs are no longer viewed as supplemental: nearly 90 percent of employers globally identify their well-being programs as a core part of their benefits strategy (Willis Towers Watson 2016a).

Conventional benefit programs have tended to use outdated technologies, designed as one-size-fits-all, and the delivery is fragmented. As a result the programs fail to live up to expectations in terms of a return on investment and do not drive sustainable changes in behavior. Even in the United States, where employers typically offer employees an opportunity to earn on average $880 per year if they voluntarily participate in the company's well-being programs, most employees only ever recoup $360 (or 40 percent) of that amount. Therefore, well-being programs of the future must leverage technology, segmentation, and personalization to be strategically aligned; focus on high-performing programs (rather than simply checking a box); personalized to life situation, culture, and demographics; and leveraged to confront the social forces within the workplace to support good habits. Leading with programs has not been a successful strategy. Instead, employers are rethinking their approaches by putting their employees at the center of their strategies.

This revitalized approach is designed to enhance well-being programs for the future. Digital developments provide opportunities to engage employees and get the most out of benefits programs, an invaluable outcome in a low return environment.

Note

1. Policies allowing temporary or early access to private pension savings have been introduced recently, for example, in Australia, Iceland, and Spain, and are being considered in Turkey. The UK has also recently lifted the requirement to annuitize retirement savings.

References

Antolin, P., and F. Stewart (2009). 'Private Pensions and Policy Responses to the Financial and Economic Crisis.' OECD Working Papers on Insurance and Private Pensions No. 36. Paris, France: OECD.

Argento, R., V. L. Bryant, and J. Sabelha (2015). 'Early Withdrawals from Retirement Accounts During the Great Recession.' *Contemporary Economic Policy* 33(1): 1–16.

Barber, A. E., R. B. Dunham, and R. A. Formisano (1992). 'The Impact of Flexible Benefits on Employee Satisfaction: A Field Study.' *Personnel Psychology* 45(1): 77–4.

Benartzi, S., and R. Thaler (2007). 'Heuristics and Biases in Retirement Savings Behavior.' *Journal of Economic Perspectives* 21(3): 81–104.

Beshears, J., J. J. Choi, C. Harris, D. Laibson, B. C. Madrian, and J. Sakong (2015). 'Self Control and Commitment: Can Decreasing the Liquidity of a Savings Account Increase Deposits?' NBER Working Paper Series No. 21474. Cambridge, MA: National Bureau of Economic Research.

Blanchett, D., M. Finke, and W. Pfau (2018). "Low Returns and Optimal Retirement Savings," in R. Clark, R. Maurer, and O. S. Mitchell (eds.), *How Persistent Low Returns Will Shape Saving and Retirement*. Oxford, UK: Oxford University Press, pp. 26–43.

Butrica, B. A., and N. S. Karamcheva (2015). 'The Relationship Between Automatic Enrollment and DC Plan Contributions: Evidence from a National Survey of Older Workers.' CRR Working Paper No. 2015–14. Boston, MA: Center for Retirement Research at Boston College.

Choi, J., D. Laibson, B. C. Madrian, and A. Metrick (2004). 'For Better or For Worse: Default Effects and 401(k) Savings Behavior,' in D. A. Wise (ed.), *Perspectives in the Economics of Aging*. Chicago, IL: University of Chicago Press, pp. 81–121.

Choi, J., D. Laibson, B. C. Madrian, and A. Metrick (2006). 'Saving for Retirement on the Path of Least Resistance,' in E. McCaffrey and J. Slemrod (eds.), *Behavioral Public Finance: Toward a New Agenda*. New York: Russell Sage Foundation, pp. 304–51.

Comisión Asesora Sobre el Sistema de Pensiones (2015). *Comisión Presidencial Pensiones Informe Final*. Santiago, Chile: Comisión Asesora Sobre el Sistema de Pensiones.

Gardner, J. (2013). 'Who Makes the Most of Matching Contributions? An Analysis of Member Choices in DC Pension Plans.' Willis Towers Watson Issue Brief. London, UK: Willis Towers Watson.

Georgetown University (2017). *Review of Potential Public Retirement Plan Options for Private Sector Employees/Employers in the State of Vermont*. Washinton, DC: The Center for Retirement Initiatives, McCourt School of Public Policy.

Guardian, The (2016). 'Thousands Protest in Chile Against State Pension Provisions.' *The Guardian World News*, August 21. https://www.theguardian.com/world/2016/aug/22/thousands-protest-in-chile-against-state-pension-provisions.

Hess, C. (2013). 'Looking Back – and Ahead – at the Pension Promise.' *Corporate Finance Matters*. London, UK: Willis Towers Watson.

Holzmann, R., and R. Hinz (2005). *Old-Age Income Support in the 21st Century: An International Perspective on Pension Systems and Reform*. Washington, DC: The World Bank.

Lusardi, A., C. de Bassa Scheresberg, and P. J. Yakoboski (2014). 'College-Educated Millennials: An Overview of Their Personal Finances.' TIAA-CREF Institute Working Paper. New York: TIAA Institute.

Ilmanen, A., and M. Rauseo (2017). "Intelligent Risk Taking: How to Secure Retirement in a Low Expected Return World," in R. Clark, R. Maurer, and O. S. Mitchell (eds.), *How Persistent Low Returns Will Shape Saving and Retirement*. Oxford, UK: Oxford University Press, pp. 81–98.

Lusardi, A., and O. S. Mitchell (2011). 'Financial Literacy and Planning: Implications for Retirement Wellbeing,' in O. S. Mitchell and A. Lusardi (eds.), *Financial Literacy: Implications for Retirement Security and the Financial Marketplace*. Oxford, UK: Oxford University Press, pp. 17–39.

Madrian, B. C., and D. F. Shea (2001). 'The Power of Suggestion: Inertia in 401(k) Participation and Savings Behavior.' *The Quarterly Journal of Economics* 116(4): 1149–87.

Munnell, A. H., A. Sundén, and C. Taylor (2001). 'What Determines 401(k) Participation and Contributions?' *Social Security Bulletin* 64(3): 1–22.

Munnell, A. H., and A. Webb (2015). 'The Impact of Leakages from 401(k)s and IRAs.' CRR Working Paper No. 2015–2. Boston, MA: Center for Retirement Research at Boston College.

OECD (2012). 'Putting Pensions on Auto-pilot: Automatic-adjustment Mechanisms and Financial Sustainability of Retirement-income Systems.' *OECD Pensions Outlook 2012*. Paris, France: OECD Publishing.

OECD (2016). *Social Spending Stays at Historically High Levels in Many OECD Countries*. Social Expenditure Update 2016. http://www.oecd.org/els/soc/OECD2016-Social-Expenditure-Update.pdf

OECD (2017). 'Growth in GDP Per Capita, Productivity and ULC,' *OECD.Stat* (website, updated March 24, 2017) https://stats.oecd.org/Index.aspx?DataSetCode=PDB_GR

Pai, Y. (2006). 'Comparing Individual Retirement Accounts in Asia: Singapore, Thailand, Hong Kong and PRC.' World Bank Working Paper No. 37432. Washington, DC: The World Bank.

PEW Charitable Trust (2015). *The Complex Story of American Debt: Liabilities in Family Balance Sheets*. Washington, DC: Pew Charitable Trust. http://www.pewtrusts.org/~/media/assets/2015/07/reach-of-debt-report_artfinal.pdf

Private Exchange Research Council (2016). *Understanding Product Offering and Choices on a Private Exchange*. Willis Towers Watson White Paper. London, UK: Willis Towers Watson.

Quinn, J. F., and K. E. Cahill (2018). "Challenges and Opportunities of Living and Working Longer," in R. Clark, R. Maurer, and O. S. Mitchell (eds.), *How Persistent*

Low Returns Will Shape Saving and Retirement. Oxford, UK: Oxford University Press, pp. 101–18.

Reilly, C., and A. Byrne (2018). "Investing for Retirement in a Low Returns Environment: Making the Right Decisions to Make the Money Last," in R. Clark, R. Maurer, and O. S. Mitchell (eds.), *How Persistent Low Returns Will Shape Saving and Retirement.* Oxford, UK: Oxford University Press, pp. 61–80.

Sethi-Iyengar, S., G. Huberman, and G. Jiang (2004). 'How Much Choice is Too Much? Contributions to 401(k) Retirement Plans,' in O. S. Mitchell and S. P. Utkus (eds.), *Pension Design and Structure: New Lessons from Behavioral Finance.* Oxford, UK: Oxford University Press, pp. 83–95.

Towers Watson (2008). 'Retirement Plan Contributions, Benefits and Assets: Highlights from Form 5500 Report.' Towers Watson Issue Brief. London, UK: Towers Watson.

Towers Watson (2014). '2014 Global Medical Trends.' Towers Watson Issue Brief. London, UK: Towers Watson.

Towers Watson (2015a). 'Pension Design Survey 2015: UK Defined Benefit Schemes and the End of Contracting Out.' Towers Watson Issue Brief. London, UK: Towers Watson.

Towers Watson (2015b). '2015 Asia Pacific Benefit Trends: Innovate to Drive Value from Benefits.' Towers Watson Issue Brief. London, UK: Towers Watson.

Willis Towers Watson (2016a). 'Employee Health and Business Success. Making the Connections and Taking Action.' Summary of the Global Findings of the 2015/2016 Staying@Work Survey. London, UK: Willis Towers Watson.

Willis Towers Watson (2016b). 'A Continuing Shift in Retirement Offerings in the Fortune 500.' *Insider* 26(2): 1–14.

Willis Towers Watson (2016c). 'Netherlands: Pending Pension Developments Moving Apace.' Willis Towers Watson Issue Brief. London, UK: Willis Towers Watson.

Willis Towers Watson (2016d). 'Japan New Legislation: A Game Changer for the Defined Contribution Market.' Willis Towers Watson Issue Brief. London, UK: Willis Towers Watson.

Willis Towers Watson (2016e). '2016 Willis Towers Watson Best Practices in Health Care Survey.' London, UK: Willis Towers Watson.

Willis Towers Watson (2016f). 'Press Release: US Employers Expect Health Care Costs to Increase 5.0% in Both 2016 and 2017.' Arlington, VA: Willis Towers Watson.

Willis Towers Watson (2016g). '2015/2016 Global Benefits Attitudes Survey.' Willis Towers Watson Issue Brief. London, UK: Willis Towers Watson.

Willis Towers Watson (2016h). 'Defined Contribution Plans of Fortune 100 Companies in 2014.' *Insider* 26(3): 1–8.

Willis Towers Watson (2016i). 'Making the Connections and Taking Action: Summary of the Global Findings of the 2015/2016 Staying@Work.' London, UK: Willis Towers Watson.

Willis Towers Watson (2017). 'FTSE 350 Defined Contribution Pension Scheme Survey 2017.' FTSE DC Pension Scheme Survey No. 12. London, UK: Willis Towers Watson.

World Bank, The (2016). 'Live Long and Prosper: Aging in East Asia and Pacific.' World Bank East Asia and Pacific Regional Report. Washington, DC: The World Bank.

Index

Note: In the main, chapters are referring to United States so this has only been indexed where it is mentioned along with other countries under the global developments chapter. Tables and figures are indicated by an italic *t* and *f* respectively, following the page number.